WILLIAM
AUGUSTUS
BOWLES:

Director General of the Creek Nation

WILLIAM AUGUSTUS BOWLES

Chief of the Embassy from the Creek & Cherokee Nations

Published as the Act directs, March 26, 1791 by T. Hardy No. 6 Great Marlborough Street

WILLIAM AUGUSTUS BOWLES

WILLIAM
AUGUSTUS
BOWLES

Director General of the
Creek Nation

By J. Leitch Wright, Jr.

UNIVERSITY OF GEORGIA PRESS · ATHENS

To FELTON

Contents

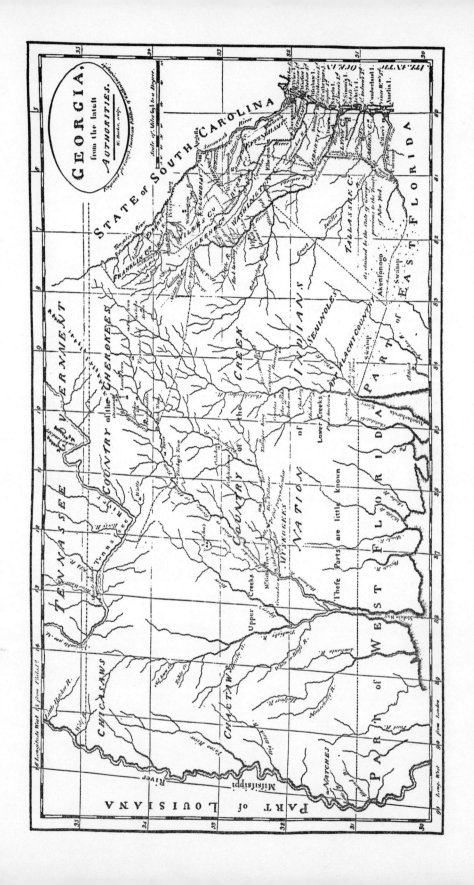

Preface

WILLIAM AUGUSTUS BOWLES'S career was short and eventful. It began in Maryland and took him to the West Indies, Florida, Canada, England, Spain, South America, the Philippines, and Africa. At one time or another—and with varying degrees of proficiency—he was an artist, actor, diplomat, navigator, soldier, musician, baker, linguist, hunter, chemist, lawyer, and Indian chief. One of his families was white, the other Indian, and he was as much at home leading an Indian war party as dining with British royalty. Contemporary accounts of his life were published alongside those of Nelson and Napoleon, and he was well known on both sides of the Atlantic. Those who knew him best either lavishly praised or vehemently damned him. His detractors customarily referred to him as a "base adventurer," "captain liar," "worthless rogue," "unscrupulous pest," and worse. But it never occurred to his detractors or to anyone else to call William Augustus Bowles, Director General of the Creek Nation, dull.

The author has been both fortunate and frustrated in trying to discover what manner of man Bowles actually was. Had the Spaniards not periodically captured, preserved, and copied his papers, it would be almost impossible to write his biography. Relying on these documents in Spanish archives and others in English and American depositories, one is able to piece together fairly accurately his public career. But his private life is another matter. Not a single letter from him to members of his family has come to light. Except for one letter from his brother, there is no record that any of his family, white or Indian, ever corresponded with him.

Bowles traveled thousands of miles, many of them against his will. In part the author has dogged his footsteps, and even today viewing the rolling mountains in Maryland, Independence Hall in Philadelphia, the dome of St. Paul's Cathedral in London, the old fortified city of Cádiz, and the ruins of Ft. St. Marks in Florida helps recapture these places as they appeared in Bowles's lifetime.

Many persons assisted in making this study—the staffs of the British Museum, the Archivo de Simancas, the Archivo General de la Nación in Mexico, the Public Archives of Canada, the Georgia Department of Archives and History, the Virginia State Library, and the libraries of the University of Georgia and the University of Florida. The personnel of the Archivo General de Indias in Seville and the Library of Congress in Washington were especially helpful. The Washington and Frederick County historical societies in Maryland, the National Portrait Gallery, the National Gallery, and the National Trust in England, the Creek Indian Memorial Association and the Museum of the American Indian in the United States, all assisted with knotty details. A grant from the Penrose Fund of the American Philosophical Society provided funds for foreign research. Mrs. Flavia Owen and her assistants at the Randolph-Macon College Library rendered countless valuable services. Professor Thomas P. Abernethy readily supplied advice and encouragement. Mrs. Sarah Wright typed the manuscript and as usual corrected many mistakes and made few. The author is also indebted to Beth.

J. L. W., Jr.

History Department
Randolph-Macon College
Ashland, Virginia

I

Soldier-Warrior

FOR THE BRITISH EMPIRE in general, and especially for the North American colonists, 1763, marking the end of the French and Indian War, was a year of triumph and jubilation. In this same year, as Britain basked in glory and France and Spain licked their wounds, William Augustus, the first child of Thomas and Eleanor Bowles, was born on the Maryland frontier. His happy parents never suspected that America soon would undergo more serious strife than in the recent war and that their helpless infant would be swept up—and indeed would try to direct—the latent forces that soon would be unleashed. During the French and Indian War Thomas and Eleanor had more than enough to worry about and to do without fretting over the future. Initially, there had been disasters for Britain's American colonists—Washington's and Braddock's defeats in the Ohio country were followed by ravages along the entire exposed frontier. Finally the tide of battle turned: first the great French fortress of Louisburg, then Quebec, the heart of New France, along with lesser French posts fell to the victorious British regular and colonial troops. The French and Indian War had been fought on a worldwide stage, and in the end Britain triumphed over her colonial rivals, France and Spain. Except for misgivings about allowing the French a share of the Newfoundland fishery, the American colonists had little complaint about the peace provisions. The signing of the definitive Treaty of Paris in 1763, following General Wolfe's storming the Plains of Abraham at Quebec and the fall of Fort Pitt and Montreal, was greeted on the Maryland frontier, as elsewhere, with bonfires, celebrations, and salvos of artillery.

Frederick, just north of the Potomac River at the eastern slope of the Appalachian Mountains, had been recently settled by Germans drifting down from Pennsylvania and by English and Scotch-Irish

1

striking out from the Maryland Tidewater; this prosperous, new town was William Bowles's birthplace. Laid out in 1745, surrounded by virgin lands and close by river and road communications, it had grown rapidly. Basically it was a German town, populated by part of the wave of Germans that had made their way to western Pennsylvania and then south into Maryland, Virginia, and the Carolinas. During the early years the houses, churches, and language more often than not were Pennsylvania Dutch. English, for a time a minority language, nevertheless could be heard in Frederick Town's bustling streets. Englishmen, associated with or dependent on the proprietary Calverts or those who had risen to prominence in the Maryland Tidewater, owned most of the land in Frederick County, whose bounds before the Revolution included all of western Maryland. They, along with a sprinkling of small English farmers and Indian traders, at first dominated the political and economic life of the frontier community.[1]

As a new western settlement bordering the disputed Ohio country, Frederick had been caught up in the turmoil of the French and Indian War. Both Washington and Braddock had passed through the town, the latter fuming because of the exorbitant prices charged for provisions and wagons by the thrifty Germans.[2] After Braddock's defeat, Frederick County, particularly that part west of South Mountain, was harassed by roving war parties that took a heavy toll in prisoners and scalps. Frederick Town, east of the mountains and the largest settlement in the West, crowded by refugees fleeing across the mountains, was spared during the war. But the Indians did not always confine themselves to the other side of the mountains, and there was good reason for rejoicing when news arrived of France's ceding the Ohio country to Britain.

Thomas Bowles had arrived at Frederick Town in the midst of the French and Indian War. He had abandoned the traditional family calling—his father, Thomas, his uncle, John, and his first cousin, Carington, were highly regarded book, map, and print sellers in London's St. Paul's Churchyard—and instead had set out for the New World.[3] Either a career as a bookseller did not appeal to him or he felt there already were too many Bowleses in this profession and that he could do better elsewhere. At first he was a teacher in the schoolhouse that was one of Frederick Town's first buildings, but the lure that drew him to the frontier, like thousands before him, was land. In the eighteenth century, in spite of the rising importance of manufacturing and commerce, land was still the most honorable source of wealth. Land was what Thomas was seeking and obtained.

Though most of Frederick County's inhabitants were German, most of the land was controlled by Englishmen. Thomas was associated with the minority English group and in a short time became a leading planter in the county. Before the Revolution he had acquired some four thousand acres, approximately one-half of which was west of South Mountain on or near Conococheague Creek.[4] As befitted the *noblesse oblige* of the English gentry, he became deputy commissary, vestryman in All Saint's Anglican Church, and a trustee of the county free school. His house was in Frederick Town, but the bulk of his land was in the county, either close by outside of town or on the other side of the mountains.[5]

It was shortly after Thomas became established as a large landowner and leading townsman that William Augustus was born, first of many children to Thomas and Eleanor. Thomas needed land to provide for his growing family: first William, then Thomas, John, Catherine, and on until there were at least a dozen.[6] A new brother or sister appeared almost annually. William spent his childhood in the frontier community of Frederick Town, which was rapidly growing and taking on more refinements of civilization. Occasionally veteran Indian fighters such as Captain Evan Shelby dropped in on the Bowles household, and the children listened in awe to accounts of daring exploits and narrow escapes during the French and Indian War or Pontiac's Rebellion; the father, however, and even Shelby himself were less fascinated by these tales and more concerned that the natives quickly be pacified so as not to hamper the fur trade and land speculation.[7] William, his brothers and sisters, and his playmates spent countless hours fishing, hunting, and riding, only half conscious of how abundantly nature had endowed the verdant rolling hills sheltered by the bluish-purple mountains in the distance. William was a handsome, muscular youth of olive complexion; he was alert, aggressive, intelligent, and gregarious; and, considering the circumstances, he received a good education. Probably he attended the local school where his father had taught and now was a trustee, or possibly there was a private tutor. William's father, as a youth surrounded by good books and aware of the advantages of a liberal education, did not neglect his children. William read widely and learned to express himself vigorously, something he was quick to do, whether in writing or orally.

The intellectual intoxication of the European Enlightenment was felt even on the Maryland frontier, and the youthful William, like Voltaire and Rousseau, interested himself in and proclaimed himself master of many fields. Literature, drama, languages, history, and the sciences all fascinated him and, true to family tradition, he painted, becoming a skilled amateur. A standard contemporary work utilized by countless potential artists was Carington Bowles's *The Artist's Assistant in Drawing, Perspective, Etching, Engraving, Mezzotinto-Scraping, Painting on Glass, in Crayons, in Water-Colours, and on Silks and Satins.*[8] It would have been surprising indeed if it were not in Thomas Bowles's library and studied by the son. Following the path set by Voltaire, William, as he matured, drifted away from orthodox Christianity and toward deism.[9] He also avidly read the classics, mastered French, and learned to play the flute and violin. In short, even in remote Maryland amid the Pennsylvania Dutch and the Indians and frontiersmen, William was caught up in part of the excitement and challenge of the Enlightenment. Though bitter future experience would turn him against the political theories of some of the *Philosophes,* this did not alter the fact that this tall, engaging, self-confident youth was becoming and always remained an ardent pupil of the European intellectual ferment.

By the mid-1770's Frederick Town was the largest and most prosperous community outside Baltimore, and Thomas Bowles was one of its most eminent inhabitants. With the increasing influence and wealth of his father, with ample opportunity to pursue his many intellectual interests—he hoped to attend a colonial or an English university—William had every reason to be optimistic. Then the fighting broke out in 1775 and at once his hopes were shattered: there was no possibility of his attending any university or of becoming a successful planter, and William soon fled his boyhood home and never returned except possibly for one brief visit. The outbreak of the American Revolution drastically altered William's career.

News of the fighting at Lexington and Concord, though not totally unexpected, electrified the colonies. For the past decade there had been colonial discontent, varying in intensity, against the mother country. Only recently William had read how "Indians" enthusiastically jettisoned tea into Boston harbor and Britain retaliated with the Intolerable Acts. At first, colonial grievances were largely economic but, as the unrest continued, inevitably they merged with the more basic political question: exactly who had the authority—Parliament, King, or colonists—to institute economic or any other policies in America? At length it was apparent that this political impasse would be resolved by war. In retrospect it can be seen that, from the Boston Tea Party in 1773 until the signing of the Declaration of Independence three years later, colonial spokesmen in the local legislatures and the Continental Congress became more and more extreme, ultimately striking out for complete independence.

The deepening crisis with the mother country perplexed most Americans. The radical followers of Patrick Henry, Samuel Adams, and Thomas Paine, a minority faction, had few qualms about violently denouncing Britain and urging measures that could only lead to independence. An even smaller group, headed by the royal governors, Anglican ministers, and wealthy merchants, was equally outspoken in protestations of loyalty to the mother country and denunciations of the colonial agitators. Most Americans, however, were caught in the middle, trying to decide whether colonial grievances were so acute that to follow Adams' and Henry's lead was the only recourse or whether a break with the mother country would bring on even more chaos and suffering. Before the outbreak of fighting in 1775, or at the latest until the signing of the Declaration of Independence the following year, Americans, if they so desired, did not have to commit themselves irrevocably to the British or the colonial cause, and in fact many were unsure of their ultimate decision. But with constant hostilities against the British regulars, with the animosity between local Whigs and Tories, and with the ultimate American resolve to fight for complete separation, not openly committing oneself was a luxury denied most Americans.

Thomas Bowles, relatively a newcomer to America, soon was caught up in the passions aroused over disputes with the mother country. The Americans did have economic grievances, and at the time of the Stamp Act crisis and the Boston Tea Party, Thomas' sympathies were with the colonists. The First Continental Congress was a direct result of the Boston Tea Party and the Intolerable Acts: the delegates drew up a long list of colonial grievances; they reestablished the policy of non-importation of British goods until the mother country redressed at least some of the grievances; and they established an extra-legal police body, the Association, to enforce non-importation. Thomas was a member of the Association for Frederick County and also a member of the local Committee of Correspondence, which by now was part of a broad, semi-legal, colonial network.[10] In the past non-importation had wrung concessions from Britain—but not now. Thomas, like many Americans, had to decide whether to remain with the Patriots, who were becoming increasingly radical, or, with misgivings, to remain loyal to Britain. Being well known locally made it hard to equivocate.

In line with the actions of some county officials but in sharp contrast to the course followed by most of the local inhabitants, Thomas in the winter of 1775-1776 refused to go so far as to support independence. This made him a Loyalist, or Tory, though not an outspoken one. It was at this point that he saw his local influence and prestige, laboriously built up over the past seventeen years, evaporate. The functions of county government were carried on by a new Committee of Observation, and Thomas had nothing to do with this group.

As the Revolution progressed, Patriot and Loyalist rancor became more intense. Early in the Revolution Tories, headed by John Connolly and Virginia's Lord Dunmore, tried to stir up the western Indians against the Americans. Connolly and his associates were captured in Frederick County en route to the West and were verbally abused, jailed, and sent back East. Later other Tory conspirators were captured and jailed in Frederick Town, but this time the leaders were hanged, drawn, and quartered—a barbarous punishment which was by then largely outmoded.[11] Thomas was painfully aware of the anti-Tory sentiment, and he had almost no one to turn to. A Tory island lost in a Whiggish sea, he knew not what course to follow and wondered how he could continue to provide for his large family. Possibly he might go east and join a provincial Tory regiment; perhaps he should remain on his lands and keep silent, hoping that soon the rebels would be defeated; or he could move to where he was less well known. Exactly what Thomas and his family did during the Revolution is unknown. Apparently at some point local anti-Tory pressure became so great that he was forced to move, because shortly after the Revolution he and his family were on their lands on the other side of South Mountain in the Conococheague Valley.[12] It is possible that during the fighting he sought temporary refuge in eastern Maryland where Loyalists were more numerous, or he might have moved across the mountains at an early date. Thomas was a moderate Tory and, undoubtedly, concern for his lands and for his large family tempered his actions; he did not actively serve in the British army, so unlike the Dulanys, Addisons, and Keys, he did not have his Frederick County lands confiscated.[13]

It was another story for impetuous William, who was indignant over the insults to his family yet not responsible for their well-being. Even as a young child he had seldom been able to sidestep issues and avoid controversy; it was no different now. Besides his father, he was the only member of the family old enough to serve, and despite his mother's misgivings, at the first opportunity he volunteered to fight and help uphold the dignity of the King. He made his way overland through miles of Patriot-dominated countryside and finally, after many hardships and narrow escapes, in the fall of 1777 presented himself within General William Howe's lines at Philadelphia. It gave him no satisfaction to quit his family circle, but at least he had put many miles between himself and those damned Pennsylvania Dutch who had not the good sense to respect their betters.

The year 1777 was supposed to be decisive for British arms: General Burgoyne, marching down from Canada, expected to crush colonial resistance in the north, and Howe, leaving a holding force at New York, resolved to take Philadelphia, seat of the Continental Congress and largest colonial city. In Philadelphia itself and in the nearby Pennsylvania, New Jersey, Delaware, and Maryland countryside there supposedly were thousands of loyal colonists eager to welcome the Redcoats and the restoration of royal authority; once offered arms, they would rally to the British banner. After a tedious voyage from New York, Howe's transports eventually made their way to the head of the Chesapeake Bay where his army debarked and marched overland to Philadelphia, entering the city after defeating Washington at Brandywine. Before winter set in there were sharp encounters at Germantown and in clearing out the rebels from the lower Delaware River. Then both armies went into winter quarters.

It was as active campaigning was tapering off and as Howe was making himself snug for the winter that the exhausted William appeared in Philadelphia. Howe had expected a warm welcome by Loyalists in the Philadelphia area and hoped for heavy enlistments in new provincial regiments. At the Revolution's onset Britain had hesitated to recruit colonial regiments, but, as the fighting continued, placing increasing demands on the British regulars and German mercenaries, she showed more interest in organizing and arming the Loyalists. Provincial regiments accompanied Burgoyne from Canada and others had come to Philadelphia with Howe. Now the call was out for more volunteers, a call that William heeded.[14]

Howe had envisioned a large influx of patriotic Loyalists into Philadelphia, but, with the rebels controlling much of the countryside, he was rewarded by only a trickle. William was part of this trickle and enlisted as a common soldier in an old infantry regiment. Soon, however, he heard about Colonel James Chalmers' new regiment of Maryland Loyalists. Chalmers, an influential Marylander from the Tidewater and an outspoken Tory, had joined Howe at the headwaters of the Chesapeake and was commissioned to raise a regiment. Chalmers was about as successful as any of the provincial colonels, and eventually his regiment totaled 336 men, the officers exclusively from Maryland; the rank and file, recent immigrants. Among the officers there was a sprinkling of Dulanys, Philip Barton Key, whose nephew, Francis Scott, would be more famous, and others identified with the Maryland large-landowner, office-holding class. The lowest officer rank was ensign—there were a total of nine—one of whom was a determined, disillusioned fourteen-year-old youth from Frederick Town. The local influence of William's father and his contacts with the Dulanys and Keys along with the exigencies of the military situation were responsible for William's commission.[15]

The possibility of adventure and military glory partially offset William's personal misfortunes. Garrisoned in Philadelphia during the winter, he had little chance to win military fame. Even so, William, happily discarding his enlisted man's uniform for a new, more glamorous one of an officer in His Majesty's forces and, infected by the excitement in crowded Philadelphia, enthusiastically began his routine duties—helping organize the regiment, drilling them in their bright red coats with olive lapels, periodically assisting the officer of the guard, and sitting on the inevitable courts-martial. There is no recorded account that this young ensign impressed anyone else in crowded Philadelphia, but William, as he went about his military duties in his bright uniform—clothes were one of his weaknesses—was impressed with himself. Like his fellow Loyalists, he was depressed when the news arrived that Burgoyne had surrendered and that the fighting would not soon be over. In many respects it was a difficult transition from the comfortable life in Frederick Town to wartime Philadelphia, though in regard to comfort Ensign Bowles was infinitely better off than his contemporaries freezing in log huts at nearby Valley Forge.

In spite of overcrowding and occasional inconveniences, Philadelphia social life was never so dazzling. The British officers considered it their duty to bring London's cosmopolitan delights to the New World, and local belles, even non-Tories, were overcome by the magnificence. There were balls, excursions, and plays put on by the officers, culminating in a lavish production, the "Mischianza," staged for Howe's departure. It began with a "grand regatta" in which warships, transports, and barges, magnificently decorated, conducted the General to the appointed landing place; Howe and his party in their brilliant uniforms were escorted between files of grenadiers to observe a "Tilt and Tournament according to the customs of ancient chivalry"; this elaborate pageantry was followed by toasts, supper, fireworks, faro, and dancing until four in the morning. To the consternation of Philadelphia Quakers, local beauties, adorned in Oriental attire, participated. No one was more awed than fourteen-year-old William, and it may have been the "Mischianza" and the theatrical productions that were responsible for his lifelong attachment to the theater—for William was a natural actor.[16]

Burgoyne, another actor, had recently surrendered, and the effects were immediately felt at Philadelphia. France decided to come openly into the war on the side of the Americans, and there was the chance that a revitalized French navy might blockade the Delaware River, cutting off British supplies. It was this possibility that made General Clinton, Howe's successor, resolve to link up with British forces in New York. As a result Ensign Bowles got his first taste of campaigning. Clinton wanted to return to New York by sea, but, after taking inventory of all the military stores and estimating the space required by the numerous camp followers and the several thousand Philadelphia Loyalists who had good reason not to stay, he concluded that not half enough shipping was available.

The alternative was an overland march through New Jersey. During the hot, humid days in the latter part of June, 1778, William, part of a vast mass of soldiers and civilians, crossed the Delaware and then, with Washington on the army's flank, headed north. The American army, buoyed by Burgoyne's defeat, the new French alliance, and an influx of volunteers, and hardened by the experience at Valley Forge, was looking for a chance to pounce on Clinton. The British army, stretched out for miles, was vulnerable, especially its enormous baggage train. Clinton entrusted its security to the entire command under the experienced German General Wilhelm von Knyphausen. The baggage train usually marched toward the front of Clinton's extended column, or wherever it would be least exposed to Washington. Some of Clinton's best troops brought up the rear and, as events proved, bore the brunt of the fighting.[17]

The German mercenaries of General Knyphausen were among the most efficient troops, and the provincial regiments under his command—the Queen's Rangers, the 2nd New Jersey Volunteers, and Bowles's Maryland Loyalists—were the newest and least experienced. Clinton feared for his baggage train, though in reality Washington in his strategy that led up to the Battle of Monmouth was shooting for higher stakes. The action involved only the British rear and, as a result, the march, gruelling as it was under the summer sun, was relatively uneventful for Ensign Bowles, except for harassment by rebel militia and repairing destroyed bridges. Despite the soundness of Clinton's tactics, Bowles never appreciated the fact that his first taste of campaigning involved guarding the baggage train. Not that there were not perils: marching with the baggage were hundreds of camp followers and soldiers' wives, so the handsome youth encountered hazards different from any he had ever run into in Frederick.[18] After Monmouth William marched without interruption to Sandy Hook, New Jersey, where shortly all the troops and baggage were ferried safely over to Long Island. Clinton was relieved at the safe arrival of his army and the fact that there had been no interference by the French fleet at Sandy Hook; whether Ensign Bowles was equally relieved by orders that now the women might rejoin their regiments is unrecorded.[19]

With the arrival of Clinton at New York most of the British army in America was concentrated there. Britain, unsuccessful heretofore in the northern and middle colonies, had to devise new strategy to defeat the rebels, a strategy complicated by the actual entrance of France and the probable entrance of Spain into the war. While Clinton, Lord George Germain, and others devised new plans, the bulk of the army had to sustain itself in the New York area. Supplies were always a problem. Many were imported; frequently gold obtained the support of local farmers; but, in addition, Britain usually was forced to "impress" provisions, as it was politely put. That now was necessary and it was no accident that this unpleasant duty usually fell on the Germans or provincials. For the remainder of the summer and on into the fall Bowles, under the command of General William Tryon, dashed about western Long Island procuring horses, cattle, and food. For many of the displaced Loyalists a chance to revenge themselves against the rebels was an opportunity not to be overlooked, and, as expected, atrocities were committed on both sides. Loyalist foraging expeditions on Long Island were as popular as Wallenstein's during the Thirty Years' War in Germany, and it was inevitable that the rebels were not always the victims.[20]

There was little glory in these expeditions, and this was no way to bring the rebels to terms. When toward the end of 1778 Britain unfolded her strategy and began deploying her forces, Ensign Bowles shared in the excitement and relief. Leaving Knyphausen to hold New York, 3,000 men, both regulars and provincials, sailed to Georgia and linked up with British forces from Florida for an assault on the southern colonies. In the late fall still another large convoy left New York, this one bound for Jamaica, with Bowles, happy to abandon his unglamorous foraging duties and ready to begin real campaigning, on board. When foul weather separated the transports from their escorting warships, William was as anxious as any until, after many days, Jamaica finally came into view.

With one Bourbon power in the war and another about to enter, the West Indies once again became the cockpit of international rivalries. The troops Britain was assembling in Jamaica could be used for several purposes: to defend the island against a French or Franco-Spanish attack; to strike at the Spanish-American mainland should Spain come into the war; or to reinforce West Florida, which was menaced by both the Spaniards and the Americans. As Britain worked out details of her strategy it was decided that the Maryland Loyalists would be in the contingent ordered to Pensacola.[21]

Because of the danger of a strong French fleet in the area, Bowles's regiment did not depart immediately. Jamaica was one of the most scenic Caribbean islands, normally a delightful place to live, but tropical sickness decimated the troops in their Kingston barracks. A violent fever killed Captain Grafton Dulany, William's company commander, and this unfortunate officer had been preceded by the regimental surgeon, who had succumbed to a malady he could not cure.[22] For those who retained their health Kingston afforded amusements: a stroll about the broad regular streets crowded with shops, an occasional visit to a tavern or the race track, an inspection of the massive Rock Fort east of the city, a short journey to the seat of government at Spanish Town and to that portion of Port Royal that had not been destroyed by earthquake, and an occasional pause merely to enjoy the beauty of the spacious bay with the low mountains in the background.[23]

Temporary removal of the French fleet's threat to Jamaica, signs that Spain was coming openly into the war, and the desire to protect West Florida and to strike at New Orleans, all prompted the dispatch of reinforcements to Pensacola. The Maryland Loyalists, weakened by fever and now ravaged by smallpox, stepped ashore late in December, 1778. For Ensign Bowles, with his regiment so sick it could not muster, Pensacola, where there was only lean beef, poultry, and pork, where it was "so d——d hot fish stinks before it can be boiled," and where the only asset was the beautiful white sand which circulated freely, was a let-down from Philadelphia, New York, and Kingston.[24] Because of sickness it was almost two months before his regiment could be mustered, and there was an excellent possibility that his diminished regiment would be merged with the Pennsylvania Loyalists, also cut down by sickness. The Pennsylvania and Maryland colonels bickered over who would command should the merger occur, and, with smallpox, yellow fever, and other diseases rampant, tempers of officers and enlisted men alike were on edge. It was in this atmosphere that William suddenly resigned his commission. Either he absented himself and insulted a superior officer when questioned, or insulted the officer first and then departed. In any case the headstrong Bowles, by temperament better suited to command than to serve, was dropped from the rolls without the benefit of a court-martial.[25] William was among the first of the provincial officers who ran into disciplinary entanglements in Pensacola. He was not the last.[26]

Defiantly throwing his regimental coat into the sea, alone in a remote outpost of the British empire, former Ensign Bowles, without revealing his innermost fears, looked to the future. Far from home— not knowing for sure where home was—sixteen-year-old William in desperation joined up with a party of Lower Creeks who had come to Pensacola for presents and began a new life with Indians in the interior. Little did he realize it at the time, but from this point on his fate would be wedded to these Indians and to Florida. Here he would spend many of his remaining years, and, because of his involvement here, they would measure far short of the Biblical three score and ten.[27]

It was not unusual for an Englishman to live among the Indians. During the Revolution Pensacola had become a focal point for British trade and authority among most of the southern tribes. Invariably there were natives in town soliciting presents and discussing some new political or economic arrangement with the British; there were old established merchants here and new ones arriving to participate in the Indian trade; more often than not there could be seen the British Superintendent for Indian Affairs; and there were numerous common traders or packhorsemen, usually white, possibly Indian or half-breed, who periodically resorted here for business and pleasure.[28]

To discover details about the rovings of the many white men in the Indian country is difficult. William's movements are as hard to follow as any. He remained among the Indians for several months; then, his curiosity about native customs partly satisfied and not enthusiastic about the skimpy diet at this time of year, he returned to the vicinity of Pensacola where he found an abandoned hogshead, with a makeshift sail fashioned it into a crude boat, and passed the days hunting and fishing about the bay—"the sky his canopy and the earth his bed."[29] In time he reached Pensacola and secured temporary lodging with a baker, but this was a short-lived arrangement because the host expected his guest to work for the bread he so liberally ate. The Creeks once more came to Pensacola and again William, for the same reasons as before, returned with them. In the tradition of Evan Shelby and others at Frederick Town who traded with the Indians and acquired vast landholdings, William expected to recoup his fortunes among the Indians through first living in and becoming the trader for an Indian village, hoping to acquire influence and wealth that could lead to more important ventures.

He went to live among the Lower Creeks on the Chattahoochee River. At first he apparently married a Cherokee girl who, along with many others, had been driven south by the Americans during the Revolution. Soon a son was born, later famous as Chief Bowles of the Western Cherokees, and there may have been other children. It is quite definitely known that when William returned to the Lower Creeks a second time he went to live with Chief Perryman, a mestizo whose village was just above the forks of the Apalachicola River, and soon married his daughter, Mary. It was not unusual for Indians or white traders to have more than one wife if they were affluent enough to afford such a luxury. William would have a son by Mary— "little Billy"—and a daughter by either her or his Cherokee wife. There probably were more children and indeed William may have taken still another wife. But it was always at or near Perryman's that William considered his Indian home to be and Mary, by Indian standards, remained faithful to him for over two decades, through good times and bad.[30]

The Creeks had a typical native marriage ritual: a female relative of the groom consulted with female relations of the prospective bride; the groom next sent a blanket and other gifts to the bride's female relations; if these were accepted then the young warrior built a house, planted and harvested a crop, brought home meat from the hunt, and presented all to the bride. Now the match was made and the girl bound to her husband—at least until a divorce was obtained, which was relatively simple. The youthful, muscular, olive-complexioned Bowles, dressed like any other warrior, must have shared in at least part of this traditional ceremony.[31]

Native customs, languages, and formal rituals interested the inquisitive William, and conceivably he might have remained undisturbed with his Indian family in his cypress-bark-covered house indefinitely. Many other whites had established themselves in an Indian village, and almost all eventually had faded away into obscurity. But suddenly the fortunes of war—the threat of a Spanish attack on West Florida—altered his manner of living. At the onset of Spanish entrance into the war Britain envisioned taking New Orleans. The energetic measures of the Spanish Governor Bernardo de Gálvez dashed this dream. First he seized the British outposts on the lower Mississippi River and then in 1780 sailed into Mobile and forced the garrison to surrender. Gálvez next turned his eyes toward Pensacola, the last and most important British post in West Florida. It was this threat to Pensacola that brought William out of the Indian country and resulted in his eventual reinstatement in the army.[32]

General John Campbell, with 1,300 British, German, and Loyalist troops and with little prospect of reinforcements, was desperate. To bolster defenses, by promising lavish presents he persuaded hundreds of Indians to come to Pensacola's aid. Benjamin James, James Colbert, Alexander McGillivray, the youthful Bowles—by now a warrior anxious to prove his mettle and share in the presents—among other white or half-breed traders, all led Creek, Chickasaw, or Choctaw war parties down to Pensacola.[33]

In order to frustrate the impending Spanish attack, to employ the Indians numbering well over one thousand, and to conserve his supply of rum, Campbell, in the midst of winter, planned a surprise raid on Mobile. The attackers consisted of almost four hundred troops, including a few British and German regulars, though they were mostly Loyalists supported by several hundred Indians, indistinguishable among whom, in his long hunting jacket, was warrior Bowles. They planned to march overland and, in conjunction with two frigates which were to sail into Mobile Bay, hoped to surprise an enemy post on the bay's eastern shore. With luck, Mobile itself might fall next. Crestfallen, William saw Campbell's plan go awry. The 150-man Spanish garrison, though temporarily surprised, rallied and drove off the white and Indian assailants. All the German officers were killed and command fell to Captain Key of the combined Maryland-Pennsylvania Loyalists. Bowles, Key's fellow Marylander and a former ensign, heading a Lower Creek war party, in vain distinguished himself by various acts of bravery and by being one of the last to quit the field of battle. Calmly firing his rifle at point-blank range, William withdrew only after a cannon ball splintered the tree sheltering him. Most of the survivors, both white and red, had already retired, and there was little joy or glory in the 50-mile march back to Pensacola.[34]

Because of his conduct at Mobile Bay and because of the danger of an imminent Spanish descent on Pensacola, Bowles, after a lapse of almost two years, was reinstated in his regiment—still an ensign, though one of the few with scalps to his credit.[35] In spite of misgivings about leaving his Indian family and friends, William, who had not made his fortune among the natives, was pleased to be back in uniform and among fellow Marylanders. He did not completely sever his contact with the Indians, however, because hundreds of them, many of whom he knew well, were still encamped around the town. For the remainder of the winter he and the rest of the garrison were on edge because of frequent rumors of enemy movements, and it was no surprise when in March he saw in the distance the sails of a Franco-Spanish fleet off Santa Rosa Island, guarding the entrance to Pensacola Bay. Gálvez put troops ashore, personally led his warships through the bay's shallow entrance in face of enemy fire, and soon was reinforced from New Orleans and elsewhere. The British, out-numbered, were gradually forced back and besieged in their fixed fortifications—Fort George and its outworks on a hill overlooking the town. There was constant skirmishing and shelling; William's Indian friends regularly returned with Spanish "sculps" while the Spaniards inched closer with their earthworks and erected new batteries.[36]

The Queens Redoubt was at the highest point on the hill overlook-ing the town, too remote to cover the town itself, but close enough, if in enemy hands, to dominate Fort George. Bowles's company was posted here, and it was against this vital point that the Spaniards directed their attack. William could look out and see hundreds of heavily guarded Spanish soldiers relentlessly dig entrenchments and mount batteries ever closer to the English fortifications. General Campbell decided on a sally to delay them and chose the provincials for the job. On the day selected for the assault British batteries com-menced a heavier-than-usual shelling; the Spaniards, protected by their trenches, were not unduly alarmed; they stacked arms and began eating their meal. Then as the British cannon fired more rapidly—but without shells—almost a hundred Loyalists rushed the Spanish trenches, caught many of the enemy unprepared, and William and the other attackers swiftly went about their grisly work, usually with the bayonet, killing nineteen Spaniards and wounding as many more before retiring.

But this sortie did not seriously hamper Spanish progress. William took cover when the shelling commenced routinely on May 8 as it had for the past several weeks. Suddenly at about nine in the morning an enemy shell entered the door of the powder magazine in the Queens Redoubt. "We saw a great column of smoke rising toward the clouds," and forty seamen from British ships in the harbor and forty-five men from the Pennsylvania and Maryland Loyalists, their bodies mutilated, were blown into the air.[37] The space of a few yards saved Ensign Bowles from being obliterated. Dazed and shaken, he had no time to ponder the horror of seeing almost one hundred of his comrades blown to bits, because the Spaniards, at first as surprised as the British, took advantage of the confusion, stormed into the flaming redoubt, and soon had guns in position to batter Fort George.

It was no surprise to the survivors who hastily retreated to Fort

George that General Campbell decided to surrender. The Maryland Loyalists, now shrunk to one-third of their original strength
through casualties, desertion, and previous capture,[38] were part of
the downcast army that on the following day filed out of Fort George,
drums beating and colors flying; then the colors and arms, except
for the officers' swords, were surrendered to the assembled Spaniards.
When William resigned his commission two years before he had wondered how he would ever get home. Now he knew; surprisingly
enough, the Spaniards would send him.

The British prisoners were treated humanely and chivalrously by
their captors. As provided in the surrender terms, the British garrison
was paroled with the stipulation that it not serve against Spain's
allies. First the prisoners would be sent to Havana and then on to
New York. The Spaniards at Havana, who almost twenty years ago
had seen the British banner waving over their city, were elated at
Gálvez's new triumph and eagerly watched the transports returning
with the victorious troops and enemy prisoners. Ensign Bowles, aboard
one of these transports, watched as his vessel sailed through the harbor's narrow entrance, guarded by the cannon from Fort Morro.
There was no particular reason for him to regard this fortress with
any more than usual curiosity. That he would spend his last days
wasting away in one of its gloomy cells never occurred to him.

The Spaniards in Havana were even more lenient toward their
prisoners than they had been at Pensacola, and one young Spanish
officer, Francisco de Miranda, was very nearly court-martialed for
allegedly parading General Campbell about the city's defenses.[39]
Though in some ways Havana with its thick walls, narrow streets,
and ancient shops was more pleasant than Pensacola, William did not
tarry here long. At the end of June the prisoners re-embarked on
transports and by mid-July once again he could see New York's familiar steeples, fortifications, and ships crowding the wharves. Three
years ago William had left New York an inexperienced, disillusioned
youth. Though still somewhat disillusioned, even at eighteen he was a
seasoned soldier and had profited and matured by his two-year sojourn among the Indians. A boy had left New York; a man returned.

The Maryland Loyalists, weakened by tropical sickness, were billeted at nearby New Town on Long Island. Since technically the
United States was not an ally of Spain, a literal interpretation of the
capitulation terms with Gálvez permitted the former British prisoners
to serve against the Americans.[40] Soon William was back at his old
task of obtaining or impressing food and wood. There were more
Loyalist soldiers and civilians concentrated here than anywhere, and

supplies were harder to come by than ever. In spite of forced attempts at gaiety—balls, plays, excursions, horseraces, cricket matches, and visits to the numerous taverns—an air of despondency began settling over the city. In the fall after William's return the impossible happened. Cornwallis surrendered! Though Ensign Bowles was part of a large, experienced army based at New York, it soon became obvious that Yorktown, following disasters at Pensacola and elsewhere, spelled independence for the United States.

William went about his routine duties on Long Island and in the lower Hudson Valley without enthusiasm as month by month the ranks of his regiment thinned.[41] As in Philadelphia, the British officers organized theatrical groups for a diversion and to benefit orphans and widows; a call was out for officers with histrionic talent, and William volunteered enthusiastically. The theatrical repertoire was commendable. The new season, beginning in January after Bowles's arrival and lasting until early summer, saw approximately four different plays by Shakespeare or more contemporary works by Richard Sheridan or George Farquhar appear monthly.[42] William, only a year before indistinguishable from an Indian, now appeared in Moorish costume as Zanga in Edward Young's *Revenge,* after having painted many of the scenes himself. Zanga, defeated in battle by the Spaniards and brought to Spain, even though befriended by his captor, was determined to revenge himself on those who brought destruction to his family and nation. This was his passion. As the lights dimmed and the audience hushed, William strode across the stage and began to unfold his hatred for all Spaniards and his resolve to seek vengeance. Apprehensive over his first role, little did he suspect that the drama being enacted at the John Street Theater was an omen of his future. His costume would change from Moorish to Indian; the enemy would be the same.[43] There is an excellent chance he painted scenes for other plays and acted other parts—that ensigns frequently were called on for female roles may partially explain the lack of details about his theatrical career. With Bowles and other officers so engrossed in the theater, one wonders why Washington tarried so long before entering New York.

Attending the theater either as a performer or spectator, attentively scanning the papers to ascertain the current status of diplomatic negotiations, and fulfilling routine military duties including sitting on courts-martial occupied most of the two years in New York. One of the frequent courts-martial was of more than casual interest—it was his own. Provincial officers prepared over twenty charges against him for conduct unbecoming to an officer; the only ones about which there are any details are that he had dressed like an Indian at Pensacola and had taken scalps. Fortunately, fellow Maryland officers rallied to his defense and the charges were dismissed.[44] Because of the animosity surrounding this court-martial or a related dispute, the hot-tempered William fought a duel.[45]

Though from time to time encouraging news reached the crowded city—that Admiral Rodney had won a decisive victory in the West Indies or that Gibraltar was being successfully defended—nothing altered the fact that Britain had made a preliminary peace with the United States and soon would give up New York. In view of the partisan feelings, William readily concurred with the other military and civilian Loyalists that they would soon have to leave.

II

Return to the Chattahoochee

AS HE wandered about the city's crowded streets or glanced over his shoulder when returning to his regiment billeted on Long Island, William was acutely conscious of the confusion and apprehension that reigned in New York in 1783. Never had he seen so many Loyalist soldiers and civilians—estimates ran from thirty to fifty thousand. This influx of Loyalists, superimposed on a city that had a pre-war population of a bare twenty thousand and that had been ravaged by two major wartime fires, created chaos by sheer numbers. All available churches, warehouses, and private dwellings were overcrowded with soldiers, refugees, American prisoners, and military stores. To make matters worse, the Americans controlled even more of the adjacent countryside, making food scarcer and prices higher. Then in March, 1783, came news from Paris of the definitive treaty of peace and the realization that almost all of the thousands of Loyalists, soldiers and civilians alike, would have to depart immediately. Never in the city's history had so many ships of all descriptions crowded into the harbor and along the waterfront's wharves; from no other American city during the Revolution would there be such a mass migration.[1]

The Maryland Loyalists on Long Island escaped little of the confusion and none of the anxiety raging in the city. Though most of the officers remained, William was not at all surprised as the ranks of the enlisted men dwindled rapidly. The crucial question confronting him and the other Loyalists was: where should they go? Or better, where could they go? To remain in New York with the American army on the verge of pouring into the city, accompanied or preceded by thousands of exiled New Yorkers, was not an attractive prospect. Few Loyalists elected to remain.

There were several possible places to go. One was to their native states, but, because of wartime passions, Washington's proclamation decreeing that Loyalists who had borne arms in the Revolution could not return home without their states' approval was almost superfluous.[2] Ruling out remaining in New York or returning home, the best alternative was to start life anew elsewhere in the British Empire—the mother country in Europe, Canada, the West Indies, or Mosquito Shore in the New World. Most Loyalists did not return to Britain; instead they pressed Whitehall to reimburse them for at least part of their losses and to provide them new lands in the remainder of Britain's American empire. Most went to Canada, either to New Brunswick or Nova Scotia on the Bay of Fundy, though a few at first and many more later made their ways to the Canadian frontier, the future province of Ontario.

The Maryland Loyalists were in the mainstream that went to New Brunswick. In the fall of 1783, after thousands had already departed but before the final evacuation, they boarded the *Martha,* part of the fall fleet bound for the Bay of Fundy. Many of the Loyalists in the convoy had formerly been in easy circumstances; the prospect of hewing a new existence out of the Canadian forest was not appealing. For the Maryland Loyalists aboard the *Martha* this was the least of their worries. The ship struck a reef in the Bay of Fundy and sank. Everyone abandoned ship, the captain and crew in the vanguard, and when all the survivors were counted it was discovered that 99 out of 174 were lost. It was scant consolation when Captain Patrick Kennedy, Bowles's company commander, one of the survivors, lodged a complaint against the ship's captain for negligence and cowardice. Fortunately, Ensign Bowles had remained in New York.[3] Unlike at least seventy-two Maryland Loyalists, his name did not rank among the founders of St. John.[4]

Only William could divulge why, in contrast to most New York Loyalists, he went to the Bahamas rather than to New Brunswick. Many factors influenced his decision. There was Dennis Ryan's theatrical company with which he had worked during the past months and which was now breaking up. Both army and naval officers and Ryan's professional group had outdone themselves in the variety and frequency of their productions almost up to the final evacuation. At least some of the professionals were bound for Nassau and it might be exciting to tag along.[5] William gave no thought to boarding with and living off a baker as he had done in Pensacola, but if circumstances forced him temporarily to become a painter, a more honorable profession and one better suited to his taste, he would have more chance for success in Nassau than in St. John, where it was difficult to hang a portrait on a tent wall. Most important of all there was William's army career, which had led him to the West Indies, Pensacola, and the Creek Indians. Starting out anew in the Bahamas, close by the West Indies and Florida, perhaps in some way he might pick up the threads of his earlier life. If the rumors that Britain was going to exchange Gibraltar for the Floridas were true, there was even more reason for heading south. William, of course, had an Indian family, and he had many memories of the months spent at Chief Perryman's village on the Chattahoochee, of his wife Mary, the chief's daughter, of his other Cherokee wife, and of his children. Perhaps it was one of these forces that drew William toward the Bahamas; probably they all did.

The Bahama Islands, stretching southeasterly some five hundred miles off the Florida coast, had been sighted by Columbus on his first voyage. But Columbus had by-passed these islands for greener pastures, and this later became the usual practice of Europeans. In the seventeenth century the Bahamas were linked with piracy; in the eighteenth century, after Britain had curbed her buccaneers, the Bahamas' small population depended on the sea for a livelihood— fishing, turtling, and salvaging wrecks. The Bahamas, or rather New Providence Island, the most important island with the best harbor, changed hands twice during the Revolution. Spain, in the wake of her West Florida victories, added Nassau, New Providence's capital, to her list of conquests in 1782. Then, just as the Revolution was coming to an end, Loyalist Carolinians recaptured Nassau for Britain, making the Bahamas available to accommodate at least some of the exiled Loyalists.[6]

Nassau was the best port in all the Bahamas, with a protected harbor guarded by two small forts; yet William in his wildest imagination could not compare Nassau with Philadelphia or New York. There was but one "tolerably regular" street adjacent to the harbor, and few of the town's houses, except that of the governor, were of any substance.[7] The entire population of all the islands at the end of the Revolution was probably no more than four thousand.[8]

It was at the period of William's arrival that there was an abrupt change in the character of the Bahamas: the population overnight nearly tripled; cotton plantations worked by Negro slaves appeared on New Providence and the Out Islands; and because of the loss of the mainland colonies, Nassau ranked higher among Britain's list of American ports. Most of the Loyalists, about seven thousand, came from Florida. There were only about fourteen hundred in the group coming from New York with Bowles.[9] Shortly after the arrival of these thousands of Loyalists the islands were split into factions—the Old and the New Settlers. The Old Settlers, or Conchs, greatly outnumbered by the Loyalists, still controlled the government, and laws were oriented to the fishing and salvaging interests. The New Settlers, many of whom were slaveowners, were concerned with establishing cotton plantations or, in the case of former Georgia and Carolina merchants, wanted to make Nassau do for Charleston or Savannah. They were accustomed to having a powerful voice in colonial legislatures and were resentful that the Conchs did not appreciate this fact. But there were many political disputes in the islands, and Bahamian parties, like those in eighteenth-century Britain, could not be divided neatly on any single issue. The ensuing struggles between Old and New Settlers frequently were as involved as those confronting Prime Minister Pitt in London.[10]

At first William was lost among the influx of thousands of Loyalists. He, along with the other provincial officers, was put on half pay (the customary pension allowed inactive or retired regular officers) and was granted six months' provisions and 500 acres on Eleuthera Island. There is no indication that he ever became, or considered becoming, a farmer. He had no slaves; the soil could not compare with that on the mainland; and worst of all he was almost isolated on Eleuthera. There was much bustle and coming and going in Nassau immediately after the Revolution. About half of the Loyalists were little more than transients and soon departed. Others, like William, remained but were restless and unable to settle down. Occasionally there are glimpses of him during his early Nassau years, wandering about town with fellow uprooted Maryland Loyalists, renewing merchant acquaintances among Loyalists from West Florida, occasionally acting in plays for the benefit of distressed Loyalists, or painting a few portraits. Never does he appear as a planter or as a person of any political prominence.[11]

All the Loyalists had come from the mainland and invariably they looked back on the continent, usually with nostalgia tempered with bitterness, sometimes with hopes of returning. In time some of the Loyalists could expect to return to their native states, or at least to another one. If this was not possible or desirable then there was the West—that vast region beyond the Appalachian Mountains stretching to the Mississippi River and on into Spanish Louisiana whose lands were immensely fertile, but which was inhabited and controlled primarily by Indians. Many Bahamian Loyalists had an avid interest in and great knowledge of this region. Some had been merchants at Charleston, Savannah, St. Augustine, Pensacola, and Mobile and were aware of the intricacies and lucrativeness of the fur trade. Fur trading frequently went hand-in-hand with the venerable colonial mania for land speculation. Less wealthy Loyalists in the past had gone to the frontier to acquire a small farm and were ready, if possible, to duplicate the process. This American frontier flowed in William's veins: there were boyhood recollections of Indians and traders in Frederick Town and recent memories of a life among the Creeks.

The Treaty of Paris awarded the West to the United States from the mountains to the Mississippi and from the Great Lakes to the thirty-first parallel. Theoretical United States sovereignty over the West was one thing; actual practice was another. The British in the north continued to occupy posts on American soil and to trade with and influence most of the Indian tribes north of the Ohio River. In the south the Spaniards claimed land north of the thirty-first parallel at least up to the mouth of the Yazoo River, possibly as far north as the Tennessee River. A majority of the Indian tribes, who in 1783, at least for the time being, controlled most of the West, considered themselves independent. Western sovereignty was far more complicated than indicated in the 1783 peace treaty.

Foreigners frequently assumed after the Revolution, as did more than a few Americans, that the United States would soon break up. One logical line of division would be the Appalachian Mountains. This notion was in the minds of some exiled Loyalists who had fled to either the Bahamas or to Canada. Their dream was in re-establishing British influence in the West by securing a protectorate over part or all of the western Indians, by co-operating with dissatisfied American frontiersmen in setting up an independent western state, or by acquiring Spanish Florida through negotiation or force. Britain, should she control New Orleans and the West Florida Gulf ports, would be able to dominate commerce in the entire Mississippi Valley. These vistas, sometimes cloudy, sometimes burning brightly, were in the eyes of New Providence Loyalists, including William Bowles. His future career would be molded by developments in the American West complicated by partisan politics which for years tore Nassau asunder.[12]

In the several years after the Revolution William could either be found in New Providence or on the mainland. There is a better than even chance that he briefly returned to his family in Maryland,[13] and there is no doubt that he spent much time among the Indians and in the settled parts of Georgia. Unlike most Bahamian Loyalists, he was not personally identified with the intense wartime passions of the southern states, nor was he well known here. He must have visited those new settlements on either side of the St. Marys River—strongly

Loyalist in sentiment—and he continued painting an occasional portrait here or in Savannah,[14] though a search for new customers could hardly have been the main reason for coming to this state. Georgia land was preferable to that in the Bahamas, and this wielded more influence in luring him to the mainland, as it did at least one fellow ensign, John Barclay, of the Maryland Loyalists.[15]

There is a fleeting picture of Bowles in Augusta, standing in the capitol intent on the work of the legislators. As he later said, the Creeks had sent him as a spy to ferret out hostile Georgian designs. Since William was in and out of the Indian country this is probably true as far as it goes.[16] Without doubt the Georgia legislature was debating legislation that would affect not only the Creeks but all of the southern Indians. Even though Georgia was under pressure to cede her western lands to the central government, she had not yet done so and therefore had claim to territory stretching to the Mississippi. Spain also claimed most of this region, and in the near future apparently the United States would take over Georgia's claim. For the time being, however, and no one was sure how long this would be, Georgia had a title to extensive western lands, largely vacant except for Indians. Long before the Revolution speculators had eyed these lands, and attention now was focused on Muscle Shoals on the Tennessee River and strategic spots on the Mississippi. Claiming these areas in 1784, Georgia established a county government for the territory around Muscle Shoals and in 1785 carved out Bourbon County, centering on Natchez on the Mississippi. Four years later the legislature lavishly granted the South Carolina Yazoo Company, the Virginia Yazoo Company, and the Tennessee Company some twenty-five million acres, or much of Georgia's western lands. The discussions of the Georgia legislature held forth the prospect of acquiring valuable land and important Indian trading concessions; Bowles, listening intently, must have wondered if somewhere there were not a place for him and other adventurous Loyalists.[17]

There is no reason to doubt William's assertion that he was spying on the Georgia legislature in behalf of the Creeks. Part, and perhaps most, of the time spent in Georgia was in the Creek country—by Georgia reckoning most of the Creek country was Georgia. At some point, either in New York or after becoming dissatisfied with Nassau conditions, William resolved to return to his Indian friends and family and to seek his fortune among the Lower Creeks. Apparently he first returned to Perryman's village on the Chattahoochee in the spring of 1785, and from this time on he was as likely as not to be garbed as an Indian. Frequently he wore a knee-length hunting jacket and buckskin leggings, but on formal occasions, since after his return he was made a chief, he donned his cloth turban with an ostrich feather plume, a half-moon silver gorget hanging from his neck, and a white man's shirt and breeches. At his side was a ceremonial silver pipe tomahawk signifying he was a war chief.

After the Revolution, disastrous for the Iroquois Six Nations to the north, the Creeks were the largest and best-organized Indians east of the Mississippi. There were numerous villages in the confederacy: some twenty-five around the forks of the Alabama River composed the Upper Towns, and approximately twelve stretched out along the Chattahoocheee River formed the Lower Towns. Further downstream on the Apalachicola River and on the Florida peninsula there were seven Seminole towns. The Seminoles were a closely related offshoot of the Creeks, and at least some of the towns were almost indistinguishable from the Lower Creeks. The Upper and Lower Creeks (and Seminoles), numbering some fifteen to eighteen thousand, were bound together in a loose confederation and periodically met together in grand councils to decide high policy. The confederation always had been a loose one, and none of the numerous chiefs or any group could dictate policy to all the towns. The chief Creek spokesman after the Revolution, Alexander McGillivray, quadroon son of a wealthy Loyalist Indian trader, lived among the Upper Creeks and, like all the confederacy, was alarmed by the designs conceived in Georgia, the Carolinas, Virginia, and the State of Franklin. If all, or any of these undertakings were executed, then the Creeks and other southern Indians would be worse off than the Six Nations.[18]

The southern Indians lived partly by agriculture and partly by hunting; profits from the latter allowed them to buy guns, ammunition, clothing, iron pots, and the like from the whites. These Indians might not starve should they lose their hunting lands but would have to alter drastically their mode of life. This they were unwilling to do; therefore, there was constant hostility on the Georgia and Tennessee frontiers. The Creeks were under no illusion that they were dependent on the whites for indispensable guns and powder, but in general they tried to limit white contacts to commerce. After the Revolution there was the pressing question of which whites would furnish the necessary manufactures. The Americans would have liked to do this, but their land hunger and inability to meet all Indian manufactured needs ruled them out. The Spaniards supplied the solution. It was not their objective nor within their power to colonize the Creek territory, and they were largely content to remain around Pensacola, Mobile, St. Marks, St. Augustine, and other Florida posts and to conduct

the Indian trade from these centers. But Spain herself was not able
to furnish manufactured goods for the Indian trade and first turned
to her Bourbon ally, France,[19] and then reluctantly to her former
enemy, Britain, for assistance. If the Indians were not satisfied with
arrangements worked out by Spain after she took over Florida, then
they would have to look elsewhere. This is what worried her and is
why soon after the Revolution she awarded the southern Indian trade
to Panton, Leslie, and Company. Formerly of Charleston and Savannah, the Company had been forced to relocate in East Florida and
Nassau because of the Revolution.[20] It was the bullets and scalping
knives provided by this firm under Spanish aegis that wreaked havoc
on the American frontiers bordering the Tennessee, Cumberland,
Oconee, and St. Marys rivers.

More closely knit after the Revolution in the face of increasing
American expansion, the Creek Confederacy, supplied by Panton and
led by McGillivray, more often than not held its own against the
advancing Americans. No theoretical scheme mapped out in Savannah
or Nashville could alter the fact that, at least for the time being, the
adjacent western lands were dominated by the Creeks who could
count on at least part of the Cherokees as allies. Early in 1788 there
was a crisis in the Creek country, and for the first time in almost four
years Bowles emerges from history's shadows.

The crisis was caused by Spain's severely curtailing presents to the
Indians, and the Creeks, pressed on several fronts by the Americans,
were desperate. Possibly, from the standpoint of over-all Spanish
diplomacy, cutting down the Indian's store of arms and munitions
was a statesmanlike move. The Spaniards, no less than the Indians,
were obsessed by the fact that Americans were pouring into the West.
One way of holding them back would be to rely on the Indians;
another way would be to co-operate and intrigue with the frontiersmen and encourage them to separate from the East and to throw
themselves into Spanish arms. The latter was now what Spain was
trying to do. By curbing Indian hostilities and holding out promise of
free navigation of the Mississippi River, she was tempting James
Wilkinson and other frontier leaders in Kentucky and Tennessee to
separate from the East and ally themselves with Spain. Whatever
the advantages to Spain or the frontiersmen, it was apparent immediately to the Indians that this policy spelled disaster for them.[21]

Having wandered in and out of the Creek country over the last
several years, William was aware of the Indian dilemma and had a
solution: he and his merchant associates in Nassau, independent of
Panton and Spain, would furnish a plentiful supply of goods to the

Indians. The Indians would have their munitions, and Bowles and his patrons would take their profits from the fur trade. If this initial arrangement succeeded, then schemes involving even larger portions of the West might be put to the test. To make extensive commercial overtures to the Indians William needed influential backers—and he had them. One was John Miller, a merchant who had been at Pensacola and Mobile since 1770, who had 2,200 acres on the Tensaw River, and who subsequently moved to Nassau after the fall of Pensacola. There is an excellent possibility that William first met Miller after resigning his commission, since they were both at Pensacola at approximately the same time, and William might well have been employed by this merchant. Misfortune followed Miller to Nassau. The Spaniards soon captured it and sent him off to Havana as prisoner. In time he was freed, came into a valuable inheritance, and returned to the Bahamas as a merchant and a member of the governor's council. It was Miller, through the partnership of Miller, Bonnamy, and Company, who now financially backed Bowles and who hoped to regain a part of the southern Indian trade, a trade heretofore blocked by Panton's monopoly.[22]

Miller's friend and fellow Loyalist was also one of William's supporters. That he was the new Bahamian governor added prestige and significance to Bowles's mainland activities. John Murray, Earl of Dunmore, was an experienced hand in the New World; he had been colonial governor first of New York and then of Virginia until the Revolution cut short his career. During the early stages of the war he enlisted and personally led Loyalists in behalf of the Crown. Dunmore knew the colonies, now the independent United States, at first hand. He was at home with eastern merchants and Tidewater planters and was well versed in frontier conditions both through leading campaigns against the Indians and even better through speculating in western lands. Duly installed at Nassau and inevitably involved in matters primarily West Indian in origin, Dunmore never forgot the West nor lost his passion for speculating in land and the fur trade.[23]

Contemporaries wondered why Lord Dunmore would accept so insignificant a post as the Bahamian governorship and suspected that in some fashion he expected to line his pockets. These suppositions were right on the mark. He did not leave London until Parliament made Nassau a free port: European colonies in America could ship colonial produce here in exchange for British manufactured goods. This was primarily an inducement for Spanish colonies, especially Cuba, to trade illegally (in Spanish eyes) with Nassau.[24] Should a lively trade develop, then Dunmore could expect, legally or not, to see filled the purses of British merchants as well as his own. Florida, whatever its boundaries, was part of Spanish America and afforded opportunities for trade. But Dunmore, like his friend Dr. John Connolly at Detroit, when looking at any part of the West could not avoid sweeping his eyes over the entire Mississippi Valley.[25]

The *Mercury,* with both Miller and Dunmore aboard, in the fall of 1787 docked at Gardner's wharf in Nassau. There were salvos from the fort, formal receptions, and fireworks lasting far into the night; and there was a sense of relief that Dunmore, a former Loyalist himself, would side with the more numerous New Settlers.[26] For reasons that are not clear, except that it was not in his economic interest to do so, Dunmore soon dashed this hope. He refused to dissolve the assembly still dominated by the Old Settlers; he flirted with ameliorating the conditions of slavery or even abolishing this institution, an institution dear to the hearts of many new cotton planters; and he instituted legal proceedings which bore heavily on some of the new merchants. In short, the latent quarrel between the Old and New Settlers was reopened in full fury, with Dunmore, Miller, and Bowles as a junior partner (oddly enough all Loyalists) pitted on the side of the Old Settlers.[27]

Immediately after Dunmore's arrival he was informed of the crisis among the southern Indians, and he and Miller, with the voluble Bowles as their instrument, determined to turn events to their own advantage. If they were successful then Spain would lose influence over the southern Indians, and obviously Panton's monopoly would suffer. But since William Panton and his associate Thomas Forbes were outspoken leaders of the New Settler faction in Nassau, any damage they suffered was all to the good. The vitriolic New Providence conflict between the Governor and his political enemies would be extended to the Florida mainland.[28]

Dunmore, Miller, and Bowles were concerned with the Indian crisis, but it was the natives themselves who were most affected. They had to have arms immediately. Spain had sharply curtailed the supply, and if Bowles could furnish quantities of ball and powder, then without question he would be welcome in the nation. With McGillivray, chief spokesman for the Creeks, thus distressed, it seemed a simple matter to confer with him and work out the details of the new arrangement. That he was Panton's friend and silent partner should not deter his co-operation. This is what Miller and Dunmore had in mind when they sent Bowles over to Florida, laden with munitions, a gold-laced suit of regimentals, and a 25-pound sterling silver sword to woo McGillivray.[29]

It was not unusual or difficult to go from the Bahamas to Florida's uninhabited coasts; Bahamian fishermen had been doing it for generations. William sailed in a 14-gun vessel from Nassau to Indian River, halfway down the Florida peninsula and one of the areas frequented by Bahamian fishermen. From here he made his way westward to the Chattahoochee River until he ultimately reached Perryman's village. Perryman, the aged Philatouchy, and other leading Lower Creek chiefs conferred with him and encouraged him in his commercial venture. Presumably Mary, her son, and whatever other children there might have been were happy to have the white warrior back in their household even for a short visit. Bidding his family good-bye and accompanied by a few native and white supporters, William paddled in a pirogue up to Coweta, the principal town of the Lower Creeks.

The Lower Creeks were in council, alarmed by the threat of Georgia expansion. McGillivray with an Upper Creek delegation was here, and Bowles, with his followers and a sampling of goods, arrived. Bowles and McGillivray had met before. The first time was at Pensacola where both had led war parties of Lower and Upper Creeks respectively to aid the British and where they had encamped for months awaiting the Spanish attack. Their acquaintance was more than a passing one. They must have crossed paths in the Indian country after the war. Now there was time to reminisce, to drink black drink in the village square, and to go through other rituals. These two had much in common: both were Loyalists who had suffered because of the Revolution and who had little use for the Americans; both had served under the British and had fought against the Spaniards at Pensacola; both were young—Bowles was twenty-five and McGillivray twenty-nine; both claimed to be the foremost leader of the Creeks or even all the southern Indians; neither was a full-blooded Indian—Bowles was entirely white and McGillivray three-quarters so; both had the dream of uniting the southern Indians with those in the north to form a general confederation to stop the relentless American advance.

Despite the similarities, these two differed in important respects. Though both claimed to represent all the Creeks, in fact McGillivray drew his main support from the Upper Creeks whereas most of Bowles's followers came from the Lower Creeks and Seminoles. Bowles was a warrior who had proved himself in battle, but McGillivray, who owned a large plantation worked by many slaves at Little Tallassie (near present-day Montgomery) and who readily admitted he had hidden in the bushes while other Indians engaged a small band of Americans, was a statesman and an administrator who had no qualms about sending out war parties but was no fighter himself. McGillivray's health was never robust, and he suffered from a variety of ailments; Bowles was in perfect health. Most important of all was that McGillivray, in fact, was the chief spokesman for most of the Creeks. He had effectively used his membership in the influential Wind Clan, his position as one of the British Indian superintendents at the end of the Revolution, his post-war relationship with Panton, Leslie, and Company and Spain, and his ability under both Britain and Spain to play a key role in providing manufactured goods to the Indians, to make himself the most important Creek leader.[30] Though it was not apparent now, Bowles at heart was McGillivray's rival; by gaining control of the Indian trade he expected to supplant McGillivray. But for the time being each had something the other needed— McGillivray had great influence among the Indians and Bowles offered a dependable supply of goods—and they got along well enough. The real business of the council was to determine exactly what goods Bowles could furnish and whether the Indians, ignoring the threats of Spain, Panton, and the United States, would accept them. To answer this question took little debate, and soon Bowles, entirely satisfied with the decisions reached at the council, was off to Nassau for a much larger supply of goods while the Indians began to assemble packhorses to receive them.[31]

Spanish officials began having second thoughts about the wisdom of curtailing Indian arms. McGillivray's belatedly informing them that a "Strange man" recently had appeared among the Indians bearing gifts from an unknown charitable society and his subsequent threat to look elsewhere than Spain for arms did little to reassure the Spaniards.[32] For the time being the Indians actually controlled most of Florida and the American Southeast. Perhaps calling off Indian raids and intriguing with frontiersmen might bring long-term benefits. But now the Indians were alienated and Spanish influence in Florida might not extend beyond the walls of St. Augustine, Pensacola, and St. Marks. It was this that worried the Spaniards.

Meanwhile, William, accompanied by Creek traders, the half-breed Randall brothers, and formally dressed as a chief, was back in Nassau, dining and riding horseback with Dunmore and Miller, arranging details of the new expedition. Miller, Bonnamy, and Company provided two vessels and freighted them with arms, powder, and provisions. Allegedly Dunmore cracked the door to Ft. Nassau's arsenal in order to help with arms. Miller subsidized the opening of a "rendezvous house" in Nassau where William provided free meals and drink to potential recruits and urged them to enlist on a semi-secret though profitable expedition. He was not swamped with volunteers, but enough restless souls were found in Nassau or jumped ship from the nearby *Sherborne Castle*—for good measure Dunmore opened the prison—to bring the total to almost fifty. William promised these adventurers 300 acres and horses on the mainland and a salary of eight dollars a month or a share of the booty.[33] Whether Georgia, Spain, or Panton would provide the booty was never spelled out, though it could easily be a combination of the three. Though the expedition was clouded with secrecy, William stated or intimated that he and the other leaders had commissions from the British government, that Dunmore gave his unofficial blessings, and that the enterprise met with McGillivray's approval. Only the latter two assertions were correct.

By stealth the vessels slipped out of the harbor one evening and dropped down to Ruth's Key where William and a few others came aboard and completed the loading. Then the entire expedition sailed over to the nearby Berry Islands where last-minute plans were made. Colonel Bowles, whose dress now was partly Indian and partly that of a British officer, saw that each man had a musket and bayonet and drilled them regularly. If it had not been obvious before it was now that this was not only a mercantile but also a military expedition. Bowles, commissioning himself colonel, was the leader; George Wellbank, Thomas Dalton, and Henry Ray were captains; Robert Milligan and William Hooper were lieutenants; Joseph Robbins headed the cavalry; John Richmond, Bonnamy's clerk, was storekeeper; and Benjamin and William Allen were interpreters. After a short stay at the Berry Islands everyone boarded the vessels, Bowles and Bonnamy aboard the larger, and after four days arrived at Indian River.[34]

Here the stores were unloaded and William continued drilling his men, all the while assuring them that McGillivray had empowered him to wage war on the Georgians.[35] The half-breed Georgia Loyalist, John Galphin, a leader among the Lower Creeks who had been at the council with Bowles and McGillivray, arrived as pre-arranged with over one hundred packhorses, and Bowles rewarded him by making him second in command with a major's commission. Galphin supervised loading the stores aboard the packhorses and departed with them for the Creeks, while William with half of his men aboard ship and half marching, made his way inland.[36] But after this initial cooperation and success things began to go awry. The Indians, not numerous in this part of Florida, were not eager to furnish the expected food and horses for Bowles's force, and this became more and more obvious as they marched further inland, generally in a north-westerly direction, but with uncertainty as to their ultimate destination. Possibly, as most assumed, they would go along with the Indians against the Georgians, or perhaps they would seize one of Panton's warehouses. The latter strategy would transfer the Bahamian controversy to the mainland with a vengeance, and, as time went on, this is what William resolved to do.

Panton had two exposed warehouses, one on the St. Johns River and the other to the west near the small, newly rebuilt Spanish post at St. Marks. The St. Johns store was closer, but reports of nearby Spanish and Georgian patrols deterred Bowles and the Indians. The St. Marks store might be more vulnerable, but it was also more distant. Uncertain whether to go to the vicinity of St. Marks close by his numerous Lower Creek and Seminole friends or to head for the St. Johns, which was closer and where he could sooner relieve his distress at Panton's expense, William changed his mind several times, alternately marching toward St. Marks or the St. Johns River; all the while his men became more disgruntled and hungry. Desertions, which had been a problem from the beginning, now got out of hand, until only a handful of the leaders remained true to Bowles.[37] Most of the deserters, after undergoing great privation, made their way to the St. Johns River where they threw themselves on the mercy of John Hambly, Panton's storekeeper, or the garrison of the small Spanish outpost. Hambly, who recently had feared for his scalp, was elated as the deserters poured in. From the St. Johns they were sent to St. Augustine where the governor imprisoned them in the barracks, interrogated them intensively, learned as much about Bowles's plans as these followers knew, and then sent a few Americans on to the United States and many of the others to Havana or Spain. A few escaped and made their way back to Nassau, which seemed far more attractive to them on their return than it had at their departure.[38]

The loss of most of his followers, even if not an elite group, was a setback, and equally serious was the reversal of Spanish policy. Spain, alarmed by massive Indian defection, once again began giving presents to the Indians regardless of the effect on the frontiersmen. McGillivray, who in desperation had turned to Bowles, along with many of the Creeks was enticed back into Spain's and Panton's arms. This reversal of Spanish policy made Bowles's overtures less attractive, and McGillivray all along may have been using the intruder as a lever to exert pressure on the Spaniards. That McGillivray, the most influential

Creek leader, was again allied with Spain and Panton was another reverse for William.[39]

But all was not lost. McGillivray was the chief but not the only Creek spokesman. Bowles, who had a hard-core following among the Lower Creeks and Seminoles on the Apalachicola, Chattahoochee, and Flint rivers, in time could hope to become McGillivray's successor. McGillivray was closely linked to Panton, and Panton to the Spaniards. At any future time Spain again might capriciously cut off supplies. Or even when presents were distributed as usual and trade carried on normally, Panton's prices for skins were never as high or Spain's presents as ample as under British rule. It was to this period, and especially to the Revolution when Britain had lavishly entertained and furnished the Indians with goods in order to induce them to fight for King George, that they looked. Bowles, a half-pay British officer posing vaguely as a British official and holding forth the prospect of a direct trade to Nassau by-passing Spanish duties, could promise the Indians a return to the good days of the past. All they had to do was follow him; he, Miller, Dunmore, and Bonnamy would do the rest.[40]

Panton, partly through necessity and partly through sharp business acumen, did charge the Indians higher prices for his merchandise. As he told the Spaniards early in 1788, it had cost him 25,000 pounds to win Indian confidence and he had not yet recouped his investment.[41] And Spain was both unable and unwilling to furnish presents as extensively as Britain. High prices and skimpy presents were Indian grievances that would last as long as Spain retained Florida. The Indian clamor for cheaper and more plentiful goods, exploited by Bowles, was widespread. Even McGillivray, heading a Creek delegation at Rock Landing in the early fall of 1789, demanded that the United States establish two free ports south of the Altahama River for the Indian trade. This would permit Panton to by-pass Spanish duties and, more important to Bowles and Miller, would give them a legal opening to compete with Panton. Negotiations failed completely at Rock Landing, and it was charged that McGillivray's "unreasonable demands" for free ports caused the breakdown. More significant for the conference's failure were American designs on Creek lands and insistence that the Indians make no treaties except with the United States.[42]

Relying on Creek discontent and the looseness of the confederacy, William hoped to emerge as an important Creek leader. Who could tell what might follow? Neither Bowles, Miller, nor Dunmore could

get it out of his mind that now the United States was weak, that
Britain traded with and controlled most of the Indians north of the
Ohio, and that, relying on western Indians and dissatisfied frontiersmen, Britain might carve a sphere of influence out of the entire Mississippi Valley and Florida. If Bowles, Miller, and Dunmore and their
counterparts in the Canadian Indian department had their way, this
is exactly what would happen.

Disappointed at the failure of his 1788 expedition but not despondent, William returned to Nassau before the end of the year to lay
plans for another, less ambitious expedition. Short-term profits from
the skin trade and the possibility of larger gains in the future was
why Miller, with Dunmore's approval, still footed the bill. By January,
1789, Bowles, Richmond, and a few other whites were back in Florida
at Perryman's village on the Chattahoochee. Here, at the heart of
Lower Creek-Seminole power, where William had lived during and
after the Revolution and where he had influential family connections,
was a logical place to begin undermining Panton's monopoly and
McGillivray's influence. McGillivray came down from the Upper
Creek villages to confer with Bowles and, as he told Leslie and the
Spaniards, could not shed the blood of his former comrade in arms
but would talk to him, take his goods, and send him on his way. Briefly
in 1788 Bowles and McGillivray had co-operated; now they were
drifting apart and future events would only widen the rift.[43]

Bowles did not heed McGillivray's "wholsom advice" and spent the
rest of the winter and spring among the Indians, usually staying at
Perryman's village and living with Mary and his Indian family.[44] He,
Richmond, and Wellbank spent their time awaiting vessels from Nassau and promoting their interest among the Creeks and any other
southern Indians. At the same time the testy New Providence dispute
was still running its course. Panton and his associate Forbes continued
to denounce Dunmore and printed articles and testimonials in John
Wells's *Bahama Gazette,* charging that not only Miller but also Dunmore was behind Bowles.[45] They also unsuccessfully tried to get a
grand jury to try anyone connected with Bowles's illegal expedition.[46]
In turn William and his associates published accounts in the rival
Lucayan Herald and Weekly Advertiser, completely exonerating Dunmore and going on to denounce Panton and the rest of the New
Settlers in terms that by now were monotonous.[47]

William, who had spent almost a decade among the Creeks, easily
could have remained among the Indians and history would care no
more about him than various contemporaries who claimed to be
leaders of the Lower Creeks or the entire confederacy. But while

Bowles was on the Chattahoochee and Apalachicola rivers during the winter and spring of 1789, unknown to him, an apparently minor drama was being enacted thousands of miles away at Nootka Sound on Vancouver Island which would threaten to alter drastically affairs in the Indian country. Soon William would be thrown into the American and European spotlight—and being at the center of the stage, even in his first appearance as Zanga, had never made him uncomfortable.

III

Nootka

THERE WERE several forces at work that were to draw Bowles from the Indian country, only some of which he knew about now and was trying to shape to his own ends. He was well aware of Indian unrest and distress, not only of the Creeks but of all western Indians. The Americans had been streaming across the mountains after the Revolution and had encroached on Indian lands. This was at the heart of Indian apprehension which was voiced by the Six Nations and other tribes north of the Ohio and by the Creeks and their neighbors to the south. Among the Indians, especially among those closest to the Americans and therefore most vulnerable, there had been talk of a general confederation to contain the whites. Emissaries from the Six Nations and other tribes above the Ohio recently had been among the Creeks to evoke interest in a confederation,[1] and southern Indians frequently had been represented at important northern councils after the Revolution.[2]

Besides the Creeks no other southern tribe was more affected by American expansion than the Cherokees. During the past they had been forced from the Piedmont to the mountains into an area stretching almost from Virginia to Georgia. Disease and costly wars with both whites and other Indians had reduced their militancy and potency, and American expansion through the Cumberland Gap to settlements on the Tennessee and Cumberland rivers was largely at Cherokee expense. A majority of these Indians, wasted by warfare, reluctantly agreed during the French and Indian War or American Revolution to cede part of their lands for peace and to hope the peace would be a lasting one; and they began to adopt more features of the white man's civilization. A faction of the Cherokees was determined to keep the Americans at bay and not to imitate so many of their ways. This group moved further west on the Tennessee River adjacent to Creek territory where, with Creek sanction, they established the Five Lower Towns. Clustered about Lookout Mountain, this aggressive branch of the Cherokees usually was referred to as the Chickamaugas, named for one of the prominent towns.[3] William's Cherokee wife probably was a Chickamauga.

The Cherokees and Creeks had not always been good friends, but the common American peril helped push their differences into the background. The Chickamaugas, living in territory formerly claimed by the Creeks, were the Creeks' closest Cherokee neighbors, and there was a good deal of co-operation—especially when American aggression was the threat. In the spring of 1789 there was an important Cherokee delegation among the Lower Creeks led by Dragging Canoe, mighty warrior, symbol of Chickamauga defiance, and founder of the Five Lower Towns, along with Little Turkey and Hanging Maw. The Americans and how to ward them off, as always, was Dragging Canoe's prime concern.[4] On the eve of the Revolution he was reported to have told the Americans on the verge of pouring into the West: "You have bought a fair land, but you will find its settlement dark and bloody."[5] Arms and powder were necessary, and obviously the Chickamaugas could not buy them from the Americans. Spain was a possibility. The Spaniards in Madrid, when discussing Florida's northern boundary with United States representatives, were likely to tap their fingers on the Tennessee River to denote the upper limits. But in spite of a theoretical claim to much of the Cherokee territory, Spain had made no significant overtures to bring these Indians into the Spanish sphere. Besides, Dragging Canoe knew that Spain had capriciously withheld Creek supplies.

Bowles had the solution. During the winter and spring of 1789 he had heard of the plight of the Chickamaugas and had talked at length to Dragging Canoe when he visited the Lower Creeks. William reasoned that the plight of the Chickamaugas was identical to that of the Creeks: arms were indispensable, and neither the United States nor Spain could furnish them on a satisfactory basis. But he, Miller, and Dunmore could. To both the Creeks and the Chickamaugas Bowles held out the prospect of their once again, in some fashion, coming under British protection and of their being furnished a dependable supply of moderately priced goods. These promises, coming at the time of mounting crisis with the Americans, were exactly what the Indians most wanted to hear. In a grand council at Coweta, the Creeks (Lower Creeks and Seminoles) listened with approval to Bowles's talks and commissioned several chiefs to accompany Bowles, who was both a chief and a half-pay British officer and now styled

Director General of the Creek Nation (Eastajoca in the native tongue), to London. Here they would present their plea directly to George III—"we stretch out our hands in vain and cannot see through the black clouds that spread over our land"—asking the British monarch to re-affirm the pre-revolutionary treaties, to issue new medals in place of the old ones that had become tarnished, and to take the southern Indians under his wing as he had the tribes north of the Ohio. Dragging Canoe and twelve other Chickamauga chiefs held a council nearby, drew up a similar petition, and authorized representatives to accompany Eastajoca to see the English King.[6] It was during this period that someone—and that person must have been William himself—painted a picture of Bowles, who was portrayed as a chief and was flanked by two Cherokee chiefs. William was represented as the military commander of the combined Creek-Cherokee nations and this portrait was displayed among the Chickamaugas for years before eventually vanishing.[7]

Bowles had set out to win an Indian following and had succeeded. He could not speak for all the Creeks and Cherokees, or even for most of them, but he did represent an articulate minority. One suspects that Bowles's idea of sending a delegation to visit George III was not conceived on the banks of the Chattahoochee River but instead in Nassau, probably in the mind of Miller or Dunmore. In any case the logical first leg of their journey would carry them to the Bahamas, and at the end of July the approximately eight Creek and Cherokee chiefs stepped ashore on New Providence. They had made their way downstream from Coweta, briefly stopping by Perryman's, before boarding a ship, probably one of Miller's which periodically had been calling at Apalachicola Bay during the past months.[8]

After arriving at Nassau, William was uncertain as to the most effective next move. Leslie, Forbes, William Wylly, and other members of the opposition had sent home bitter denunciations of Bowles's buccaneering expedition, which they insisted was organized in Nassau by the governor solely to plunder Panton's St. Johns store and which could lead to a rupture with Spain.[9] Dunmore assumed he still was in favor with Whitehall and denied complicity: "I declare upon my honor that I am ignorant of the whole affair except that of the 2 Irish convicts."[10] He could assume that the ministry would believe him, but perhaps Bowles had better delay until he made sure. A better reason for waiting was that there already was a Creek emissary in London, none other than Thomas Dalton, one of Bowles's captains. After the failure of the 1788 expedition, Dalton, weakened by sickness, remained among the Indians for several months, finally making his

way to Pensacola. Either in disguise or personally escorted aboard ship
by McGillivray and Panton—there is one version by McGillivray and
another by the American Caleb Swan[11]—Dalton sailed from Florida
to England. There is some question as to whether he stopped by the
Bahamas, but there is no doubt that at some point Bowles, Miller, or
Dunmore suggested that he represent the cause of the southern Indians
to the home government. He carried a petition of the kings, chiefs,
and head warriors of the Creek and Cherokee nations adopted at the
general council "over black drink" at Coweta's square "last Windy
Moon," denouncing the Spaniards and Panton's abuses, urging an
open trade with Britain via free ports to be opened and defended by
the Indians, and insisting that the southern Indians, along with their
northern counterparts, were still loyal to Britain. "As I came so many
hundred miles to make the talks strate, I hope you [Lord Sydney]
will be pleased to receive them." Since Dalton, dressed as an Indian
and unprepared for the British climate, by necessity was confined to
his room, there was an added air of urgency.[12] With Dalton's trying to
get the ear of the British ministry at the same time that Bowles arrived
in Nassau, he and Dunmore considered it wise to wait word from
London before sending the full-fledged Creek-Cherokee delegation.

Another reason for delay was that Bowles was undecided over the
best route to take to London. Political and economic considerations
dictated that the quickest way to achieve his objectives was not necessarily the shortest distance between two points; it might be worthwhile
first to stop by Quebec, almost doubling the length of his journey.
A powerful Indian objective was to have the British government,
through the Canadian Indian Department, embrace not only the
northern but also the southern Indians. In the near future over-
enthusiastic Shawnee emissaries, without authority, would promise
Canadian arms for the southern Indians.[13] Bowles, Miller, and Dunmore reasoned that the Canadian Indian Department needed Nassau's
help. Britain's retention of the northern forts and continued Indian
hostility in the Old Northwest, allegedly instigated by Britain, made
for a fluid and dangerous situation that at any moment might get out
of hand. Should this occur, aid from the southern Indians would be
most valuable.

While Bowles was in Nassau conferring with Miller and the Governor and anxiously awaiting the latest word from London or the
mainland, he and his fellow chiefs were the focal point of the political
controversy rocking the tiny island. Wells's *Bahama Gazette* was full
of derogatory articles portraying him as a rogue, plunderer, and petty
chief with no following among the Indians, and many of these charges

were levied against Miller and Dunmore as well—"let Dunmore refute [these allegations] if he can."[14] Bowles countered in the opposition *Lucayan Royal Herald and Weekly Advertiser,* insisting that deserters from his Florida expedition first robbed him and then fled to St. Augustine and Nassau where they gave false testimony. In his diatribes against William Panton, John Leslie, and Thomas Forbes, Bowles was equally flexible with the truth.[15]

He carried the defense of his past actions and denunciations of Panton, Leslie, and Company to the Spaniards. In letters to Florida officials and even to Secretary of State Floridablanca in Madrid, Bowles insisted that statements made by his deserters at St. Augustine were false to begin with or were altered by Leslie, who helped in the interrogation. It was Leslie's firm, profiting from Spain's misguided policy, that was responsible for Florida's difficulties. This company kept the Spaniards at St. Augustine and Pensacola well supplied but was gouging the Indians. To restore Indian tranquillity Panton must have competition; there must be one or more free ports in Florida where reasonably priced goods, by-passing Spanish customs at Cádiz and Florida, could be furnished the Indians. Bowles stopped here but assumed that Floridablanca could easily read between the lines: Spain was losing her influence over the southern Indians as a result of Panton's oppressive monopoly and had better make room for Bowles and Miller. Further squinting by Floridablanca suggested that officials at St. Augustine and Pensacola were bribed by Panton and Leslie, not that this would set them apart from their counterparts elsewhere in Spanish America.[16] Leslie had recently married at St. Augustine, and one suspects that Bowles's denunciations and hostile actions must have cut short his honeymoon.

Eastajoca and the other chiefs remained at New Providence until the early fall of 1789, waiting to hear the outcome of Dalton's mission in London, to make doubly sure that Dunmore was still in favor, and to decide whether a Canadian visit was worthwhile. All signs pointed to a Quebec visit. Dalton had made little headway with the British ministry; establishing contact with the Canadian governor, Lord Dorchester, and, it was hoped, winning his support would insure a more favorable reception when the Indian delegation eventually reached London.[17]

As time passed Bowles was encouraged by still another reason for visiting Quebec—the possibility of an Anglo-Spanish war in which the Creek and Cherokee Indians might play an important role. The cause of the dispute was Spanish seizure of British merchant vessels at Nootka Sound on Vancouver Island. Nootka Sound was one of the more remote places on the globe and it took time for the news of the seizure to trickle back to Mexico and the West Indies and ultimately to Europe. There was an interval before it was apparent that this was something more than a capture of British merchant ships by another Spanish *guarda costa*. As details of the dispute became known, each side became more rigid in its stand. Disposition of the captured ship itself became relatively unimportant, and instead whether a ship flying the British flag had a right to be anywhere near Nootka became the key issue. The question of ownership of the entire Pacific Northwest was raised, and each nation began to assert its title more forcefully. If neither backed down, war was likely. In the fall of 1789 there were only vague rumors about the Nootka crisis and the possibility of war. Bowles already was committed to a Canadian visit; the possibility of an Anglo-Spanish war provided just another reason for going.[18]

It was one thing to decide to go to Canada and Britain; it was something else to get there. William persuaded Miller and Bonnamy that it was in their interest to furnish transportation. These merchants wrote one of their Florida ship captains to take the delegation to Canada, and in September Bowles and the Creek and Cherokee Indians sailed over to the mainland to join the captain. William was annoyed to learn that the captain had to return to Nassau to pick up a cargo for Halifax and was more furious to discover subsequently that Miller and Bonnamy, for some reason, had changed their minds about sending this particular vessel to Canada at all.

Bowles, who apparently had remained in Florida, was determined to get to London without delay. If he could get there via Canada, fine; but get there quickly he must. Since apparently it would be some time before Miller would furnish passage to Canada, William resolved to strike out on his own to Jamaica, which was closer, and to urge the British governor there to send the Indians on to England. After some time Bowles and his Indians, who had been subsisting on little more than venison, acquired a small vessel and with Eastajoca as captain and the chiefs as crew members, made their way south along the Florida coast. When they reached the Keys they ran upon a windfall—a small abandoned vessel wrecked on a reef. As, in the tradition of the Bahamian wreckers, they proceeded to salvage part of the cargo, the captain of the wrecked vessel appeared and offered to buy what had been salvaged, an offer that Bowles and the Indians readily accepted. After haggling over details, Bowles reached an agreement with the captain whereby he would transport all the Indians to Canada in return for the salvaged cargo. Bowles again changed direction and as originally planned headed for Halifax.

The confusion was not over yet. Before leaving Florida waters, Bowles was overtaken by another vessel chartered by Miller to take the Indian delegation to Canada. Making a new agreement with the captain of the salvaged ship and writing Whitehall that, after dropping by Canada, the southern Indian delegation would soon be in London, Bowles boarded Miller's ship and, after an eight month's delay since leaving Nassau, sailed for Canada. The delegation was now reduced to six—two Creeks, three Cherokees, and Bowles. All dressed and looked like Indians, but most, and probably all, had some white blood. Bowles was pure white; the Cherokees, Moses Price and Richard Justice, were half-breeds; and it is likely that the remainder were not pure-blooded. By temperament William was a man of action and chaffed at delay. His recent prolonged stay on the Florida coast was only one of many periods of frustrating inactivity which tempered his impulsiveness.[19]

The Creek and Cherokee chiefs began their voyage aboard Miller's ship. It was apparent now that Dunmore still enjoyed Whitehall's favor but that Dalton had failed to win support from the government in London.[20] Quebec, the Canadian capital, was Bowles's immediate objective. He later asserted that Miller had paid the ship captain to carry them all the way to Quebec but storms and headwinds forced him to drop the Indians off at Halifax. Chances are he let the Indians off here because this is all he had been paid to do. As in the past Bowles had only the unofficial blessings of Dunmore. Should the Indian delegation cause any controversy or unpleasantness, the Nassau governor could not be implicated. To a considerable extent William was on his own; certainly this was the case when he set foot in Halifax with little money and almost no official reason for being there.[21]

As leader of the delegation, he was eager to rely on his wits for his mission's success. The chiefs, their faces painted, wearing their turbans adorned with multicolored feathers, their silver medals, gorgets, and beads hanging from their necks, some with long hunting jackets brightly decorated around the edges, others with European shirts and silver arm bands, attracted attention and comments from the minute they stepped ashore. Halifax was a relatively new post, established just before the French and Indian War to help keep Nova Scotia out of French hands. After the Revolution many Loyalists went to Nova Scotia, some to Halifax, and William renewed wartime acquaintances and visited William Sabatier, an old friend of his father.[22] The Maryland Loyalists were settled across the Bay of Fundy at St. John, though there is no indication he saw any of them. Bowles's objective was Quebec; his problem how to get there. One of his first calls was on John Parr, the governor of Nova Scotia. With dignity, but with enthusiasm and eloquence, Eastajoca showed the Governor the Indian petitions to George III and urged that, because of the American threat to the northern Indians and the northwest forts and because of the possibility of a British attack on Louisiana and Florida, it was desirable to call on the Canadian governor, Lord Dorchester. Dunmore was in full sympathy with this Indian mission. Bowles also presented his case to Admiral Richard Hughes, the ranking naval officer at Halifax. Both Parr and Hughes were favorably impressed; Parr drew a draft on the Canadian Indian Department to pay for the Indians' passage up to Quebec, and Hughes provided a schooner.[23]

The impressive view of Quebec, a city protected by thick stone walls and situated on a high bluff overlooking the St. Lawrence, greeted Bowles in the distance as he and the Indians approached the Canadian capital early in July, well over a year since they had drawn up their petitions on the bank of the Chattahoochee. Dorchester had no inkling that this Indian delegation was about to descend on him. As soon as there were reports of the arrival at Quebec of a small party of strange Indians, he dispatched a representative of the Indian Department to fathom their business. This agent talked to them at length, discovered they were southern Indians but had no official message for Dorchester either from the Indians or from Dunmore— the Indian petitions were to the British King, and Dunmore, as always, was careful not to commit himself in writing to Bowles's schemes. The Canadian governor reasoned, however, that they had made a difficult journey, had been encouraged by Parr and Hughes, and merited at least a minimum of hospitality. The Indians were offered simple lodgings in governmental quarters, but Eastajoca deemed them too rustic for his delegation's dignity and refused for them. In general the officials at Quebec had no knowledge of or interest in the southern Indians; those north of the Ohio were problem enough. But Bowles's delegation always attracted interest and was surrounded with an air of secrecy. Dorchester could hardly refuse to see them.[24]

This was not the first time William had seen Dorchester. In 1783 Lord Dorchester, then General Guy Carleton, had come to New York to take charge of the evacuation. Bowles doubtless saw the General as he busied himself with details of the evacuation, though there is no reason to assume that Carleton had met or had reason to remember the provincial ensign. In the audience with the Governor, Bowles confirmed that he bore no official message but repeated what he had told Parr and Hughes. At any time the Americans, in their zeal in fighting against the Indians, might forcibly try to take possession of the Northwest posts and once again plunge Britain and America into war. Should this occur the southern Indians would be invaluable allies. Their cause was the same as the northern Indians', and their warriors should be taken under the same British protection as those north of the Ohio. If not, thousands of Creek and Cherokee warriors and a thousand Loyalists received into the southern Indians' bosom would be lost to Britain forever. Though Eastajoca had no official message for Dorchester, it had seemed only natural to the chiefs and to Dunmore that the Canadian governor would want to confer with them, especially since now there was chance of a rupture with Spain. The Governor's French predecessors at Quebec never stopped at the Ohio when gazing southward; neither should Dorchester.[25]

Dorchester was an able governor and by nature a cautious man. The vision of a western state, dominated by Britain, did not burn as brightly in his mind as in Bowles's. The Governor had agents in the West, Vermont, and New York to advise him of frontier dissatisfaction and weakness of the United States and he, like most, was convinced that New Orleans would become "the great emporium of North America."[26] If the United States began to break up, then maybe Vermont, the Old Northwest, and even the Old Southwest might naturally gravitate toward the British in Canada. Until then he was inclined to follow a course that would not precipitate hostilities; indeed these were Whitehall's instructions.[27] The Governor listened politely to Bowles's presentation, offered to send on any communication the Indians might have for the King and in the meantime to record their address so that the King's answer might be forwarded, and hoped this would conclude matters. Dorchester knew that southern Indians had sat in important councils in the North—other Creek and Cherokee representatives were near Detroit at this instant,[28] and Wellbank, representing the Creeks, was corresponding with Sir John Johnson and his subordinates in the Canadian Indian Department[29]—but Dorchester did not respond to Bowles's suggestion that he supply the southern Indians to save the West for both the Indians and Britain.[30]

Bowles, now and in later conferences and written exchanges, was adamant that his delegation did have good reason to come to Quebec, that they were not young men wandering about for the sake of adventure, and that they should not be politely pushed aside. Bowles was disturbed by Dorchester's lack of enthusiasm and was getting desperate for money. There was a question whether the draft drawn by Parr on Indian Department funds would be honored and whether Dorchester would pay for passage to London—or anywhere. Bowles's most telling argument was that he and his Indian and Loyalist allies could be of great service in a Spanish war. With only limited naval aid New Orleans and Florida would fall easily. Dorchester was less interested than Bowles in New Orleans, but it would be a natural wartime target and valuable prize should hostilities occur. Since Eastajoca would not leave his address and quietly disappear, perhaps it would be best for Dorchester to send him on to London, thereby avoiding the risk of alienating potential allies. The Governor procured a small schooner and stocked it with provisions so that these versatile Indians, who would man the ship themselves, could continue their journey to England.[31]

One aspect of Bowles's Canadian visit is, and perhaps always will be a mystery: did he see Dr. John Connolly, who was employed by Sir John Johnson in the Canadian Indian Department?[32] There is no evidence of such a meeting, but it is illogical to think one might not have taken place. Connolly was Dunmore's old friend, and both before and during the Revolution they had co-operated in fighting Indians or rebels and especially in land speculating. After the Revolution both were working along the same lines to bring the West in some fashion under British control. One suspects, though it cannot be proved, that Connolly must have exerted pressure to help insure the success of Bowles's mission, or at least that they conferred with one another.

Bowles's unexpected visit and the attending publicity had embarrassed Dorchester. Public accounts of southern Indians' being entertained at Quebec could undermine the Governor's negotiations in the United States. The Americans naturally wondered what the Creeks and Cherokees were up to so far from home. Informal Canadian-American conversations had been going on in New York for some time; the chief topics were violations of the 1783 peace treaty and more recently what would be the United States' attitude in an Anglo-Spanish conflict. The Canadian agent in New York was George Beckwith, who had served in New York during the Revolution as an intelligence officer and who in recent months had held a series of confidential talks with Alexander Hamilton. One of the main issues now was what would the United States do should Britain launch an attack on Spanish Louisiana from the northwestern posts on American soil. Would she go to war with Britain if troops marched over American territory? Or would the United States join Britain?[33]

The latter was a possibility and was the chief reason that Dorchester considered Bowles's visit untimely. The United States had reason to go to war with Spain: dispute over the Florida boundary, alleged Spanish incitement of the Indians, and above all the fact that Spain refused to open the Mississippi without restriction. There had been talk of the necessity of New Orleans to the West, and it was sometimes predicted that the United States might take it by force before the 1790 crisis. The United States and Britain could relieve Spain of Louisiana and Florida with little difficulty. Dorchester, with excellent reason, felt the United States would doubt his sincerity if he intrigued with the southern Indians at the same time he was trying to secure American co-operation. As the Nootka crisis deepened Dorchester recognized more and more that both the United States and the southern Indians could be valuable allies. But there was little likelihood that the two would work together if Dorchester held the reins.

Beckwith's chief function in New York was to advise Dorchester of events taking place in the American capital, especially those points that related to the probable Spanish war. One such point was the treaty being negotiated by McGillivray with the United States. While Bowles's delegation, representing the combined Creek-Cherokee nations, was in Quebec, McGillivray, with a larger, more impressive all-Creek delegation, was in New York. The United States genuinely wanted peace with the Creeks, a peace which would finely balance the extreme positions of the Indians and the Georgians. A quick settlement was desirable, if for no other reason, to keep the southern frontier quiet so the United States could devote its full efforts to the north.[34]

McGillivray was a British Loyalist. What were his feelings toward Britain; what accord would he reach with the United States; and did he or Bowles really speak for the Creeks? These were questions that Beckwith tried to answer. The Spaniards also sent Carlos Howard, whose health was "delicate," up from St. Augustine to answer these same questions.[35] Whatever arrangements McGillivray made naturally were of greatest importance to Bowles and Dunmore, and they did not lag behind Spain or Dorchester: their man was on the scene also. The ubiquitous Dalton had returned from London, had read newspaper accounts of McGillivray's forthcoming treaty, and was on hand to greet McGillivray's entourage. McGillivray "was very much surprised to find him here on my arrival; we met in public on my landing, he has been plaguing me very frequently by messages and notes from day to day, and I was not able to get rid of him."[36] Dalton had met with little success at Whitehall and reasoned that he could be of more value to Bowles in America—though there is no reason to assume that his idea of coming to New York was any more original than that of going to London. In the American capital Dalton did everything in his power to discredit McGillivray and to lure away some of the chiefs. This adventurer made a nuisance of himself both to McGillivray and to American officials. General Henry Knox even threatened to throw the pest in jail. The treaty eventually was signed, but Dalton had little influence on the terms.

Considering everything, the treaty was about as favorable as McGillivray could expect: "I have been obliged to give up something in order to secure the rest."[37] Part of the disputed land east of the Oconee River actually settled by the Georgians was ceded, though the boundary was something less than the Georgians had demanded. In turn the Creeks received presents amounting to $10,000, while McGillivray took an oath of allegiance to the United States, was commissioned a brigadier general, and was given a pension. There were vague arrangements whereby the United States might take over Panton's trade should it be disrupted by war.[38] Throughout the negotiations Dalton in vain insisted that McGillivray was selling the Creeks short. In a formal ceremony the chiefs and high American officials witnessed the treaty signing; there was another round of entertainment for the Indians; then they all set sail for Florida.

In the long run this treaty was both advantageous and unfavorable to McGillivray and Bowles alike. McGillivray was not excessively vain or avaricious, but he was favorably impressed by the attention the Americans bestowed on him and by the pension and commission. But he would soon discover that ceding Creek lands alienated many of his Indian followers and that the Spaniards, because of the American commission and pension, distrusted him more than ever. After his return to Little Tallassie he found that his control over the Indians was weakened and that the Spaniards paid more attention to the idea of replacing him. For the time being, however, Bowles, to his chagrin, realized that because of the publicity surrounding the treaty there was a widespread impression that it was McGillivray who currently spoke for and was directing affairs of the Creek nation. Bowles was well aware of this and when he reached England was careful to see that the papers referred to him as the leader of a Cherokee (or Cherokee-Creek) delegation to set himself apart from McGillivray who in the popular mind was identified as head of the Creeks. But Bowles knew, or soon discovered, that there was serious Indian and Spanish dissatisfaction with some of the treaty terms, and he was confident that in the long run he could use this discontent to discredit McGillivray and to further his own ends.

At almost the same time that McGillivray's Creeks were sailing out of New York, Bowles and his Indians were sailing down the St. Lawrence River, and confusion reigned in Quebec, New York,

St. Augustine, and even Mexico City over which chiefs represented
what nation.[39] William paid little attention to the narrow, rectangular
farms reaching down to the edge of the St. Lawrence still worked by
the industrious French. He was preoccupied with the immediate
details of commanding the tiny schooner, with the future course to be
steered and possible hazards in crossing the Atlantic, and with the
most effective moves to make as soon as he arrived in England. It
was required by law that his vessel stop at St. Johns, Newfoundland,
before sailing to Europe, and it was there that disaster suddenly
struck. The schooner's former owner owed money to a St. John's
inhabitant who had the authorities attach the vessel for debt. William fumed but could do nothing. He did not have funds to redeem
the schooner and was stranded. After prolonged, heated discussions
he and the Indians were provided transportation back to Halifax.
There they recounted their misfortunes to Parr and Hughes, stressed
the importance of the Indians' quickly reaching London, and im-
plored assistance. From the beginning Parr and Hughes had supported Bowles's mission; Dorchester, with some hesitation, had done
the same thing; and it was only natural that the Governor and the
Admiral used their influence and government funds to obtain the
Indians' passage to England on the merchantman *Dorchester* now
anchored at Halifax.[40]

As Bowles, hopefully assuming there would be no more delays,
was sailing for Britain aboard the *Dorchester,* the Nootka crisis was
at its peak. Britain was aware of the Spanish dilemma and was determined to make the most of it. Each side had been feverishly arming, and Britain's demands were worded so that Spain soon would
have to fight or back down. France held the key. Would she, beset
by revolution, be willing or able to come to Spain's rescue? No one
was sure of the outcome, but it was obvious that the issue could not
long be in doubt.[41]

The *Dorchester* carefully made her way into Spithead Roads at
the end of October, and Bowles eagerly watched the dropping of
the anchor and scanned the multitude of masts, steeples, and docks
that stood out in Plymouth's historic harbor. The first messages from
shore warned that war seemed imminent. It was not surprising that
word was soon out that aboard the *Dorchester* were Creek and
Cherokee chiefs anxious to lead thousands of warriors against Spain.
The captain of the *Alcide,* a 74-gun man-of-war anchored nearby,
sent over his barge, and with great ceremony Eastajoca and the other
chiefs were taken ashore where they attracted much attention.[42]
Garbled accounts circulated—many of the distortions came from

Bowles—of how twenty thousand Creek and Cherokee warriors, easily
reinforced by an equal number of Chickasaws and Choctaws, could
conquer Florida and Louisiana. From here an overland march to
Mexico was within the realm of possibility. Bowles was offering the
English what they wanted to hear. By reviving the glories of Drake,
Hawkins, and even Henry Morgan it was always easy to whip up
enthusiasm for a Spanish war, especially since Spanish plunder should
more than pay the cost. Englishmen, reading newspaper accounts
of the Creek and Cherokee chiefs, were likely to take at face value
assertions that Florida, New Orleans, and even Mexico were easily
within grasp. It was generally assumed that Spanish successes during
the American Revolution had been an accidental stroke of luck; now
was the time to prove this point.

William could not have been more pleased or confident. Everywhere he was treated with marked attention and deference—how
could Dorchester have had doubts about a London visit? It was
necessary to get to London quickly, but there was one minor problem
—money. Dorchester's and Parr's funds took the chiefs to Portsmouth and no further. Bowles promptly called on a leading merchant
with Canadian connections and reaffirmed what the papers had said
about the importance of his Indian mission. Bowles insisted that
Dorchester had sent him on this important undertaking and that
the government would make good any advance.[43]

The Indians got fifteen guineas and were off to London. After
getting settled in Osborne's Hotel at fashionable Adelphi on the
Strand, close by the Thames and Whitehall, and after conferring
with various officers interested in the American campaign, Bowles
contacted Home Secretary William Windham Grenville.[44] He would
know how best to weave Creek-Cherokee tactics into the broad anti-
Spanish fabric and would determine the most appropriate manner
for the Indians to present their petitions to the King. Dorchester
had informed Grenville all about Bowles, but Grenville, unlike Dorchester, had no misgivings about these Indians' coming to London;
indeed, because of the delay he was alarmed that they might have
decided not to come.[45] Grenville, engrossed with affairs of the forthcoming Spanish war, was primarily concerned with Indian military
usefulness. Bowles's Indians were not the only Americans in London
offering their services to Britain. Levi Allen had been there for some
time intimating that dissatisfied Vermonters might throw in their
lot with Canada should the United States break up or should the
Nootka crisis bring about a break with the United States.[46] And
Francisco de Miranda, a Venezuelan creole, was negotiating about

liberating his homeland in particular and all of Spanish America, including Louisiana and Florida, in general.[47]

Grenville, confident of a Spanish war, considered that it was only natural that these Indians should personally present their petitions to George III. These petitions, drawn up in councils on the Chattahoochee, asked that once again the Creeks and Cherokees be taken under British protection, that the pre-revolutionary treaties be re-affirmed, that new medals be bestowed, and above all that arms be supplied. In turn these Indians, as in the past, willingly would take up the hatchet in behalf of the English King. Within a few days after Bowles's arrival a time was set at a royal levee for the audience with George III. The English nobility, foreign diplomats, and assorted spectators were curious to see the King receive homage from the chiefs painted and dressed in their native costumes.[48]

The distinguished guests arrived for the levee, but the Indians were conspicuous by their absence, and the reason soon was apparent: news had arrived of a Spanish capitulation and there would be no war. Publicly receiving these Indians obviously would irritate both Spain and the United States. Since it appeared there would be no war it was senseless to make this unnecessary public affront. Eastajoca was crestfallen. Success was within his grasp and had slipped away. There was far less chance that his Indians would be taken under the British wing or receive British arms. And a Spanish war might have spelled the downfall of Panton and McGillivray, though whether Florida were lost or not Panton's difficulties would have been compounded. Either the war would cut off his commerce, or if it were tolerated by Britain and Spain even in wartime, then Bowles could easily charge that Panton's munitions were destined for the Spaniards and not the Indians. The Spanish ambassador in London had delayed granting passports to Panton's ships; now that the crisis had passed they were allowed to proceed as usual, and no one was more relieved than Panton in Nassau or more dismayed than Bowles in London.[49]

The Spanish capitulation was a major setback for William, but perhaps he could salvage something; in any case London society was more diverting than that of Coweta's great square. His Indians had received an undue amount of publicity—it had rankled the American minister in London that the press had paid as much attention to Bowles's mission as to that of the ambassador extraordinary of the Holy Roman Empire who arrived at the same time[50]—and even though after the Nootka crisis had passed it was jubilantly reported in Nassau that the savages "are now quite out of fashion,"[51] they continued to be an attraction. Invariably these young Indians, living proof of the concept of the "noble savage" eulogized by contemporary writers, drew crowds when they toured the sights of London, visited the theater, or even attended a masquerade at Ranelagh.[52] The Indians naturally were spared the expense of obtaining a costume, and theirs was the most authentic, if not the most original.

They remained in London until spring, and they found much leisure time. The excitement, the dismal English climate, or some other cause made many of the chiefs sick, and it took them time to recuperate in their new quarters overlooking Brompton Park. Eastajoca, with or without the other chiefs, was introduced to the highest society and was received by the Prince of Wales, the Duke of Gloucester (both members of the royal family), by Lord Townshend, and other nobility.[53] Bowles also attended Dr. George Pearson's Chymical Lectures, struck up a close friendship with the prominent doctor, and on his advice purchased chemistry and mathematical works for future study, though in the diplomatic and social whirl the Director General overlooked paying the bookseller.[54] Another admirer, gratuitously presenting Dr. Lewis' *Philosophical Commerce of Arts, Trades, and Manufactures* to Bowles, at least did not further complicate his accounts with the bookseller.[55] It is safe to assume this was a more sensitive issue for Carington Bowles than for his cousin. At some point William met George Browne, who may have been a displaced Loyalist living in London but about whom little is known. In any case, William frequently visited Browne, his wife, and children and was warmly received into the family circle. Throughout William's adult life the Brownes would be among his closets friends and in part became a substitute for his Maryland family.[56]

Captain Benjamin Baynton, a Loyalist who had escaped being blown up at Pensacola and who had first seen Bowles bobbing about in a hogshead, was in London and dropped by Osborne's Hotel on several occasions.[57] In addition to reminiscing and posing while William painted his portrait, Baynton took many notes about Bowles's career and, urged by Bowles's admirers, in early 1791 published an account of the Indian leader's life.[58] This work, *The Authentic Memoirs of William Augustus Bowles, Esquire, Ambassador from the United Nations of Creeks and Cherokees, to the Court of London,* along with Bowles's portrait by Thomas Hardy which was on display, kept the Indian chiefs in the news. They received many invitations and were responsible for introducing "Cherokee fricassee" to London gourmets.[59] The handsome Bowles, confident in his bearing and surrounded by an air of mystery, captivated more than one cosmopolitan belle. There is no record that he saw any of his London relatives, but his cousin, Carington Bowles, who had bought William's grandfather's business, was still managing the book, map, and print shop next to the Chapter House in St. Paul's Churchyard. It is difficult to conceive that Carington and his children were not visited, though William probably knew no more about his family in Maryland than Carington.

Despite a strenuous social calendar, Bowles still had pressing official business. Upon his arrival he had every reason to be confident of a favorable reception, but after the Nootka crisis passed the presence of the Indian chiefs proved an embarrassment. Any official encouragement now could only indicate a lack of sincerity in dealing with Spain or produce still another issue with the United States. Grenville hoped that the Indians, taking into account the altered diplomatic situation, would return home and offered 500 pounds as an inducement. William was indignant. He informed the government that he had not made this tedious voyage for presents and that he had already lost more than this sum in America on behalf of the King.[60] Though he had received an equal share of his father's estate when Thomas died in 1787, William would have been far better off financially had he never joined the British forces in Philadelphia and had his father not been a moderate Tory. William's assertion about his loss probably was no exaggeration.[61] His Indians, he maintained, had made a difficult journey from the banks of the Chattahoochee. They would have to present their petition to the King—hopefully in person—and have him exchange the 1764 medals, or else Britain would be abandoning them entirely.

Grenville was in a predicament. He would like to see these Indians vanish and leave him be, but Bowles was not one silently to disappear, and there was something to his argument for a British connection with the southern Indians. The Nootka settlement with Spain might break down, or some other pretext for war arise, or outstanding Anglo-American disputes might lead to hostilities. In any of these cases the southern Indians could prove valuable allies. Grenville kept open negotiations, though Bowles, as he busied about Whitehall, fumed about having to wait in the Common Attendance Room exposed to idle curiosity. The Creek chief, determined to salvage something from his mission, indicated he had a new proposal: perhaps it was best that the Indians not publicly see George III and it was not really mandatory that he bestow new medals. For the time being, if Britain would still sympathize with the Creeks and Cherokees and in some secret or unofficial way succor them, this would be satisfactory. Negotiations along this line could best be made in private.[62]

Bowles had been forced to lower his sights. What he was aiming for now was British approval of a direct trade between Nassau and the Creek-Cherokee country without reference to Spain. Ordinarily this was not an unusual or difficult request. Parliament's Free Port Act of 1787 was designed to encourage this type of commerce, especially contraband trade with Spanish America. Colonial produce from any American territory under European control could be brought to Nassau in foreign European ships and exchanged for English wares. For Florida, a portion of Spanish America, Panton had permission to carry on this commerce in British ships. It was these arrangements which Bowles felt were injurious to southern Indians. He maintained that the Creek-Cherokee nations, which he called Muskogee[63] were independent and that he was their Director General. There was confusion as to whether a vessel flying the colors of the state of Muskogee could legally be admitted to Nassau. If Muskogee were independent, then its ships and territory would not be under control of a foreign European power and therefore could not be admitted to Nassau. And Panton's concession obviously would be of no value. What Bowles now was hoping to obtain was either a liberal interpretation of the Free Port Act or a Parliamentary amendment that would serve the same end. He argued that, as things stood, the Creeks and Cherokees who had supported Britain during the Revolution were on a worse footing than Spain, who had been an enemy, and that the southern Indians could furnish not only deerskins but, since they were increasing and adopting more and more of the white man's civilization, they could also soon provide naval stores, tobacco, indigo, dyeing wood, drugs, and the like.[64]

Bowles also continued negotiations with Spanish officials which began in Nassau in 1789, though up to now the Indians had a monopoly on the negotiating. In his previous letters to the Florida governor and Floridablanca in Spain, Bowles had insisted that the Indians were master of all Florida except the several Spanish presidios and that the southern Indians were strengthening ties with the northern Indians. These southern Indians, victimized by Panton and not so convenient to Canada, had to have ports for a free trade to Nassau. With such pretensions it was small wonder that Spain had made no answer. But a year and a half after writing these letters Bowles was in London, and regardless of exactly how much influence he had as a chief, he was a figure of some consequence. It was more difficult to ignore him, and, with misgivings mingled with curiosity, the Spanish ambassador, the Marqués del Campo, entertained him at his residence in Manchester Square. Bowles made a number of visits there; sometimes he and the chiefs attended a formal dinner; sometimes he dropped in on his own.[65] These visits had few tangible results: Campo gleaned no new information and could only assume that Dunmore was behind it all, and there was never an answer from Madrid to Bowles's earlier letter to Floridablanca. In the course of the conversations Bowles made it plain that he expected to negotiate seriously with the Spaniards about the ports no later than upon his return to Florida. If an accommodation were not reached by then, the Indians would use force to open an independent trade.[66]

More headway was made with Grenville than with Campo. Bowles informed Grenville of all details of his Spanish negotiations and stressed that in no fashion had Britain been involved, except that he had asked that future Spanish communications be forwarded through Whitehall and that he was a half-pay British officer posing as the Director General of Muskogee. Bowles made it as clear to Grenville as to Campo that the Indians were bent on establishing their own ports and apparently would have to fight Spain to get them. Once he returned to America, the Florida posts, along with New Orleans and even Mexico, should fall to his thousands of Indians, Loyalists, and frontiersmen. After becoming master of a considerable territory, he would seek an open British alliance. Britain had lost the great game during the American Revolution; unofficial encouragement of the southern Indians, he warned, was one of the last cards she held in America and should not be tossed away.[67]

These arguments had their effect. The Indian leader was informed that under existing legislation Nassau could be open to Muskogee's ships—an indirect recognition of Muskogee's sovereignty.[68] But in Florida Eastajoca would be on his own: he would have to make his own arrangements with the Spaniards, either by negotiation or, apparently, by force; and, assuming it were possible, he would have to make his own accommodation with the United States. But should Bowles make himself master of Florida and especially New Orleans, then Britain would reconsider her position in America. It might evolve that these areas could be linked more strongly to Canada and the West Indies. For the time being everything was up to the Director General. Once again he paid a visit to Downing Street, had a final breakfast with Grenville's first secretary, then bid the government and his friends farewell and prepared to return to America.[69]

IV

Militant Muskogee

THE THAMES was dotted with ships of all nations as the Indian chiefs made their way down to the docks and boarded the *Mercury*. Despite this vessel's name it would be a long voyage, and many thoughts ran through William's mind as the *Mercury,* taking advantage of the ebb tide, weighed anchor and slowly sailed down to Deal and on into the English Channel.[1] There was good cause for disappointment. When he had arrived at Spithead five months before he had every reason to assume that the government, bent on a Spanish-American attack, would openly back him. Settlement of the Nootka crisis ruined these hopes. Now bound for the Indian country, he had misgivings about leaving London where he had been feted, had his portrait painted, had an account of his life published, and where he had conferred with the highest British and Spanish officials. But diplomatic reverses and melancholy aside, he was glad to be returning to America and was optimistic about the future. Only twenty-eight years old, he was already an international figure and could expect to have more prestige and success among the southern Indians. In recent decades there had been abrupt diplomatic and territorial changes in America; perhaps, after consolidating his position among the southern Indians, future developments would allow him to play a more prominent American role.

The *Mercury* arrived at Nassau in the latter part of June. The captain had been most agreeable and courteous to the chiefs, and the Indians had made the long voyage less tedious. Dorchester had paid the fare to England, and there is every reason to assume that Grenville paid the passage home—one reason the captain was so accommodating.[2] After going ashore and obtaining lodging Bowles had frequent conferences with Dunmore and Miller, who were anxious to know exactly what Grenville and Campo had said. This information, added to Dalton's reports about the terms of McGillivray's treaty and their subsequent effect on the Creeks, would make it easier to plot the next move.

The Indians remained in Nassau for three months, and controversies surrounding their presence did not calm the island's political turbulence. Immediately after their arrival Dunmore notified Grenville that the chiefs had had a pleasant voyage, that they would contribute to a profitable commercial connection with Florida, and that now, as always, Eastajoca was zealous in the King's service.[3] The Governor could not imagine what conceivable reason there was for delay in reimbursing Miller, who had underwritten Bowles's expenses in previous expeditions. These expenses, totaling some fifteen hundred pounds, though not authorized, had been advanced by Miller to further British interests. Legally Bowles owed the money to Miller and upon demand could be thrown into prison. But for Miller to demand it now would damage Britain's reputation among the southern Indians and was unthinkable.[4] Dunmore neglected to mention that Miller had received cargoes of skins from Florida, though there is no way to tell if they were of sufficient value to reimburse him for his investment; and Miller, of course, had loaned Bowles funds primarily in behalf of Miller's rather than Britain's interest. Bowles joined Dunmore in urging the exchequer to reimburse Miller but was careful not to implicate the Governor, who had "declined aid in any *effectual* manner." Bowles argued that it would be desirable for the government to pay this bill so that Miller would suffer no loss, so that there would be no excuse to throw the Director General of the Creek-Cherokee nations into jail, and so that Miller would continue to liberally underwrite Bowles—which for the time being he was still doing.[5]

One reason for William's delay in Nassau was that he was arranging transportation to Florida, and again Miller was instrumental in securing a vessel and stocking it with trading goods. "A new flag was displayed here on Wednesday, that of the Creek nation, worn by the vessel carrying General Bowles and the Indian chiefs to the American continent."[6] Some time between 1789 and 1791 Bowles had been promoted from colonel to general; it was never clear who authorized this commission, but from ensign to general in a decade was no mean achievement. Another reason Bowles lingered in Nassau was to procure a flag for his vessel. The local shops were quite out of Muskogee banners, and one had to be made to his description: he specified that a blue cross be superimposed on a red background; the blue background of the upper left hand corner had a sun with human features

resembling both an American Indian and Bowles himself.[7] Legally
only vessels flying this banner or authorized by Panton's concession
could trade with the Florida Indians. Miller had successfully sent
several vessels to Florida in the past, but there was always the question of how they would be received by Bahamian customs. While
Bowles was waiting, he conferred with a number of the local inhabitants, of whom almost all were Loyalists, and with some success
urged them to come to Muskogee as soon as he had put his Indian
nation on a firm footing.

By August Bowles had completed his preparations and, boarding
Miller's ship laden with boxes and barrels of trading goods, set sail
for Florida. He had chafed at the delay and was relieved to see the
sails fill, Muskogee's broad pennant wave briskly from the top of the
mainsail, and New Providence sink below the horizon. As he steadily
made his way westward his thoughts more and more turned to conditions on the mainland. The western Indians from Florida to Canada
were agitated. In Florida there was resentment over Panton's high
prices and McGillivray's New York treaty, while the neighboring
Americans, through the Yazoo grants or similar concessions, were
actively encouraging carving up Indian lands. To the north General
Arthur St. Clair was moving against the Indians with a large army.
Talk of a general western confederation to protect Indian lands was
more prevalent than ever, and William was impatient to be on the
scene. Out of all this uncertainty he should be able, at the very least,
to open up a lucrative trade with the southern Indians who would
have to have a reliable supply of guns and powder.[8]

The Muskogee vessel took the usual course from Nassau to Indian
River, successfully eluding several vessels sent out by the Spaniards.
Here Bowles probably unloaded some of his goods which, according
to exaggerated accounts, were valued at 50,000 pounds.[9] Profiting
from his 1788 failure, he did not venture inland but reboarded his
vessel and sailed around the tip of Florida to Apalachee Bay. His
first stop was at the Indian villages near the forks of the Apalachicola
River where chiefs Philatouchy and Perryman enthusiastically received him—and his gifts. One can only assume that Perryman's
daughter, Mary, was just as overjoyed. The Director General's prime
objective was to secure the support of the Lower Creeks, Seminoles,
and Chickamaugas and, he hoped, many more southern Indians.
Soon a general council was to be held at Coweta, the principal Lower
Creek red (or war) town, with representatives from the Seminoles,
Upper and Lower Creeks, as well as a Cherokee delegation. Of greatest concern to the Florida governors, Panton, McGillivray, and James

Seagrove, the United States Indian agent, was whether these assembled Indians would accept Bowles's talks.[10]

The Indians began arriving at Coweta in the early fall of 1791, and soon the deliberations began. There were the usual preliminary formalities, the ceremony of the black drink, long speeches; ultimately Eastajoca had his turn to address the Indians. Here he was at his best. He was always at home on the stage, but there were few times when he more wanted to impress his audience. Twelve years among the Indians had given him an easy command of the native languages—Muskogee, the Creek language proper; Hitchiti, spoken by some of the Lower Creeks and Seminoles; and he had acquired a smattering of Cherokee. There were many points that Bowles wanted to drive home, and among the foremost was that McGillivray had outlived his usefulness. He had played the traitor in New York by ceding Creek lands on the Oconee, and, even worse, he was in American pay. These charges were not new: the treaty's terms, probably even the secret ones, had been known for some time, but that did not make these specific provisions any more palatable. It might have been that Bowles's telling the Indians that McGillivray was in American pay was the first notice of this secret provision to some of the delegates. Another example of McGillivray's duplicity was that he was a member of the Yazoo companies who were bent on despoiling the Indians of most of their lands. Directors of these companies had made overtures to McGillivray—and to Bowles—and there were rumors, apparently groundless, that the Upper Creek chieftain was allied with the land speculators. Bowles outwardly took these rumors at face value and used them as another example to demonstrate how McGillivray had gone over to the Americans. Or even if this were incorrect he was still Panton's silent partner, and what had Panton or Spain done for the Indians?[11]

These natives, beset by land-grabbing Americans, defrauded by Panton and Spain, and deceived by McGillivray's forked tongue, had no recourse, Bowles argued, but to follow his lead. Only he could effectively protect them from the Americans, and at his bidding six thousand Bahamian Loyalists would eagerly join the Indians in their struggle against the advancing frontiersmen. Should he, in some miraculous fashion, have been able to transport six thousand souls from the Bahamas to the mainland, he would have removed almost every man, woman, and child, black or white, from the islands, and even then he probably would have had to scour the Out-Islands or rob a few graves. An exactness with figures, however, was never one of William's characteristics.[12] Regardless of whether these Loyalists came to the Indians' aid, Bowles contended it was mandatory to co-operate with the northern Indians. These Indians had been fairly successful against the Americans, and, if joined by their southern counterparts, would force the United States, already allocating most of its budget for frontier defense, to become conciliatory. And the British both in Canada and the Bahamas stood behind the Indians. It was arms, powder, ball, and knives supplied directly by the British that were restraining the Americans in the north, and Britain easily could play the same role in the south.

Muskogee was independent: neither the Americans nor the Spaniards had any rights to its territory. It was both legitimate and advantageous, Eastajoca continued, to open two Indian ports that would afford free commerce with Nassau. Panton's oppressive monopoly would be done away with, and the western Indians, united and supported by British Canada in the north and British Nassau in the south, with or without an influx of Loyalist volunteers, could contain the Americans. Bowles asserted he was no mere adventurer or transient but spoke with sincerity and authority. Had he not lived among the Creeks for over a decade, was he not a proven warrior, and did he not have an Indian family and know their problems at first hand? Had he not conversed at length with the highest British authorities in New Providence, Canada, and London? As was widely known he was a half-pay British officer and only recently had been authorized by Grenville to speak to the southern Indians. Exactly what authority Bowles, speaking in the native tongue, told the Indians he had from Whitehall will never be known. Without question he told them he had just come from London and that George III wished them well; perhaps, as it soon was widely circulated, he asserted that Britain had commissioned him superintendent of the southern Indians and that with a little effort the clock could be turned back to pre-Revolutionary days.[13]

The Indians listened with interest and mixed reactions. His denunciation of McGillivray alienated many of the Upper Creeks and they began to drift away from the council and to return home. Because McGillivray's influence was less and Bowles's arguments seemed plausible, a majority of the Lower Creeks and Seminoles remained. His arguments seemed to point out the only course to follow. For the present it was an open question who had more influence among the Creeks, and outward appearances tipped the balance toward Bowles as far as Secretary of War Knox, who had helped negotiate the Treaty of New York, was concerned: "It seems probable, that either Mc-Gillivray or Bowles must fall."[14] McGillivray was furious and distraught. He considered the New York treaty, in spite of its shortcomings, the best that the Indians could hope for. Now many of the Creeks, even Upper Creeks, had been taken in by Bowles's talks. The Upper Creek chieftain publicly tore up Bowles's letters and set out for Pensacola to seek consolation from Panton. There was reason to believe that Bowles was not exaggerating when he characterized McGillivray's journey to Pensacola as "a flight."[15] Not only Bowles, but LeClerc de Milfort, McGillivray's French brother-in-law, substantiated this charge.[16] McGillivray was a young man, only four years older than Bowles, but drink, syphilis, rheumatism, and now Bowles's attacks would bring him little solace in the remaining years of his short life.

Bowles's immediate objective was to take advantage of McGillivray's plight and to entrench himself among the Creeks and Cherokees. Then from a position of strength he could proceed to link the southern Indians with those north of the Ohio and with the British in Canada, and he could deal with the Spaniards and, with good fortune, could bring the Florida presidios and even New Orleans under his sway. But now it was mandatory that an uninhibited trade be opened with Nassau. Bowles set about what he had told both Grenville and Campo he expected to accomplish in Florida: the establishment of two ports. One, at Indian River, was easily reached from Nassau; it was an Indian village containing a few whites and it had had a continuous illicit commerce with the Bahamas since the Revolution. A fortified warehouse at Indian River could conveniently serve those assorted Indians who lived on the Florida peninsula, the Seminoles, and, if necessary, the Upper and Lower Creeks. The other post would be near the mouth of the Ochlockonee or Apalachicola rivers, either of which could provide convenient communication with the Seminoles, Creeks, Chickamaugas, and possibly other Indians. Like almost any spot in Florida, these posts had the advantage of being remote from strong Spanish settlements. Bowles should have little difficulty in establishing these posts, because, as Dunmore notified Whitehall, "I am happy to inform you that Bowles was well received in the Indian country and has entire command of those natives."[17]

Bowles's return had not surprised the Spaniards. Timely reports from Florida authorities, Panton, Campo, and British and American newspapers had allowed the Spaniards to follow Bowles from Florida to Canada and London and back again. They accurately surmised that, with the abatement of the Nootka crisis, Britain, at least for the time being, would not openly support this adventure.[18] But during the Nootka controversy Britain belligerently reaffirmed her doctrine of effective occupation, and whether most of Florida and Louisiana was effectively occupied was open to question. Regardless of whether Bowles was authorized by Whitehall or not, he was an unwanted and potentially dangerous intruder.

While his preparations to return were underway in Nassau the alarmed Florida and Havana governors armed swift, light-draft vessels for his interception. John McQueen, an American who had gone to Florida to escape his creditors, subsequently became a Catholic and enjoyed the favor and confidence of both the Spaniards and Panton. He commanded one of the several vessels that were outfitted on the St. Johns River in the late summer of 1791 to search for Bowles, and there was talk of building a Spanish fort at Indian River. No fort was ever built, and McQueen was no more successful than any other in preventing Bowles's return.[19] In the near future he would have good reason to fear for the safety of his two hundred Negroes and would be forced to keep them concentrated on the coast where they could leave on short notice.[20]

The Spaniards, unsuccessful in preventing Bowles' return, were more disconcerted when they realized that the Indians were listening to his talks. Should he make further inroads among the natives, Spanish control over Florida's interior, based on Indian loyalty secured by Panton and McGillivray, threatened to collapse. This was as obvious to the Spaniards as to Bowles and is why he proffered them both the sword and the olive branch. He insisted in Florida, as he had to Campo in London, that the Indians had title to Florida and had every right to establish two ports. Force would be used if necessary. But why resort to arms? Both Spain and Bowles's Indians had common objectives: to restrain the Americans and to prevent the surveying of the boundary line conceded by McGillivray at New York. This deceitful Upper Creek leader, Bowles avowed, had gone over to the Americans, and it now was in Spain's interest to back the Director General of the Creek-Cherokee nations. If not, necessity, Bowles threatened, might drive him into American arms.[21] He never considered a permanent Spanish alliance, but for a start it would be no mean achievement if he could supplant McGillivray and Panton. The Spaniards always had misgivings about Panton's monopoly and currently were debating whether to continue it; and they never wholeheartedly trusted McGillivray. They weighed the logic of Bowles's arguments, but that Bowles and Miller would be more solicitous of Spanish interests than McGillivray and Panton was unlikely.[22]

While consolidating his position among the Lower Creeks, Seminoles, and Cherokees and making overtures more or less in good faith to the Spaniards, Bowles was also negotiating with the Americans, though he was not optimistic about an accommodation. He insisted he wanted peace—but peace on Indian terms. Bowles claimed McGillivray had not represented the Creeks at New York and had been a traitor to his nation. He gave away Indian lands without authority and was bribed by the American pension and commission to do so. The Creeks had been pushed back from the coast further and further into the interior; the way was paved by numerous treaties, many fraudulently negotiated and invariably broken. The natives, with Eastajoca as their champion, would retreat no more: restrain the Yazoo speculators who had carved up the Indian country and do not attempt to run the 1790 boundary line. Then there will be peace; if not, "we still have friends and warriors sufficient to stain your land with blood. . . . It is our solemn determination to sell our lives with our country."[23] Bowles avowed he was the legitimate Creek spokesman and that McGillivray had taken flight and run off to "some other country." For the time being he would restrict Creek warriors to the Oconee's west bank, and the Americans must withdraw to the east. Then, if they sincerely wanted a treaty, they could come to him at Usachees below Coweta in the heart of the Lower Creeks.[24] That none showed up to pay homage to the Director General and receive his terms was hardly a surprise.

On several accounts Bowles was an issue at the new American capital of Philadelphia. The 1790 Creek treaty was a cornerstone of American Indian policy, and Bowles was the chief instrument in preventing surveying the boundary line. This alone was enough to perturb President Washington and Henry Knox, the portly secretary of war. Another concern was the relationship of Bowles to the British government. Was he, as was current in the newspapers, the new British superintendent for the southern Indians? If not, what was his connection with Whitehall? These questions were frequently raised; confusion abounded; and no one was more perplexed than George Hammond, the new British minister to the United States. He was pointedly asked whether in fact Bowles were a new superintendent, whether reinforcements were on the way to help the Creeks maintain their ancient boundary, and whether Britain was supplying powder, guns, and even cannon. Hammond's dilemma was that he did not know. He reasoned that in view of the Nootka settlement it was unlikely that Britain would back Bowles. This could lead to a rupture with both Spain and the United States, and if such a crisis were imminent certainly he should know about it. He was positive Bowles had no commission but could prove it only by "implication and analogy"—something less than satisfactory to Knox.[25] Only Whitehall could speak with authority, and both Hammond in Philadelphia and Dorchester in Quebec, for the same reasons, immediately wrote for clarification. Grenville replied with the truth—almost: Bowles had no commission and no right to speak for Britain. She was not even encouraging the Indians north of the Ohio and would not think of tampering with those farther south.[26] Despite this reply relayed by Hammond, Americans, considering Bowles's visit to Quebec and London, found it "curious that the King of England should be at so much trouble and expense for no other purpose but to advise the Indians to be at Peace."[27]

Hammond had been reassured of a fact that Bowles well knew: despite the financial assistance and encouragement he had been given by British officials in the Bahamas, Canada, and even in London and despite the permission Muskogee vessels had to trade in British West Indian ports, as far as Whitehall was concerned technically he was on his own. Nevertheless, William had made considerable headway on his return. McGillivray had "fled" the Creek country; there was some prospect that the Spanish negotiations might bear fruit; and chances for a general western Indian confederation after General Arthur St. Clair's defeat seemed better than ever. If an effective confederation came into being and if there were an adjustment of the 1783 Anglo-American peace treaty, then the western boundary might be modified—and not only north of the Ohio. To promote a western confederacy Bowles and his friends encouraged northern Indians when their delegations arrived in the south; Richard Justice, who had accompanied Bowles to London, joined other Cherokees in a scalp dance at Lookout Mountain Town and helped tear a fresh Cumberland scalp with his hands and teeth;[28] and the youthful Director General tried to keep open communications with Canada.

The Canadian government had just been reorganized and split into two provinces: French Lower Canada with its capital at Quebec, and English Upper Canada with its capital at Newark on the Niagara River. John Graves Simcoe was the energetic new lieutenant-governor of Upper Canada and was an old comrade-in-arms of Bowles. It is questionable how much in common the provincial ensign had had with dashing Colonel Simcoe, commander of the Queen's Rangers. The Colonel had been wounded in the fighting at Monmouth, and later his Queen's Rangers were part of the New York garrison. It was here, or possibly earlier at Philadelphia, that Bowles became at least casually acquainted with the Colonel in the period before the

Maryland Loyalists left for the West Indies. It was not until the summer of 1791 when he was on the verge of leaving for his new Canadian post that Simcoe again heard from "that Active Adventurer, Bowles: he had served when a boy under my command. I inculcated to him peace, and to settle a boundary, and a system of colonization which I thought practicable and might be eventually of great utility to this country. You will perceive, to my surprise he talks of visiting me in Upper Canada."[29] There is no telling what system of colonization or what boundary Simcoe meant, but there is every reason to believe he was not thinking of Ensign Bowles whom he had not seen probably since 1778 but the Director General of the Creek-Cherokee nations who had recently attracted so much attention in London.

Simcoe, because of his position, was more concerned with western affairs and by nature was more aggressive than Dorchester. Should Bowles visit Upper Canada he might expect more encouragement than at Quebec. Simcoe, like most westerners, was interested in New Orleans, and after arriving in Canada indicated he would furnish the American frontiersmen arms for a New Orleans attack.[30] Indian hostility prevented any such Canadian-American frontiersmen's co-operation, and one of Simcoe's main concerns was whether the northern Indians, jubilant after their recent successes, could continue to hold off the Americans, and if, in turn, the boundary might be adjusted in Canada's favor. "The Northern Confederacy will strengthen in the meantime, and if Bowles is not idle the treaty to the Southward may be broken."[31]

A journey from the Lower Creek territory to Canada would be a time-consuming undertaking, and events dictated that William would be too occupied ever to make such a journey. Leadership of the loosely confederated Indian towns demanded constant attention. The minute that an Indian spokesman could not provide for basic needs was likely to be the instant that his influence waned, especially if another were eager to take his place. And there were a half-dozen or so individuals in Creek territory currently or in the immediate future claiming to be head of the Creeks. John Galphin, like McGillivray a half-breed son of a wealthy Loyalist Georgia and Carolina Indian trader, was one; Milfort, McGillivray's brother-in-law, was another. Rivalry for leadership had hurt McGillivray and could easily injure Bowles. His concern, as McGillivray's, was in providing an ample supply of goods. Patrolling Spanish vessels off the Florida coast, aided by Panton's tips as to when Miller's vessels were leaving, were a cause for anxiety. And McGillivray, though infirm and with diminished popularity, could not be discounted.

The Creek nation was in turmoil. Bowles was desperately trying to maintain or increase his influence, but opening a free trade with Nassau in face of determined opposition was proving difficult. He expected to establish two ports, one at Indian River and the other near the mouth of the Ochlockonee River. Though the latter was more distant from New Providence and was only thirty miles from the fort at St. Marks, in William's mind this port was to be the most important because it was near the heart of the Creek-Seminole country and only a little further from the Cherokees. Shortly after his return Seminoles and Lower Creeks, supervised by Wellbank and a handful of whites, laid out a town, hoisted the Muskogee flag, and began constructing log warehouses and other buildings necessary for trade. Though occasionally a Nassau ship reached Bowles, Indians in the interior began wondering if he would be able to furnish supplies in the quantities promised. Arms, powder, blankets, iron pots, and the like were indispensable for the Indians. There was another solution, and what he suggested was not new. Some six miles upstream from the small Spanish St. Marks fort was one of Panton's principal warehouses. It was heavily stocked with goods, out of sight of the fort, and in the area where Bowles's following was strongest. Why not appropriate Panton's goods until Miller's vessels began regularly arriving? Given the opportunity Bowles would have seized one of Panton's warehouses in 1788, and since Panton recently had placed a price on William's head, there was even more reason in 1792.[32]

Bowles could not allow his influence to dissipate and resolved that appropriating Panton's warehouse was the only recourse. Accompanied by a handful of whites and about one hundred Indians, he made his way in January to the vicinity of Panton's store. One of the whites with the Director General was a newcomer, William Cunningham. Later when he was in the hands of the Spaniards Cunningham maintained he was merely trying to return to Detroit from the defunct state of Franklin. But since General St. Clair's army was between the Tennessee and Detroit it seemed expedient to head southward through the Indian country and to try to secure passage to Nassau and Canada. Supposedly it was only by chance that Cunningham, journeying through the Creek nation, for the first time came upon Bowles. The Director General insisted he had a British commission and urged Cunningham to join—an offer that was accepted and Cunningham was appointed major.[33]

It is hard not to agree with the Spaniards, who later suspected Cunningham's story. Was it merely coincidence that Cunningham was originally from Washington County (formerly Frederick County), Maryland—Bowles's birthplace—that he was a Loyalist in New York before the evacuation—when Bowles and Wellbank were there—and that he had been employed in Detoit in 1790—when Bowles had been in Quebec urging Dorchester to take the southern Indians under his wing? Indications are that Cunningham knew of Bowles's desire to unite all western Indians into a general confederation and that he came into the Creek country to seek out the Director General.

Both Bowles and Cunningham, accompanied by a few Indians, visited Panton's store, had lengthy discussions with Edward Forrester, the storekeeper, and unsuccessfully tried to wean him away from his employer. On one such visit Cunningham, this time alone, was even invited to dine. After dinner and after exchanging pleasantries, the Major, startling everyone at the table, rose to his feet, drew his sword, thrust it into the wooden floor, declared that Forrester and the warehouse were in Bowles's power and that anyone who moved would be cut to pieces. Immediately Bowles and his Indian followers appeared, relieved Forrester of his keys, began distributing powder, ball, guns, blankets, shirts, and boots and later at night celebrated their success by "dancing and hooping round the fire." The status of the bulk of the undistributed goods and skins, valued at up to fifteen thousand dollars, was yet to be decided.[34] Some of the Indians felt Eastajoca had gone too far in seizing Panton's store. One was Thomas Perryman, Bowles's wife's kinsman. It is difficult to tell if there was more to the dispute, but in the end Bowles chased Perryman, his brother, and a few others across the Wakulla River. Thomas Perryman never forgot this insult.[35] It was always hard for Bowles to disagree mildly with anyone, whether it was his superior officer at Pensacola in 1778, his antagonist in the New York duel, or now Mary's relations.

Only a few miles away was the Spanish St. Mark's garrison; it would have appeared that Bowles had taken a great risk. Actually the danger was slight. The garrison was small and to defend the fort and Panton's warehouse simultaneously was not at all feasible. A 24-man patrol, half of the garrison, had set out after Bowles, but learning of the many armed warriors—newly armed to be sure—returned to the fort's sanctuary.[36] The Spanish commandant's main concern, despite Bowles's assurances of restricting hostilities to Panton's warehouse, was for the fort's security. Panton's partner, the distraught Leslie, within the fort and getting frequent reports of how Bowles was helping himself to the captured stores, was furious but could not prod the commandant into action. Leslie had no recourse but to write Panton about the details of the capture, about how the supposedly friendly Indians indebted to their firm had joined Bowles, about the lack of resoluteness of the Spanish commandant who would not risk all to recover the store, and about concern over McGillivray's inactivity.[37]

News of Bowles's action quickly reached Pensacola, and it was difficult to tell whether the Spaniards or Panton were more furious, though Panton, who immediately dispatched a letter to McGillivray demanding Bowles's scalp, seemed to have the edge.[38] It was not Panton's loss that overly concerned Governor Arturo O'Neill at Pensacola and Baron de Carondelet at New Orleans but that Bowles might make good his bid for Indian leadership to the detriment of Spain. After news of Bowles's triumph, Carondelet armed the packet boat at New Orleans with eight cannon, and early in February, under the direction of the experienced sailor, Pedro Rousseau, the *Galga* set sail for St. Marks. Aboard were twenty-three soldiers, commanded by José de Hevia. This tiny force was not likely to overwhelm Bowles, but it and the armed vessel could make the St. Marks garrison more respectable and could interdict commerce with Nassau.[39]

Bowles was true to his word in not molesting the Spaniards. He considered taking St. Marks—this is exactly what he told Grenville he would do—and there was an even chance he could have succeeded. At this time, however, the Director General hoped to supplant Panton with Spanish approval. He had been hurt by the loss of his St. Marks store; McGillivray had not come to Panton's aid; and Bowles reasoned that this was the ideal time for Spain to overthrow both Panton and McGillivray. Bowles remained at the warehouse, insisting on the justice of his action, all the while loading ammunition on packhorses for distribution to the various towns.[40] At the same time he was completing work on his own warehouses on the Ochlockonee, only thirty miles away but relatively safe from the fort's tiny garrison, and he was wondering why there was no word from Dunmore or Miller. Maybe now the Spaniards would tolerate this commerce; maybe he could put into effect the plan of government he envisioned for Muskogee; maybe he could draw the southern Indians into closer relations with Canada. Maybe. There were many possibilities, many dreams, and William had to rethink his strategy almost daily.

Hevia, cautiously making his way up the St. Marks River in the *Galga,* helped Bowles make up his mind. The Spanish captain would like to capture the intruder, and the infuriated Leslie was in enthusiastic agreement. There were some forty friendly Indians at the fort, and they, along with a detachment of soldiers could go after their

quarry—but at considerable risk. As it turned out, there would be no
bloodshed. It suited the convenience and capability of each party to
negotiate. Bowles, dividing his time between supervising the distribution of Panton's goods, building his own warehouses, and watching
the Spaniards at the fort, had timely information of the *Galga's* arrival. Hevia, looking out from the newly built, triangular-shaped,
hewn-stone fort, discerned a small party of Indians approaching, four
chiefs on foot and a tall figure on horseback wearing a plumed turban—the latter it was disclosed was the author of the recent disturbance.[41] Bowles was a familiar figure to the garrison, and in the past
both the Spaniards and Leslie without success had tried to entice the
Director General into the fort. He had returned now to see if Hevia
had anything to offer.

This time William entered the fort and was greeted by familiar
faces: Leslie, Forrester who had "thought proper to take a dark night
and come to the fort," and, surprisingly enough, William Cunningham. After the capture of Panton's warehouse Cunningham and
Bowles had quarreled. Perhaps, as Cunningham alleged, he discovered Bowles had lied about a British commission, or perhaps, as
Bowles insisted, Cunningham had disobeyed orders. Whatever the
cause of the dispute it was a violent one, and Cunningham, who was
tied up by the Indians and feared for his life, escaped and counted
himself lucky when he reached the fort with hardly any clothes.[42]
Leslie was both relieved and apprehensive at Bowles's arrival: relieved because at last Bowles apparently was in Spanish clutches but
apprehensive because of the Director General's protracted conversations with Hevia. Could by any chance the Spaniards be negotiating in earnest and believe that this madman had replaced McGillivray? Without question Bowles believed the Spaniards at last were
ready to treat with him. Naturally they distrusted him, but in the
present circumstances each might be able to serve the other. Should
Spain ever want to come to terms, now was the time. Many of the
Creeks were following his lead, and McGillivray had yet to show his
face.[43]

From the beginning Hevia indicated that Spain was ready to
negotiate in earnest and to consider the points mentioned in the Director General's earlier letter to Floridablanca. But such important
conversations, involving the fate of Spanish Florida and even Louisiana, could not effectively be carried on in the inelegant setting at
St. Marks. To reach a satisfactory understanding it would be desirable
for Bowles to come to New Orleans and negotiate directly with Carondelet rather than to deal with Hevia, who was only an ensign. Hevia

was a gentleman and pledged his word and that of his government that Bowles would be dealt with honorably. He would be given a safe-conduct pass, and, regardless of the negotiations' outcome, would be allowed to return to his Indian friends within forty days. Despite Wellbank's warnings and some misgivings, Bowles accepted the Spanish offer. He believed circumstances would force the Spaniards to make extensive concessions to Muskogee and before departing left a letter explaining his decision for the captain of the merchant vessel expected to arrive any day at the Ochlockonee from Nassau: "I am obliged by business of a publick nature to go to New Orleans . . . you may land what goods you have . . . [if you await my return] then you may depart with more satisfaction than before."[44] Bidding his followers farewell, Eastajoca boarded the *Galga* anchored alongside the fort and soon began to sail downstream out into the Gulf. The relieved Leslie jubilantly informed his partner that "we have at last prevailed on Squire Bowles, to pay a visit to the Governor of Louisiana."[45] Leslie assumed that Carondelet would have the good sense to insure that Bowles never returned to Florida.

The St. Marks commandant was delighted to see Bowles leave but was disappointed that Hevia's men departed. Even with this adventurer out of the way, conditions around St. Marks had not changed. Wellbank now was in charge of the Indians and, supported by some two hundred natives, was still master of Panton's store. The Spanish garrison dared not venture far from the fort and in reality was in a state of semi-siege. There were rumors, having some foundation, that armed vessels were outfitting in Nassau to take possession of the fort, and for this and a number of other reasons the commandant did not care to contemplate his fate if he did not receive reinforcements or if Bowles did not return within forty days.[46] In addition to watching over the fort and Panton's store, Wellbank was responsible for the crude huts erected near the mouth of the Ochlockonee River. Only a few days after the *Galga's* departure, the New Providence vessel heavily laden with merchandise that Bowles had been expecting—this time Dunmore was the chief owner of both the vessel and its cargo—arrived. The crew went ashore but was disappointed in learning that the huts were not brimming over with deerskins, that there were only a few Indians about, and that Bowles was bound for New Orleans.[47]

A passenger aboard Dunmore's vessel was John Bowles, William's younger brother. John probably had not seen his brother since they had hunted, fished, and gone to school together during the early stages of the Revolution. But John, reading the public accounts of the Director General and probably directly encouraged by his brother, had sailed from Maryland to Nassau. Miller and Dunmore took the younger Bowles in hand, and in turn John helped the Governor get his ship outfitted. When it was learned at the mouth of the Ochlockonee that the Director General had sailed for New Orleans, no one was more disappointed than John. With Wellbank and the bulk of the Indians at St. Marks, with the *Galga* or some other enemy vessel cruising about, it was dangerous to unload the cargo or to linger. John returned to Nassau and, with Miller's aid, eventually to Maryland, having failed in his bid for glory among the southern Indians. Miller, who had been on the verge of dispatching his own vessel to Florida, decided to wait until there was word from New Orleans.[48]

Wellbank was disturbed that no merchandise was unloaded at the Ochlockonee huts, but even so he had his hands full guarding the remaining goods at Panton's store. Many already had been distributed, and packhorses from the Indian towns were frequently arriving for more. Wellbank had to keep most of his armed Indian followers here, or the St. Marks' garrison might repossess the warehouse. Over a month after Bowles's departure Milfort, McGillivray's brother-in-law, modestly asserting that, as McGillivray's right-hand man, he was Tastanegy or Great War Chief of all the Creeks, arrived with a party of Indians. There were numerous conferences and much haggling but no hostilities; and in the end Wellbank's followers agreed to return home peacefully. By now there were few goods to guard at the warehouse, and Panton's claim that his loss was fifteen thousand dollars was no great exaggeration.[49] Wellbank retired to the village of Usachees on the Chattahoochee with Bowles's papers and personal belongings, continued to intrigue with Perryman and Philatouchy, raised the Muskogee flag, and awaited the return of his chief; Dunmore, Miller, Panton, McGillivray and a host of others remained deeply concerned about the outcome of the New Orleans negotiations.[50]

V

Spanish Duplicity

AS THE *Galga* steadily made its way toward New Orleans, Hevia was relieved that the troublesome Indian chief was aboard and thankful that it was not necessary to decide between treating his passenger as the head of an independent state or as a prisoner. Hevia was not sure of Bowles's official status because his superiors—themselves uncertain what to do with Bowles—had given Hevia no detailed instructions. And Bowles, wondering what the Spaniards at New Orleans intended, watched as the *Galga* sailed into the mouth of the Mississippi and up the meandering river to New Orleans. Hevia delivered his passenger to the new, forceful, Louisiana governor, Baron de Carondelet, who lodged his guest in the regimental barracks, treated him courteously and with respect, but, ominous for the future, made it clear that Eastajoca was not allowed to leave his quarters at will. Nevertheless, with Bowles now in New Orleans, negotiations could begin in earnest.[1]

The Baron and other officials were fascinated by this controversial adventurer who had stepped ashore wearing his plumed turban and Indian dress. The energetic Carondelet had recently been installed as governor and had ambitious plans for his province. He was determined to maintain Louisiana's and Florida's integrity in face of American expansion by building more forts at strategic locations or repairing old ones, by continuing to intrigue with dissatified westerners, by encouraging Americans to settle on Spanish soil and become Spanish subjects, and especially by organizing the southern Indians into a tighter Spanish-dominated confederacy. In this latter regard Eastajoca might be of service, and it was more than idle curiosity that prompted the Baron to visit the Director General.[2]

With forcefulness and logic Bowles, making a determined bid in behalf of Muskogee, explained why there should be an alliance. He claimed that the sickly, grasping McGillivray had sold out to the Americans and had alienated the Creeks by territorial concessions at New York. Spain, no less than Eastajoca, should be insistent that the 1790 boundary line not be run. Moreover, Bowles, in contrast to Mc-Gillivray, was in excellent health, held no American commission, and was not in American pay. In addition to being a leader of the Creeks, Bowles argued that he had an important following among the Chickamaugas, and it was in Spain's interest to bring these warriors, implacable foes of the Americans, into the Spanish orbit. The idea had occurred earlier to Carondelet and was in accord with his plan of forging an effective southern Indian confederation. Bowles maintained that he was not only the leader of the Creeks and Cherokees, the Director General of the combined nations' affairs, but also he had recently negotiated a treaty with the northern Indians that would be instrumental in containing the Americans.[3]

Both Panton and McGillivray, William repeatedly emphasized, had lost their usefulness to Spain and to the Indians. Panton's high prices, partly because of Spanish duties and partly because of the Scotsman's avariciousness, were a prime source of Indian discontent; and McGillivray had lost his influence and in no way had been able to impede Bowles. Should the proposed alliance come into being, Eastajoca, magnifying the number of his followers, promised that twenty thousand Creek and Cherokee warriors, and probably other southern Indians, would combine with Spaniards against the Americans. Through his Canadian contacts and existing treaties with the northern Indians, he would promote a western Indian confederation to serve both British and Spanish interests. In return Spain must allow him at least two free ports in the Indian country to keep the Indians content and amply supplied. Spain would not have to, and indeed should not, indiscriminately throw open the Florida trade— except to his Providence Island merchant backers.[4]

Carondelet and the Indian leader held a series of interviews as the voluble Director General argued for an alliance. For the most part Carondelet concurred with Bowles that Spain ought not to allow the 1790 boundary line run; that McGillivray had lost his influence or even had gone over to the Americans; that there were serious faults with Panton's monopoly; and that the southern Indians should remain content and friendly to Spain. Where the two never reached agreement was whether Bowles would be more zealous and effective in Spain's behalf than Panton was. The Director General was a half-pay British officer, so it was not only McGillivray who was subject to the charge of serving two masters. It was an open question who—

Britain or Spain—would profit most from a general western Indian confederation stretching from the Gulf to Canada subsidized exclusively by British merchants.

Bowles was never able to convince Carondelet exactly how Spain would benefit by sanctioning free ports in Florida for commerce with Nassau. It could be argued that there were advantages, but these points aside, asking Spain to permit free trade anywhere in her American empire was no insignificant request. It is true that she had just enacted many "free trade" reforms for her empire, but these reforms reduced internal rather than external commercial barriers. The writings of Adam Smith and the physiocrats had influenced the Spanish Bourbons, but the king of Spain was hardly more willing now than in the sixteenth century to allow foreigners to traffic freely in Spanish America—not if it could be avoided. William knew that Spain had been forced to make an exception to her traditional restrictive policy in Florida by allowing Panton to dominate the southern trade, and conceivably she could make another exception in his favor. But should the Spaniards allow a free commerce between Nassau and the Creeks and Cherokees, would these Indians be any more dependent on Spain and solicitous of her interests?

Bowles remained in New Orleans for only two weeks before going on to Havana for further negotiations. Even in this brief period his charges—others vented them as well—that McGillivray had gone over to the Americans and had lost his grip on the Creeks were disturbing to Panton and Leslie. Even more alarming was that Carondelet might throw caution to the winds and reach an agreement with this adventurer. If Eastajoca and his Nassau backers, Miller and Dunmore, won concessions from Spain, which they might legally do, what room would there be for Panton, Leslie, and Company? This possibility was more disturbing than any inactivity or deception by McGillivray and is why Panton, in his letters to Carondelet and other Spanish authorities, outdid himself in denouncing Bowles. "I never saw that Jockey, in my life, but what I have heard of him, his volubility of Speech Can only be equalled by his Empudence, in uttering the grocest falsehoods."[5] The Scotsman's anxiety was not decreased when Carondelet was adamant that the Americans not run the 1790 treaty line: if McGillivray did not reverse his New York agreement and take steps to insure the line was not established, then Spain would have no choice but to support Bowles.[6] Speaking bluntly, Carondelet held the threat of Bowles as a replacement over McGillivray's head, hoping this would force the Upper Creek leader to sever his connection with the United States. Panton, quick to defend and make ex-

cuses for McGillivray, insisted that his recent supineness was due to
sickness and dissipation rather than any intent to betray Spain and
was quick to point out that McGillivray's brother-in-law, Milfort,
eventually had arrived at St. Marks and had helped disperse Bowles's
followers—"which altho' too late to come at Bowles was not the less
meritorious, and was at last of great service; because it disperced those
plunderers, who were still in a body sufficient to comit mischief."[7]
Panton had nightmares over the possibility that Bowles might effectively oppose McGillivray and contended that it would be folly
for Spain should she "estimate that scoundrel's abilities at too high a
rate."[8] McGillivray, himself, was just as adamant that Bowles was a
base adventurer who had deluded the Indians with false promises of
goods and British troops.[9]

Cunningham was equally vehement in his denunciations. Pres-
ently he was a Spanish guest in New Orleans and, like Bowles,
quartered in the regimental barracks, though unquestionably a prisoner. The Spaniards became convinced that Cunningham was a
worthless intriguer not to be trusted, and there is no indication they
were deceived. All along he maintained that he had known Bowles for
only a brief period, that he had been commissioned major under false
pretenses, and that he had been forced to draw his sword and demand
the keys from the St. Marks storekeeper. Cunningham went into
detail about Bowles's plans. He disclosed that he had made a thorough examination of Bowles's papers and that the Director General
had no British commission and no commitment from Dorchester. He
then made the damning charge that Bowles was part of the sordid
Yazoo speculation and was in collusion with Dunmore, General Elijah Clark of Georgia, William Blount, governor of the Southwest
Territory, Colonel David Ross of Virginia, William Cocke, an
organizer of the State of Franklin, and George Hancock of Botetourt
County, Virginia. Both McGillivray and Bowles were accused of collaborating with the Yazoo speculators, though no authoritative judgment can be passed until the intricacies of the Yazoo speculation are
unraveled. In assessing Cunningham's lengthy testimony and charges
one cannot escape the opinion—the one held by the Spaniards—that
his loquaciousness was primarily to ingratiate himself with his captors
in order to secure his release.[10] To accept all of his testimony at face
value would be questionable.

While interrogating Cunningham and negotiating with Bowles,
Carondelet was observing closely developments in the Indian country.
One of his main concerns was Wellbank. What was he up to? Would
he be able to retaliate should Eastajoca not return within forty days?

Before retiring to the Chattahoochee with Bowles's belongings, Well-bank and the Indians remained at the huts on the Ochlockonee awaiting word from Bowles and supplies from New Providence. Wellbank became anxious and wrote to his chief.[11] At this point Carondelet had not decided what to do with the Director General and considered it possible that it might be in Spain's interest to employ him and to acquiesce in at least part of his demands. Until a final decision was reached certainly he should not be turned loose. To gain time and to calm Wellbank, Bowles was allowed to answer his subordinate's letter and to disclose that, at Carondelet's suggestion, it would be necessary to go to Havana to conclude the negotiations. Despite misgivings, Bowles had accepted Carondelet's proposal. In reality the Governor was not sure what to do with his prisoner—there were risks regardless of the decision—and, since Bowles would not accept a Spanish commission and put aside Muskogee's extensive demands, he was passing along both Bowles and the responsibility of reaching a decision to Luis de las Casas, the Baron's brother-in-law and governor of Cuba.

Bowles had realized he was taking a risk when he first boarded the *Galga* and sailed to New Orleans, but he had assumed the stakes justified such a move; besides, gambling was part of his nature. Yet as he now sailed down the Mississippi into the Gulf of Mexico out of sight of Louisiana and Florida, he had serious doubts that his gamble would pay off.

The voyage to Cuba was routine, and by mid-April Havana was in sight. As eleven years before, William sailed through the harbor's entrance, the somber Morro, ageless and indestructible, guarding the passageway. Even from the superficial inspection permitted, he could see that Havana had changed little. As the Spaniards lodged him in the inhospitable Morro, Bowles realized, much to his chagrin, that he now was definitely a prisoner; that Las Casas treated him with all decency and respect was of little comfort. It was not yet apparent, but in fact Bowles had begun a long odyssey which would take him thousands of miles from the Creeks, always a prisoner. Whether Spain treated him more like a common felon or regarded him as an important political prisoner of state normally varied in direct proportion to his distance from Florida.[12]

Negotiations with Las Casas in an abbreviated form were a replica of those with Carondelet. William unleashed all his old arguments: that McGillivray was in the pay of the United States; that this American protégé also was collaborating with the Yazoo speculators; that if Spain did not make a satisfactory treaty with Muskogee then the

Creeks would be forced to look elsewhere; and that Panton's avariciousness was undermining Spain's control over the southern Indians. Las Casas, like Carondelet, would privately concur with most of these charges, but the Cuban governor was far more convinced than Carondelet that replacing McGillivray and Panton with Bowles and Miller would be going from bad to worse. The Governor knew Bowles was a British half-pay officer and felt his visit to Quebec and London had not been in vain. If there were a western buffer state dominated by British merchants in Canada and New Providence, exactly how would Spain benefit? Would not the Floridas be swallowed up and would not the whites who settled in the West under British auspices be just as covetous of New Orleans, and infinitely closer?[13]

If by chance there should be an Anglo-Spanish rapprochement—an eighteenth-century rarity—then Bowles might be of some service, and it might be worthwhile to agree to some of his demands. Las Casas was remote from the fluctuating European diplomatic scene and resolved to send Bowles to Spain for an ultimate decision. For the time being he would be out of touch with Wellbank, and if the government wanted to employ this adventurer they could return him on the same ship with new instructions; if not, good riddance.[14] Carondelet had been careful to maintain the illusion that Bowles was not a prisoner, but the Cuban governor did not fret over such a distinction. Recent events in the Indian country indicated that such deferential treatment was no longer necessary.

News that Milfort had induced most of Bowles's followers to return to their villages was encouraging and in some measure restored Spanish confidence in McGillivray. And the Upper Creek leader apparently was willing not to run the 1790 boundary line—or the combined pressure of Pedro Olivier, the Spanish agent sent to "advise" McGillivray, and Bowles's following forced him to adopt this position. Moreover, Carondelet, partly through Panton, was attempting to bring the Chickamaugas into the Spanish sphere, reducing their dependence on Bowles, Wellbank, Miller, or their Canadian counterparts. Las Casas reasoned that Bowles was merely a non-recognized adventurer, that the safe-conduct pass was not binding, and that it was perfectly justifiable to send him on to the *rey católico* in Spain.[15] Bowles could only wonder whether servants of the Catholic king relied primarily on the Gospels or the principles of Machiavelli's *Prince*.

Escorted by Spanish soldiers, Bowles took leave of Fort Morro and made his way down to the *Mississippi* anchored in the harbor. Much to his surprise he found that his traveling companions were Louisiana's former Governor Estevan Miró and his charming wife Celeste, return-

ing to Spain after capably serving the province for some years. Miró
knew about Bowles and considered him a menace to Spanish interests
in Louisiana and Florida. Yet Miró and Celeste were not sorry to have
the prisoner aboard. Among whites as well as Indians Bowles always
elicited controversy, and he was called every name conceivable in a
variety of languages. But frequently those who denounced him most
or had the best reason to fear his designs were the ones who were
most captivated by the ingratiating Indian chief. This had been true
with Carondelet, who was impressed by Bowles's bearing and his ability
to converse on a wide range of subjects—in reality their personalities
were not dissimilar—and this was also Miró's reaction. The long
journey would be less tedious with the Indian chieftain aboard. Celeste,
more than her husband, was intrigued with the youthful Director
General, whose impressive carriage, Indian costume, and conversa-
tional abilities were a welcome shipboard diversion. When the sea
was calm Bowles, borrowing paper and brushes, painted a pastel
portrait of Celeste, though, according to her devoted husband, the
results indicated that the sea was still too rough[16]—or that William
should have studied Cousin Carington's *Artist's Assistant* more carefully. In his free time he wrote an account of his life for Miró, similar
to the one published in London. The former Louisiana governor was
too sensible to believe everything in this narrative or to be taken in
by the captivating adventurer. But Bowles was excellent company;
he had charmed Celeste; and should conditions warrant Spanish employment, he could expect Miró's influential support. As soon as the
former Louisiana governor landed in Spain he sent to Madrid authorities the account of Bowles's life and subsequently conferred with
them at length about the desirability of utilizing him in Florida.[17]

At some point in the voyage a Spanish infantry captain, who had
been one of William's guardians and who could not swim, fell overboard. William, who was on deck and witnessed the accident, immediately dived in and, according to his admiring biographer, dramatically
addressed his struggling victim: "Wretch! it is in my power either to
leave you to your fate, or to precipitate you at this very moment to
the bottom of the ocean—live, however (added he, raising him up),
if life can be desirable to such a man as you, and from my hands!"[18]
Simultaneously to deliver a Periclean oration and to save a full-grown
drowning man is impossible. One suspects that Bowles, desperately
trying to keep the officer's head above water, was not as eloquent in
the ocean as he was on land.

Panton's store had been captured in January 1792, and by June
Bowles was in Spain. In this instance the Spaniards had moved with

more than customary dispatch and, other considerations aside, were anxious to put as much distance as possible between Eastajoca and the Indian country. They were afraid he might communicate with Wellbank and incite the Indians to hostilities. There was some basis for their fears, because Wellbank was not idle. Resplendent in his scarlet British uniform, he journeyed from the huts on the Ochlockonee, to Coweta, to the Chickamaugas, and even to Nassau to keep alive the influence of Bowles, Miller, and Dunmore: "I will gladly obey any person sent . . . to replace General Bowles."[19] At one point Panton, alert to every opportunity to discredit the Bahamian governor, sought out Wellbank and attempted to buy Bowles's papers, though the Scotsman was aware that Dunmore was "too keen a *Rascal*" to leave incriminating letters.[20] Wellbank's main concern, like Bowles's, was in maintaining a dependable trade with Nassau, and he informed Miller and Dunmore that, though Panton had burned Bowles's warehouses on the Ochlockonee, he was rebuilding them, and that supplies must quickly be sent lest in desperation the Creeks and Cherokee turn to the Spaniards.

Dunmore did not acknowledge defeat with Bowles's capture. There was always the possibility the Spaniards might reach an accord with the Director General, and there were still Lower Creeks, Seminoles, and Cherokees who formerly gave their allegiance to Bowles and now to his lieutenant, Wellbank. All the old projects might be carried out even though Eastajoca was no longer on the scene. While unsuccessfully pressing Whitehall to intervene in Bowles's behalf, Dunmore was still encouraging the southern Indians, giving presents to Creeks and Cherokees who occasionally visited Nassau, and who invariably had been Bowles's enthusiastic disciples, and urging the government to provide these presents on a permanent basis as in Canada. Those Indians who indicated they were willing to cede lands to the Governor were singled out for special attention. Philatouchy was one of those who came to Nassau, and in 1793 Dunmore gave him a commission authorizing him to train the warriors in his village and be ever ready to serve George III or the Governor.[21] Though Bowles was gone, he could return at any moment; in the meantime there was something to the reports that one of Dunmore's sons was to be his replacement.[22]

As of old, Miller and Dunmore loaded Indian goods aboard a ship, the *Resolution*, bound for the Ochlockonee. The Spaniards for obvious reasons had become concerned with illicit Bahamian commerce and had commissioned more armed vessels to patrol the coast.

These vessels harassed Bahamian wreckers and turtlers on the Florida peninsula and, more important, captured the *Resolution* and the party of eleven Creek and Cherokee Indians aboard, including Phila-touchy, the Tiger King, and the half-breed Tom Lewis, all of whom were Bowles's old friends.[23] This recent setback cost Dunmore dearly. The lure of profits from western fur trade and land speculation was still there, and a change on the diplomatic front might yet bring success; but for the immediate future he would be more circumspect —at least where his own money was involved. Now he concentrated on having the British government reimburse him for the "illegal" Spanish seizure and at the same time insisted that Bowles, "judaised [*sic*] by the Spaniards," be released.[24]

United States officials, including the Creek agent, James Seagrove, on the fringe of the Indian country at Coleraine, and Washington, Jefferson, and Knox in Philadelphia, had observed with attention Bowles's capture and its effects on the Indians. Though the Director General was thousands of miles away his influence was still felt in the Indian country, and many questions remained unanswered. The American cabinet was never sure whether Bowles had an official commission and exactly what were Britain's designs on Louisiana and Florida. Were the newspaper reports that Bowles had been hanged in Spain correct; if not, why had the Spaniards gone to the expense of sending him there?[25] Was this not a ruse to get him to Spain to negotiate a treaty? With Britain and Spain apparently drawing closer together was there not some Anglo-Spanish plot brewing to restrict American expansion in which the Director General would play a prominent role?[26] And there was John Bowles who had returned to Maryland. Could he not be arrested, as some were suggesting, to insure William would stay in line? John had never had an opportunity to commit any treasonable act or to violate American neutrality, and Washington was not able "to lay hold of him."[27]

Another question was why, with Bowles in Spain, was the 1790 boundary line not run? Was his following still so powerful that Mc-Gillivray dared not execute the treaty and was Spain on the verge of abandoning the Upper Creek leader? The distraught McGillivray, with only months to live, bemoaned the fact that Bowles's faction was still agitated and that Spain was putting undue pressure on him not to allow running of the boundary line: I find I am "in the situation of a keeper of Bedlam, and nearly fit for an inhabitant."[28] Would by any chance Spain return Bowles to Florida to make doubly sure the line was not run? With the passage of time and still no sign of Bowles, with McGillivray's apparently regaining control of the Creeks, and with the death of Dragging Canoe in 1792, Washington could rest easier regarding the southern Indians.

Bowles, either imprisoned in his Havana cell or enjoying relative freedom aboard the *Mississippi,* was cut off from developments in the Indian country, a circumstance which became even more acute in the years ahead. Charles IV's advisors, the Conde de Aranda and the youthful guardsman, Manuel de Godoy, though they disagreed on vital issues, were in complete accord that for now Bowles should not return to Florida and should be closely guarded. When the *Mississippi* anchored at Cádiz, William bid *adiós* to Miró and Celeste and soon the former governor and his wife left for Madrid to lobby successfully for a high army appointment and to give more details about Bowles.[29] William went directly to the gloomy royal prison of this ancient port. Spain had many prisons for those who violated her detailed colonial regulations, and the Director General was to inhabit more than his share. Before he reached Spain there had been some question whether he were a prisoner; at Cádiz there was none, and looking up at the clear sky and out on the blue ocean from his humid cell, thinking about his friends and family in the Indian country, he realized, unless he could persuade the Spaniards to change their attitude, he had blundered by walking into the St. Marks fort.

After being installed in Cádiz' prison, and even before leaving the *Mississippi,* he began bombarding leading Spaniards with detailed reasons why a treaty should be negotiated and why he should be allowed to return immediately to the Indian country. He had wrested control of the natives from McGillivray; Panton was serving his own and not Spain's interests; and only Eastajoca could induce the Indians to support key Spanish objectives. In contrast to McGillivray, William avowed he would have nothing to do with the advancing frontiersmen and Yazoo speculators. On several occasions, including early in 1792, he asserted he had turned a deaf ear to American entreaties that he lead an attack on Florida and New Orleans. Spain would benefit if the Director General were in the Indian country—and delay was dangerous. How long could it be concealed that Spain had violated his safe conduct pass? Bowles's followers had received no word since New Orleans; what would they do when they learned he was being treated as a common criminal?[30]

Future diplomatic events might dictate that Spain would agree to some of Bowles's terms and negotiate a treaty, or it might be equally expedient to try him for seizure of Panton's store and other crimes. There was no possibility, however, that he would quickly be returned to Florida; for the time being it was convenient that he be sent to

Madrid. And so William continued his long journey. Guarded by a
Spanish officer and a small detachment of soldiers, he was escorted
inland across the hot Andalusian plain to Seville, up onto the Meseta,
until ultimately the Spanish capital was in sight. Frequently in the
distance Bowles saw ancient castles silently guarding arid hilltops.
Zanga had been brought to a castle such as these, and William had
painted scenes of the battlements himself. It was natural that he
compared his present plight to Zanga's—except that Don Alonzo,
Zanga's captor, freed and befriended his prisoner. Excluding Miró,
who now was gone, Bowles had no Don Alonzo in Andalusia or in
Castile. The soldiers deposited their prisoner in Madrid's prison, the
last in a series stretching halfway across the country.[31]

Bowles did not know what the Spaniards were up to, nor were they
sure themselves. Europe in 1792 was in a state of confusion, much of
which was related to the effects of the French Revolution. Charles IV
was disturbed about the French upheaval, about the constitution and
semi-imprisonment forced on his Bourbon ally, and about the seepage
of republican ideas across the Pyrenees. Louis XVI's execution and
the beginning of the Jacobin reign of terror the following year were
causes for further alarm. It seemed probable that Spain would have to
sever her traditional French alliance and join other European mon-
archies in stamping out Jacobinism. This happened when in 1793
Spain joined Austria, Prussia, and even Britain in a loose anti-French
coalition.

In the eighteenth century France had been Spain's traditional ally
and Britain the common enemy; now these alliances were reversed, a
circumstance which Bowles knew might work in his favor. Spain and
Britain both had a common interest in restraining western American
expansion, and the Indians, united in a general confederacy, could be
of the greatest assistance. Bowles vainly proposed that to strengthen
the Anglo-Spanish alliance and to further their joint interest in the
Mississippi Valley he should be sent back to America. The fluctuating
European scene was one reason why Bowles's Madrid sojourn was
prolonged. Another was the domestic political confusion and the
question whether the veterans Floridablanca and Aranda or the youthful Godoy enjoyed royal favor. Bowles no sooner opened negotiations
with one of these ministers than he was replaced.[32] This was not the
only perplexity. Some Spaniards, especially Carondelet in Louisiana,
were anxious to utilize the Indians to contain the Americans and were
more willing to employ Eastajoca; others, especially Godoy who was
to win out over his rivals, were becoming more concerned with the
risks rather than the advantages of utilizing the Indians.[33]

The Spaniards, reviewing the changing international and domestic picture and watching the continued American expansion, kept Bowles for a year and a half in his Madrid cell, debating whether to employ him on his own terms or imprison him indefinitely. The Director General was not the only one in this predicament—not that it made a great deal of difference. His lieutenant with whom he had quarreled earlier, William Cunningham, was here also. Cunningham had dogged Bowles's footsteps: from St. Marks to New Orleans, Havana, Cádiz, and ultimately Madrid. These two, assuming Spanish orders were enforced, were never allowed to communicate with each other. Even though Cunningham denounced his ex-comrade, disclosed that the Director General was bent on attacking Spanish possessions, and asserted that Wellbank was a close friend of the American land speculator William Blount and that the Indians ridiculed Bowles and called him the Lying Captain, the Spaniards never believed that Cunningham had known Bowles for less than three weeks and had been compelled to help take Panton's store.[34] If by chance Cunningham were telling the truth he would have many lonely months to rue the consequences of a chance acquaintance. He had arrived in Cádiz some weeks after Bowles, shirt torn and in a common laborer's trousers, with no Miró or Celeste to ease his plight. Like Bowles, Cunningham, guarded by a small detachment, was sent to Madrid for a prolonged imprisonment, never convincing the Spaniards that his incarceration was a gross miscarriage of justice.[35]

Both Bowles and Cunningham, alone in their cells, were cut off from developments in the Indian country, even though William emphasized the danger to Spanish Florida of keeping him secreted in prison. This threat had caused concern. But Bowles's followers eventually had dispersed from St. Marks, and though they insisted they would have nothing to do with Olivier or any other Spaniard until Spain returned "our father . . . once more [to] our land to revive our drooping spirits,"[36] and though John Galphin and small parties of Lower Creeks continued to molest the settlers on both the Spanish and United States side of the St. Marys River,[37] the Creeks did not take up the hatchet in force. It appeared that McGillivray was regaining control and that, after changing his mind, he supported the numerous Creeks who were determined not to see the boundary line run. Meanwhile, Panton, prodded by Spain and in spite of the risks, was taking steps to initiate or improve trade with the Chickamaugas and Seminoles, making them less susceptible to outside agitation.[38] Soon Little Turkey and other defiant Chickamaugas, having little alternative, went down to Pensacola for munitions; and even Moses Price, who had accompanied Bowles to London, became a Spanish interpreter. A few Chickamaugas, refusing to come to terms with either the Spaniards or Americans, moved west of the Mississippi. Bowles's Chickamauga son, now almost full grown, soon to become famous as a leader of the Western Cherokees, was in this group.[39] Except that McGillivray died early in 1793 and Spain needed a successor to manage the Creeks in her behalf and barring the possibility of close Anglo-Spanish co-operation in the Mississippi Valley, there appeared no reason why Eastajoca should ever return to Florida.

Wellbank, after trying over a period of months, for the most part unsuccessfully, to keep open commerce with Nassau via the Ochlockonee or Indian River—Robbins, one of Bowles's lieutenants, was near the latter[40]—eventually was forced to retire to his friends among the Chickamaugas. The opposition of Spain, Panton, and the Creeks had been too great; and the Perrymans, still resenting the humiliation of being chased across the river, joined in.[41] From the vicinity of Lookout Mountain, Wellbank now looked more to Detroit than Nassau and urged Simcoe to take the Chickamaugas under his protection. In the recent past French traders from Detroit had brought their wares to the Tennessee River, and they should be encouraged to continue this commerce. Or else Simcoe should use his influence to see that a satisfactory trade with Nassau was maintained.[42]

With a small party of Creeks and Cherokees Wellbank in 1793 made the long journey to Detroit and Niagara to confer with the northern Indians and Simcoe, and such missions by southern Indians to the north or vice versa were not uncommon. Wellbank explained in detail the plight of the southern Indians, the effect of McGillivray's death and Bowles's imprisonment, and the hope that either via Detroit or Nassau—and not Pensacola or St. Marks—the Chickamaugas could be supplied with British goods. He obtained no positive commitment, only unofficial encouragement. Times were not appropriate for Britain to intrigue with the southern Indians, but in the future, possibly the very near future, all this might change. Simcoe, who knew Bowles was conducting negotiations in Spain and who believed that Bowles had the best chance of becoming leader of all the Creeks, gave Wellbank and his Creek and Cherokee chiefs presents, a few pounds, and encouraged them to bide their time.[43]

Before Simcoe would seriously involve himself with the southern Indians, he wanted to see just how far Anglo-Spanish co-operation would extend in the Mississippi Valley and what would be the fate of General Wayne's army, organizing to go against the northern Indians. If Wayne met Arthur St. Clair's fate, if the bonds of the Anglo-Spanish alliance grew tighter, and if Britain signed a Spanish treaty whereby she would be allowed free navigation of the Mississippi River and a Florida port, then Wellbank might expect far more than ten pounds. Should all this occur, then Bowles, as Simcoe was quick to point out to Carondelet, would be of great service to both Britain and Spain and should be released from his "unfortunate situation."[44] To some extent Carondelet concurred but, as always, mistrusted any western Indian confederation under joint Anglo-Spanish supervision. These reflections were academic because in 1794 Wayne roundly defeated the Indians at Fallen Timbers, and Wellbank ventured among the Upper Creeks, put up at an "improper house," first was robbed, and subsequently had his brains bashed out with a "lightwood not."[45] Because of the death of Wellbank and the earlier loss of Dragging Canoe, because of Wayne's victory over the Indians, because the Anglo-Spanish alliance was weakening, and because Godoy was becoming reconciled to granting sweeping concessions to the Americans, the despondent Bowles realized there was less reason for the Spaniards to negotiate with him as head of an independent state and more reason to proceed against him as a common criminal for robbing Panton's store.

He had hoped that the Anglo-Spanish alliance might result in his release and threatened that his continued imprisonment would embarrass Spain's relations with Whitehall and would result in British intervention in his behalf. According to Bowles, who was becoming desperate as he saw his last chance of outside intervention slipping away, he had powerful influence both at Whitehall and with the British royal family.[46] All along, however, Campo had been assured in London that Bowles had greatly exaggerated and had no commission and that he was only casually acquainted with some members of the royal household; and the Ambassador was convinced, far more than the Spaniards in America, that these assurances were true. In the past during the Nootka crisis Britain would have utilized Bowles, but by 1793-1794 the diplomatic wheel of fortune had turned completely about; Whitehall was primarily concerned with seeing the fall of the French Jacobins and wanted Spain's assistance. Flirting with Bowles without Spanish approval could only weaken the alliance. The ministry made this clear to Campo in London and Dunmore in Nassau: "If the Spanish complaints are true, Bowles's actions are criminal and mar Anglo-Spanish amity."[47] To Dunmore's further chagrin, Home Secretary Henry Dundas indicated he would lodge no protest about the *Resolution's* capture and certainly would make no reimbursement for its loss.[48] These developments were as disheartening to Dunmore as to Bowles, though Bowles, from his cell's isolation, frequently had to imagine what was occurring in the outside world.

While William was in Madrid, Mississippi Valley affairs were of the greatest concern in both London and Madrid; indeed, this was one of the reasons for his extended stay. Had Britain, because of her seizure of numerous American vessels in the West Indies and because she allegedly was encouraging the northern Indians, not made a minimum of concessions to the United States in the Jay Treaty, war would have been probable. This minimum concession—abandonment of the northwestern posts on American soil—coming on the heels of Wayne's victory at Fallen Timbers, resulted in Britain's being far less involved in the Old Northwest. It was circumstances surrounding the Jay Treaty that were of such interest in London.[49]

These developments and related ones leading to a Spanish-American Treaty—the Pinckney Treaty of 1795—were of great concern to Spain. The ambitious Godoy, having won out over his rivals, in the face of Spanish defeats by France and with a mounting distrust of Britain, first made peace with France in 1795, even a republican France, and the following year openly entered the war against Britain. In the aftermath of the Jay Treaty it seemed more probable that Britain and the United States might draw together, increasing the chance of American militia's joining the British navy in an assault on Florida and Louisiana. With this possibility and in view of Spain's failure to contain American expansion, Godoy considered it expedient to make concessions to the United States—the thirty-first parallel as West Florida's boundary, free navigation of the Mississippi River with the right of deposit at New Orleans, and a promise to restrain the southern Indians—to prevent any Anglo-American combination.[50] With chances of a close Anglo-Spanish alliance fading and instead the prospect of a British war, there were the best of reasons why Bowles should not return to Florida. It was in the same year as the Pinckney Treaty that Spain, after vacillating for almost three years, finally sent Bowles on his way—not to Florida but to the Philippines.[51]

He had spent a year and a half in his Madrid cell and another year in Cádiz when he was transferred there early in 1794, not a pleasant experience for anyone, especially for the thirty-one-year-old Bowles. There was leisure for reading and study; both in Madrid and Cádiz the Spaniards were aware that they might make an alliance with Bowles, and the tortures of Torquemada's Inquisition were not unveiled. But Bowles, like the bald eagle, was not designed for a cage. Accounts of his imprisonment are meager and frequently from his own pen. Subsequently discussing his Spanish imprisonment, he maintained he was at the heart of the sordid intrigue between Floridablanca, Aranda, and Godoy in their struggle for royal favor. On several occasions Godoy's underlings, courting his favor by returning his impounded papers and by promising freedom and a favorable treaty, solicited him to make false statements against Floridablanca and Aranda. Bowles, stoutly maintaining his integrity, refused. Again, according to his own account, Spanish officials, both in New Orleans and in Spain, offered him a commission so long as he would become a Spanish subject and forget the nonsense about Muskogee's sovereignty. But Bowles regarded himself as a subject of Britain or Muskogee and hoped there soon would be no distinction. He had already sacrificed much on behalf of his British citizenship and on no account would abandon it. He protested that Spain could not legally imprison him for taking Panton's store, because it was located in sovereign Indian territory and did not belong to Spain: the Spanish "pretence is idle and unjust"; furthermore, he asserted, the manner of his imprisonment was "cowardly and unbecoming the character of His Catholic Magesty's officers . . . the conduct of His Magesty's Ministers in detaining me still a prisoner, altho' they are acquainted with these unjust circumstances, is truly strange . . ."; as for the offers of a commission and other bribes: "I shall ever treat with the contempt that such offers to me justly merit." This was the tenor of his arguments while he was in Spain, and it is not surprising he reached no agreement with the Spaniards.[52]

While he was at Havana the Spanish governor had recommended that, unless there were a close British alliance, the English adventurer be sent to a remote colony such as the Falkland Islands where few ships called and there was little chance of escape.[53] Soon after Bowles reached Madrid the Council of the Indies seconded this recommendation, substituting the more distant Philippines for the Falkland Islands: to turn him loose would be like freeing a rabid dog.[54] It was not until 1795, after tangled European and American affairs became clearer, that he actually left the Iberian Peninsula. His future had never looked blacker.

VI

Exile

BOWLES'S SECOND Cádiz imprisonment had been the most depressing: he was cut off more than ever from the outside world; his cell was insufferably hot, and it was apparent he would reach no agreement with the government. Since boldly entering St. Marks in 1792 he had spent three years in prison or aboard Spanish ships and there would be no change for the better. William, after delays and frustrated attempts at negotiation, was ordered aboard the *Reyna Louisa,* bound for he knew not where; ahead were months of confining shipboard life. He was not chained in the hold; he enjoyed limited freedom aboard ship, but his baggage had been "artfully tho' purposely detain'd" in Spain, and he had only one suit of clothes and three shirts. The shirts, as they became worn and soiled, were thrown overboard, though it can be presumed modesty forced him to hold on to his one suit. At length the Spanish captain assisted with a few minimum necessities.[1]

Bowles knew he was going to the Far East, but exactly where was open to question. A century earlier a Spanish voyager bound for the Orient would probably have sailed to Veracruz or Portobello, made his way overland, and boarded the Manila galleon for the Philippines. Toward the end of the eighteenth century Spain relaxed her restrictive maritime regulations, and vessels normally did not have to follow prescribed routes when sailing anywhere within the Spanish Empire. For this reason and because of nautical improvements since Magellan's day, Bowles made the long passage around Cape Horn into the Pacific. Although there is no record, it is logical to assume his vessel stopped for provisions at Buenos Aires or the Falkland Islands before sailing around the Horn. At the tip of South America he could see desolate Tierra del Fuego in the distance, but the vessel never came close to shore—a circumstance that would have disappointed neither

Bowles nor the crew. After six months of hard sailing, to the relief of everyone aboard, Lima, eight miles inland and capital of the Vice-royalty of Peru, came into view. Here Bowles disinterestedly watched the crew stow away additional supplies before sailing to higher latitudes to catch the westerly trade winds.[2]

William, except for his skimpy wardrobe, found shipboard life not physically unpleasant—merely boring. There was no Celeste or Miró to while away the hours or to become his benefactor, and, except when land was occasionally sighted, there was little to mark one day or week from another. Accounts of his months aboard ship are primarily from his own pen, and if he is to be trusted, he was still the hub of political intrigue. The Spanish captain, alleged Bowles, was careful never to make conditions too harsh because there was always the possibility that William might relent and accept Spanish offers— offers which included accepting a Spanish commission and within narrow limits serving Spanish interests in Florida. At Lima William avowed that he merely had to indicate a change of heart, and the Spaniards soon would have him back in the Indian country via Panama and Portobello.[3]

Bowles had always assumed that Copernicus was wrong and that the world revolved not about the sun but around himself. At Lima there was every reason to believe his astronomical computations were faulty. Godoy currently was signing the Pinckney Treaty and was being pressured by France for a retrocession of Louisiana and West Florida; therefore, because the Spanish statesman was not inclined to follow Carondelet's lead and adopt an aggressive policy in a Florida of diminishing importance, he was not disposed to employ the spirited Englishman. There was less reason than ever to return him to Florida and more than ever that he reach the Orient. William, with time on his hands and thinking about earlier Spanish offers made in New Orleans and Madrid, wished and even encouraged the Spaniards to drop him off at Panama; later when writing about his experiences he asserted, without any qualification, that they made such an offer. There is every indication his longing to return quickly to Florida and his overemphasizing his importance to Spain induced him to take liberties with the truth.

The long voyage continued and Bowles, "without changing three words with any person on board," by now was aware of what he earlier had suspected: the Philippines were his destination, though not necessarily his ultimate one. After months of sailing, this archipelago, long ago discovered by Magellan and now the most important Spanish possession in the Far East, appeared on the horizon. Even

Bowles shared in the relief and excitement and eagerly watched as his vessel sailed into Manila harbor, and as the ancient walled city of Manila, with regular paved streets, numerous convents, and a population numbering three thousand, came into view. What the future would bring was uncertain, but anything was better than almost a year at sea. He was not kept in suspense about his status: upon landing he was immediately taken to the governor's palace and "in a most formal manner" notified that he was to be held indefinitely in the Philippines. If he behaved himself and reported to the magistrate daily, he would be allowed the freedom of the island of Luzon. After the Spaniards "indecently housed" him the first night he was on his own. He could seek employment and provide for his own maintenance, but the governor did not elaborate on job possibilities for former Creek chiefs.[4]

Spanish authorities—and for some reason officials of the Royal Company of the Philippines—provided him with a few necessities, but basically he was penniless and desperate: "I live almost like [a miser] in order to keep out of debt."[5] At first a Spanish noble, the Count of Avilés, offered William a country house, an offer which he accepted. But he soon became convinced that the Count had been forced by the government to extend this hospitality, and Bowles immediately departed. In no way could "I be subservient or in the employ of Spain."[6] From his early childhood William was fiercely proud of his British citizenship: this loyalty had cost him dearly during the Revolution and was now partially responsible for his treatment in the Philippines. He was always ready, however, to use the threat of British intervention in his behalf to advance his own interests and was quick to intimate now, as in Spain, that there would be dire consequences if Spain did not treat him honorably or meet his terms.

His primary source of ready money during his fifteen months in the Philippines was a fellow Englishman, Pendock Niel, an East India Company merchant resident in the free port of Manila. It was not long before Bowles, insisting on his importance as a Creek chieftain and playing up Spanish perfidy, ingratiated himself with Niel. This merchant advanced Bowles 100 guineas, to be repaid by William's half-pay accumulating in London. It was Niel's hospitality, liberality, and sympathy that made Bowles's exile tolerable.[7]

Though many thousand miles away, William, carefully protecting his plumed turban, silver gorgets, and arm bands, never abandoned hope that he would return to Europe and America and that again he would play a leading role among the Indians. Only in a general way did he know what was happening among the Creeks, though it was common knowledge that McGillivray was dead and times were ripe for someone to take his place. Bowles also was aware of the Jay Treaty, which made it less likely that the southern Indians could look to Canada, and of the Pinckney Treaty, which divided Creek lands and weakened Spain in Florida and Louisiana, and of France's desire to acquire Louisiana and Florida. In any attempt to return to Florida Bowles reasoned he could try to prevail on the Spaniards to employ him on his own terms or he might escape and persuade Britain, already alarmed by possible French expansion in Spanish America, that it was in her interest to acquire Louisiana and Florida from tottering Spain or at least to encourage a direct trade with Florida.

To a limited extent Bowles still negotiated with the Spaniards in Manila, and much of the negotiation concerned finances and Bowles's indignation because Spain would not provide funds to support him in a manner appropriate for a distinguished prisoner of state. At any time, he avowed, bribes were readily available if only he would become a pliant tool of Spain in Florida, or if he would denounce the Duke of Alcudia, "but I paid no further attention to the Governor upon that head or indeed any other."[8] Surprisingly enough he continued to correspond with and to press his ideas on the British government. There is little doubt that his friend Niel, in spite of the risks, provided the means of communication. Bowles's most important London correspondent was John Reeves, founder of the newly created, ultra-conservative, anti-French Association for Preserving Liberty and Property against Levellers and Republicans, over the past years having filled several official posts below cabinet rank, soon to become the King's Printer. It is impossible to say when the close friendship with Reeves began. He was born in London and, except for a brief term as Newfoundland chief justice, spent most of his life there. He probably knew Carington Bowles and his family. It is likely that Bowles first met Reeves in London during the Nootka crisis before the Chief Justice left for his new post in Newfoundland. Regardless of where or how the friendship began, it became a firm and lasting one, and Reeves was William's most constant advocate in the government. It was Reeves whom Bowles kept informed about the details of negotiations in Manila, and, though Bowles penned lengthy memorials to the cabinet about his unjust treatment, it was through Reeves especially that William tried to insure that Whitehall did not lose sight of Louisiana and Florida.[9] Bowles could smuggle out frequent letters to Reeves and others in the government, but little that the

Director General proposed had relevance unless he were on the scene in London or Florida.

It is impossible to recapture his daily routine during his fifteen months in Manila, though a fragment of his diary survives and sums up his treatment:

11th [January], I was taken out of my house at ten at night by the Corregidor of Tondo and lodged in the gaol of Santa Crux . . .; 13th Mr. Nuñez visited me and told me that the Governor had issued his orders that morning for my liberty; 18th, Nunez's strange manner; 19th, the Corregidor at 12 o'clock sent a servant to desire me to come to him. I desire him to tell his master to come to my room. At one o'clock the Corregidor and his wife with her servants come to my room; he delivered me a message from the Governor touching a representation to His Majesty . . . . He told me I was at liberty to retire to my house whenever I thought proper; 21st, at half past 11 o'clock the Corregidor entered my house attended by a number of people and without any ceremony ordered them to register everything belonging to me . . . seized my papers, books, etc. and removed all the remainder with myself to the Casa Hall or gaol of Santa Crux where I am at present under a sentinel; 22nd, still remain; 23rd, still remain without hearing a word except my escritoire has been sent to the Governor; 24th nothing new.[10]

It is certain that Bowles was true to form and generated turbulence. He denounced the Spaniards in general and the Philippine governor in particular, was not meticulous about daily reporting to the authorities, and as a result was occasionally thrown into prison. Bowles, threatening at the first opportunity to repay the Spaniards for his unjust treatment and utilizing his special talents for inciting the natives against the Spaniards, was regarded by the governor as an English Jacobin—a label that made William wince.

Since Manila was a free port at this time, British and American ships called at the Philippines, and Bowles, when he was not in prison, always considered the possibility of escaping. The Manila governor had his fill of worrying over this animated Creek and resolved to return him to Cádiz and let the officials of the Casa find a more isolated spot for imprisonment.[11] Another reason for sending Bowles to Spain was that he had become ill, though there is no reason to assume that the governor overly fretted about Bowles's dying. There is a chance—a slight one—that either Bowles or the Spanish government suggested that, in view of the possible cession of Louisiana and part of Florida and in view of Spain's alliance with and dependence on France, he might be induced to serve the Directory; or Spain, for reasons of her own now putting up a bolder front to the Americans in Florida and Louisiana, again might have considered employing Bowles.

Whatever the reason—probably that he had made a thorough pest of himself—Bowles late in February, 1797, again resumed life aboard ship, the *Concepción,* formerly the *Clive,* presumably either bought or captured from the British East India Company and now a part of the fleet of the Royal Company of the Philippines. He was on the verge of a long voyage resulting in an enforced circumnavigation of the earth. It was in the Philippines that Bowles and Cunningham finally parted company: after William reached Manila, Cunningham, true to schedule, arrived several months later. But now Bowles was returning to Europe while Cunningham had been exiled to Cavite, forever fading into history and severing his ruinous connection with the Indian leader that began when they plotted against the Spaniards in Florida.[12]

Relieved at leaving the Philippines under any pretext, William watched with enthusiasm Captain Martinez hoist anchor in February, 1797, as the *Concepción* began her long voyage across the South China Sea, through the Dutch East Indies into the Indian Ocean. A raging storm developed before they reached the Cape of Good Hope; Martinez had to put into the tiny French island of Mauritius, and as a result there was considerable delay.

This island's populace had been agitated before Bowles landed. French merchants and settlers here, though remote from Parisian tumults, had watched with greatest concern political changes in the mother country. Here as in France there were shades of opinion ranging from monarchist to Jacobin, though the conservative monarchists, fearful that their Negro slaves would become infected with republican notions about liberty, were in the ascendancy. They had no use for the Jacobins and not much more for the Directory, which currently held power.[13] During his stay at Mauritius Bowles won the confidence of a number of the French inhabitants, many of whom were monarchists, or Masons, or probably both.

Here the same problem followed William that had beset him in the Philippines—he was penniless. He fumed when he discovered that the Manila governor had not realized that storms might drive the *Concepción* into a foreign port and that financial provisions had not been made in advance for the distinguished prisoner: "He must have given you [Martinez] the necessary orders . . . to supply me with what I should stand in need." As a gentleman and a prisoner of state Bowles demanded that he be allowed ashore and that Spain provide for his maintenance.[14] Martinez did not fret over the alleged negligence of the Philippine governor; Bowles could go ashore, apparently giving his word not to escape, and would have to provide for himself. He was on his own and had to appeal to local inhabitants. Either in New York, Nassau, or London, Bowles had become a Mason, and he now appealed to the lodges in Mauritius, explaining that Spanish perfidy was responsible for his distress: "as your memoralist has upon all occasions, when in his power, afforded assistance to all brothers who have approached him in want, so, in the present, he with confidence represents his destitution." The French brothers, or possibly other residents in Mauritius, charmed by accounts unfolded by this stranger and sympathetic to his plight, advanced money and a few necessities and were the counterpart of Niel in Manila.[15]

In Mauritius there was definite word of the Anglo-Spanish war, though it would have taken no astute observer to predict the rupture. But for Martinez and the captain of another Spanish ship anchored here there was the increased risk that their ships, laden with specie and oriental wares, would be captured before reaching home. It seemed logical to ask their French allies for two frigates to convoy the Spanish ships, and upon payment of $60,000, it seemed just as logical for the French to accept.[16] Preparations complete, the four ships bid *adieu* to mountainous Mauritius and began a voyage which with luck would soon bring them to Cádiz or Toulon and Brest. Bowles reboarded the *Concepción*, even though Martinez was no more solicitous than ever about the dignity and welfare of his passenger, and the voyage around the Cape of Good Hope and up the West African coast was routine—until midway up the continent in the vicinity of numerous French, British, and Spanish colonies and slave-trading posts. Here, according to Bowles, he attempted a plot which he had been contriving for weeks—with the aid of miscellaneous Frenchmen aboard, to overpower the *Concepción* and to sail her to a nearby British African post. Premature alarm thwarted his design; Spanish soldiers seized all the ringleaders and imprisoned them aboard the two French frigates. William, briefly scenting freedom, was discouraged as he was transferred to the French frigate where the captain, unconvinced by Bowles's arguments that he should be deferentially treated as head of an independent Indian nation at peace with France, imprisoned him as a common felon.[17] Having restored order, Martinez and the rest of the convoy again had to battle the elements and eventually were forced to put into Gorée, a tiny, though strategic, French island post close by present-day Dakar. It may have been more than coincidence that storms arose every time the Spanish vessels approached a French port, yet Martinez and the other Spaniards must have wondered whether officials in the Casa de Contratación would attribute their stopping at foreign ports solely to Divine Providence.

There may have been smuggling going on—it would be surprising if there were not—but contraband trade and storms aside there was good reason to put into Gorée. British cruisers were about and would like nothing better than to take a rich Spanish prize or two. This is exactly what the 32-gun frigate *Pearl* attempted. She sailed boldly into Gorée, opened a furious fire on the land battery and French ships, and in the confusion hoped to bring out a Spanish prize. The *Pearl* failed in this attempt but could not have been more successful in creating havoc. All eyes were on the *Pearl* when she commenced the cannonade. Confined below deck, William, at the first sign of hostilities, dashed to the porthole and witnessed the drama being enacted in the harbor. The thoughts that ran through his mind were far different from those of the other spectators. Here was an opportunity to escape! During the tumult, while the smoke of battle was thickest, and encouraged and aided by French officers, Bowles popped through one of the French frigate's portholes and swam to a nearby American merchantman.[18] Hardly catching his breath, he urged the merchantman to catch up with the *Pearl* so he could reveal how to capture the Spanish ships. But the American captain, concerned about his cargo's safety, wisely decided to steer clear of all foreign frigates and soon continued his regular course, occasionally stopping to trade or take on supplies. Free at last and temporarily ashore in a nearby harbor, Bowles castigated his most recent captor, the French captain: "I am now safe on shore and set down to tell you that your treatment to me on board the *Virtue* was extreamly unjust and impolite . . . you ought [not] to insult me in a public manner and treat me as a criminal. . . . I can never forgive and [unless you quickly apologize] shall mention you upon all occasions as a poltroon and a wreck." Bowles, standing on shore and lashing out at the captain, made the same impression as King Canute when he ordered the incoming tide to recede.[19]

In time the American merchantman put into nearby Sierra Leone, and Bowles debarked early in June, 1798. Though this was one of the most remote and godforsaken British colonies, he was overjoyed at his arrival as, after seven years, he again set foot on British soil. Thanking the American captain and bidding him farewell, Bowles began to inspect the British colony. Sierra Leone with its capital of Freetown formerly had been a slave-trading factory, but recently British abolitionists had tried to make it into a model colony where freed

Negroes from Britain or America could be settled. Attacks by the
French, malaria, and discontent among the freedmen themselves had
contributed to the colony's lack of success. But the newest governor,
Zachary McCaulay, was able to report substantial progress, and it
was to this governor that Bowles reported straightaway and unfolded
his story: how in good faith he had gone to Spain to negotiate a
treaty and instead had been thrown into prison; how he had been
exiled to the Philippines; and how subsequently fortune allowed him
to make a dangerous escape at Gorée. He was determined to make
his way back to the Creek country and would seek passage on the
next vessel bound for the West Indies—in the meantime would the
Governor advance him a small sum to be repaid out of his half-pay?
McCaulay throughout was sympathetic, assisted William in a number of ways, and willingly advanced him ten pounds. At this stage
even this paltry sum looked good to Bowles.[20]

He secured passage on the *Elizabeth Anderson* bound for Tobago,
wrote the foreign secretary, Lord Grenville, to inform him that he
was free and again ready to serve the King, that he was prepared to
resume his role among the Creeks, and that he would follow Whitehall's suggestion and either wage an active war against Spain in
Florida or instead negotiate with her and, since she was hard-pressed
in the present war, wring extensive concessions from her.[21] But more
hardships and delay were in store before he again saw Florida. The
Elizabeth Anderson ran into a storm that splintered her masts and left
her drifting dangerously. Fortunately a British convoy from St. Helena
bound for London overtook the crippled ship; and Bowles, wracked by
fever, was taken aboard *H.M.S. Isis.* The officers were charmed by the
accounts of the Creek chieftain who had wandered so far from home,
and as always he won admirers and made lasting friendships.[22] Life
aboard the *Isis* was as pleasant as could be expected under the circumstances, though it was a relief when Bowles spotted the chalk
cliffs of Dover. Prime Minister Pitt happened to be at nearby Walmer
Castle, and Bowles obtained an audience. There is no record of the
conversation, except that orders were given to aid the distressed Director General so that he could continue to London, and by late August
the massive dome of St. Paul's Cathedral was in view.[23] His gaze
automatically descended to the cathedral's base to catch a glimpse of
his cousin's book and print shop, although the elder Carington had
died years ago and the business was now managed by his son, Carington, Jr.[24]

London newspapers reported that "Bowles, the famous Creek General, who was in this country in the year 1791, is again arrived at the

Hotel in the Adelphi. He is only attended by a Negro servant. . . . He seems to be in a very bad state of health, and is supposed to be consumptive."[25] At the end of the eighteenth century anyone who was sick and did not have venereal disease was likely to be considered consumptive. There is no telling the exact nature of his illness except that it was a respiratory one, apparently contracted in the Philippines; it had plagued him at Mauritius, Sierra Leone, and was worse than ever in London. He had a million pressing things to do but had to defer almost all until he regained his health. His good friend Dr. Pearson, whose lectures he had attended and whose company he had enjoyed in 1791, demanded that William leave London and recuperate in the country at Ealing outside the city in Middlesex. Bowles, much against his will, had no choice but to obey. It took several weeks under Pearson's solicitous care before he would be strong enough to return to London.[26]

Though he was making satisfactory progress, William grew impatient. He had been put off or imprisoned by the Spaniards for the last six years—enough inactivity to last a lifetime—and was relieved when in the early fall he was able to return to Osborne's Hotel in Adelphi on the Strand. His objective was to return to the Creek country and to resume his role as Muskogee's chief of state. Encouragement from the government, official or not, was indispensable; and he was optimistic of obtaining backing because of his past "steady, stoic like manner in which I rejected [Spanish] offers, disregarded their threats, and bore the ill treatment they thought expedient to exercise . . . if I had my price . . . they were not able to come up to it, with all their mines of Mexico and Peru."[27]

Surveying the international situation, he was heartened to see that it had changed materially since his last visit to London. Then there was only the possibility of a Spanish rupture; now a war with Spain was an actuality, and Whitehall, whatever it did, would not have to spare Spanish sensibilities. Florida and Louisiana were fair game, and Bowles's ambition was to make the Duke of Portland, Pitt, and the rest of the cabinet realize that a blow against the enemy could best be delivered in Florida. As in the past he assured them his "twenty thousand" warriors were eager to serve the English king, and he unleashed all his old arguments. Florida's advantages were its strategic location and the furs and naval stores it could provide; New Orleans more than ever was the growing market of the Mississippi Valley and should be in Britain's hands; even though Britain had abandoned the Northwest posts, Canada still could be linked to Florida and New Orleans via Louisiana on the Mississippi's western bank (and if dis-

satisfied American frontiersmen joined forces then both banks of the
Mississippi could be a bridge between Canada and Florida and
lower Louisiana); and acquiring Spanish Florida and Louisiana could
be the first step in acquiring or setting free the rest of Spanish
America.[28]

Bowles's arguments were not original; they had been and would
still be considered at Whitehall whether he had returned to London
or not. On several occasions in the past when Britain threatened or
actually went to war with Spain the cabinet had planned moves
against Louisiana and Florida that could implement Bowles's proposed policy. The war breaking out in 1796 was no exception, and
several possibilities were considered: Canada might be reinforced
for an assault on St. Louis and points south; in all probability a
British fleet would simultaneously co-operate in the Gulf of Mexico;
and possibly the Indians and American frontiersmen would assist.[29]
That Britain had designs on Louisiana and Florida was no secret, and
that just before the outbreak of hostilities she insisted that Canadians
have the same privilege of navigating the Mississippi and the right of
deposit at New Orleans as the Pinckney Treaty guaranteed the Americans, was one of many indications.[30] Canadians had journeyed to the
Ohio and approached frontier leaders,[31] while in turn assorted Americans, notably Senator William Blount of Tennessee and John Chisholm, veteran Indian agent, had secretly sounded out the British
about the southern Indians' and frontiersmen's co-operating with the
British fleet against Spanish Florida and Louisiana. Chisholm held
several conferences with Robert Liston, British minister at Philadelphia, who sent Chisholm on to London where the Indian agent spent
two months unsuccessfully trying to obtain support from the ministry.[32] Exposure of an incriminating letter resulted in Blount's expulsion from the Senate and his disassociation from the project. And
Liston, after the publicity surrounding the Blount affair, instead urged
that Canadian traders organize Indians on American soil for a
Louisiana attack and subsequently recommended that a formal understanding be made with the United States and that they jointly
attack Spanish and French American possessions.[33]

What Bowles was advocating in 1798 was not radically different
from what the British cabinet had been considering on and off for
sometime and from what Liston and Chisholm had been proposing
less than a year before. Chisholm and Bowles both had intimate contacts among the Cherokees and Creeks and undoubtedly knew of each
other—and may have been acquaintances. Unfortunately, time has
cast a shadow over their relationship. Bowles's current argument—

which Blount, Chisholm, and Liston had used before—was that acquisition of Louisiana and Florida would only be the first step in Britain's becoming master of the rest of Spanish America. Bowles's entreaties were joined by those of Miranda who also had returned to Britain, though Miranda was urging the liberating of all Spanish America, with emphasis on Mexico and South America, where in the aftermath Britain would enjoy favored commercial treatment.[34] The argument was appealing since, as the war continued to disrupt traditional continental markets, more than ever Britain was forced to seek new colonial markets and sources of raw materials; inevitably she was drawn to consider Spanish America and even Louisiana and Florida on the periphery.

Bowles argued that another advantage of acquiring Florida and Louisiana—a negative one but probably the most important of all—was that if Britain did not take the initiative and relieve Spain of these provinces by force, then France would acquire them through diplomacy. There was no lack of indications of French designs on these colonies: the Genêt Affair, the unsuccessful attempt in the 1795 Franco-Spanish Treaty to obtain them, and the suspicious activities of French General Victor Collot and others in the Mississippi Valley.[35] Just before Bowles reached London there were incorrect reports that the French flag was actually flying over Pensacola.[36] Were there no more than Louisiana and Florida to consider there would not be so much cause for concern. But would France stop here any more than Britain? There was every reason to assume that this would be but the first step toward Mexico and South America and, though in fact French troops were not yet in Florida, the French menace was emphasized by Bowles, Miranda, and a host of others in London.

There was a recent development which Bowles carefully followed and which was of great consequence for both Britain and Muskogee: the United States was on the verge of war with France. He avidly read newspaper accounts about French seizures of American merchant vessels, about the subsequent XYZ Affair in France, and about Britain's sympathy over the injustices inflicted on her former colonists. There would be many ramifications of a Franco-American war. One was that inevitably Britain and the United States would draw together, and there were indications that already this was occurring.[37] The question concerning Bowles—and Miranda—was what would be the nature of this co-operation? Would there be a joint enterprise against Louisiana and Florida? Such an undertaking was contemplated not only in London but also in Philadelphia. Rufus King, the American minister in London, was for it; Timothy Pickering, the Federalist secretary of state, was an advocate; Alexander Hamilton, who envisioned himself leading an American army into Florida, Louisiana, and possibly further south, could have wished for nothing better.[38] In any combined expedition against these colonies Bowles stressed it would be logical to assign him a role even though Benjamin Hawkins, the American Indian agent, would turn green at the thought of Eastajoca at the head of the Creeks.

Since the Director General had been absent from the Creek country for over six years, Whitehall had reason to question whether he still retained any influence and whether thousands of natives would eagerly follow him into battle. His assumption throughout was that, should he make satisfactory arrangements with the British government, he could quickly revive and even strengthen his prestige once he returned to Indian soil. Bowles's contemporary, Louis LeClerc de Milfort, McGillivray's French brother-in-law, at this same time in Paris was asserting that he was the true leader of the Creeks and was pressing most of Bowles's arguments on the Directory.[39] Bowles's goal in London, like Milfort's in Paris, was to ingratiate himself with the government and to win high officials over to his point of view. Bowles was more successful than Milfort. In Reeves William had an ardent, influential, ultra-conservative champion. For Reeves nothing was more detestable than a passionate republican, whether in France, Britain, or elsewhere. The prospect of the tri-color waving over Florida, Louisiana, and the rest of Spanish America was anathema. The British ensign, or some friendly banner, must be placed here at all costs, even—and the very idea made him wince—if it meant encouraging a revolution. A friend of Reeves's, just as conservative and determined on an aggressive campaign against the French, was William Windham, secretary at war and one of Edmund Burke's leading disciples.[40] But Pitt and most of the cabinet, though decidedly anti-French, were more moderate in their opposition, more willing to take the Directory's utterances at face value, and, committed in Ireland, Egypt, and India, were less anxious for a Spanish-American campaign. It was Pitt and a majority of the cabinet whom Bowles, Reeves, Windham, Miranda, King, and Hamilton hoped to win over to an aggressive policy against the diffusion of Jacobin principles in America.[41]

Throughout the world conservatives were alarmed by the export of French liberalism. This was true in Britain—it was to the arch-conservatives here that Bowles looked—and it was also true in the United States. The Federalists, especially the Hamiltonian faction, were the ones who most feared Jacobinism. Through the newspapers

and political confidants, Bowles attentively observed Philadelphia affairs and was encouraged when it appeared that the most militant
Federalists were in the ascendency and that, following their lead, the
United States soon would be openly at war with France. Should this
happen, then American Federalists and British Tories, emphasizing
their common dread of French doctrines, might reconcile their differences regarding Florida and Louisiana. It was conceivable that the
United States might agree that the former Tory ensign should come
to the Old Southwest. Such American co-operation was possible, and
Bowles made overtures to the American minister in London; but if
William had his way he would prefer not to need Philadelphia's
stamp of approval.[42]

After recovering his health, he was more confident than ever of
support from a variety of sources and of resuming his role among
the Indians. What he wanted most of all was an alliance or official
connection with Whitehall. This is what he had sought in his letters
to the government from Freetown, as soon as he arrived in England,
and throughout his entire stay in London; and Reeves, Windham,
and even the aged Lord George Townshend were his eager advocates.
But plead as they might they could never convince the ministry to
adopt a resolute campaign against Florida and Louisiana and to
employ Eastajoca. One reason for hesitation was concern over how
much authority the Director General wielded over the Indians after
so long an absence. A more important cause for delay was the need
to decide whether in any attack against Spanish America it would be
desirable to co-operate with the United States and, if so, whether
Bowles would retard or improve Anglo-American amity. With Napoleon's Egyptian campaign and the threat to British India and with
a revolt in Ireland, would it be judicious for Britain to launch a
blow against Spanish America? In the long run Bowles got only unofficial encouragement from the government. He knew, however, that
the government was considering the possibility of an attack against
Louisiana and Florida and was given the impression that it might
authorize such a campaign in the near future. This is why the government paid part of his London expenses and his transportation back
to Florida; Reeves made doubly sure William's back salary was
brought up to date; West Indian governors were ordered to assist
Bowles; and he was unofficially assured that Muskogee's ships would be
welcome in West Indian ports. More positive aid would depend on
the future.[43]

Bowles also bid for the support of merchants who would be given
an opportunity to crack Panton's monopoly. There was the fur trade,

and timber and naval stores were an added enticement. The demands
on the British navy were greater than ever, and there was a direct
relationship between ample supplies of naval stores, masts, and the
like, and national security. Bowles was quick to point out that Florida
was full of oak and could furnish a variety of naval stores and that
merchants could benefit themselves and their country by investing in
Muskogee. Some did. One was John Miller, still on the Bahama
Council and still a storm center of the tiny island's partisan politics.
Another was John Brickwood, friend of Reeves, a merchant who had
traded with various parts of America, who was Miller's London fac-
tor, and who now advanced 200 pounds for the erection of a sawmill.
Should this limited investment pay off at all it was likely to pay off
handsomely—at the expense of Spain and Panton, Leslie, and Company.[44]

Meanwhile, Leslie, whose firm had suffered at Bowles's hands in
the past and who now was in London, readily appreciated this fact.
He could scarcely believe his eyes when reading newspaper reports
that Bowles had miraculously escaped, that he was conferring with
high officials in the government, and that he soon would return to
Florida, apparently with a commission. "When I first heard of his
being in London I paid no attention to it, thinking it impossible and
that the report proceeded either from mistake or some interested mo-
tive of deception. Being, however, after a while, assured of the truth,
I thought of having him arrested, either on an action of debt, or on
a criminal information, but was dissuaded." Leslie rushed to see
George Chalmers, secretary to the Board of Trade and a fellow Loyalist, attesting that Bowles was a liar and a thief in no way deserving
favors from the government.[45]

The distraught Leslie had one consolation: Dunmore was no
longer governor, and, if nothing else, this should clip Bowles's wings.
The controversial Scottish earl recently had been relieved of office,
either because of mounting reports of nepotism, corruption, and de-
spotism or because new faces at Whitehall were responsible for a new
Bahamian governor. Whatever the reason Dunmore was furious:
"that I should leave the Bahamas by the same vessel that brought my
successor" was an unprecedented action by the Duke of Portland, the
home secretary.[46] This prompt departure, alleged Dunmore, resulted
in considerable loss to him and his large family and, if the government did not make good all his expenditures, many innocent people
would be ruined. Heading the list was the former governor himself,
and he demanded compensation and reward for a half-century in the
king's service. He was not one to accept enforced retirement grace-

fully and bombarded the government with memorials and petitions. But he made little headway and, as Chalmers observed, "he will bustle awhile . . . and he will disappear forever"—a pension at Holyrood will "keep him out of trouble."[47]

The former governor was in London early in 1799 personally presenting his case. Also in London was Dunmore's old friend, Dr. John Connolly, who had run into difficulties in the Canadian Indian Department because he considered the "King's stores as well appropriated to the use of white people as of Indians." The doctor was pressing the government to take New Orleans and other Spanish territory. Since Bowles frequently was in Dunmore's company, it is as probable that he conferred with Connolly now as in Canada during the Nootka crisis.[48] But Dunmore, however, was no longer governor, was getting old, and though a good friend of both Connolly and Bowles, had lost his influence and had too many problems of his own to afford the luxury of overly concerning himself with their schemes.

Bowles was disappointed by Dunmore's dismissal and realized this venerable prop was no more. But even though he had not reached a formal understanding with Whitehall, the government had not been unfriendly, and Brickwood's interest was encouraging. No source of support, however, could be overlooked, so William turned to the Church Missionary Society. It was a new association designed to bring Christianity to the natives in Africa, the Orient, or, as Bowles suggested, America. His stay at Freetown, which was a haven founded by Christian reformers for freed slaves, secured him an introduction to members of the society. In glowing terms Bowles described how the southern Indians were on the threshold of civilization and how they would be receptive to the teachings of Christ. Though he leaned toward deism, he regarded himself as a Christian and was aware that the flag might follow hard on the heels of the Bible. Bowles's pleas for the Creeks' spiritual well-being fell on sympathetic ears, but the society's directors judiciously decided to withhold financial contributions until the Director General returned to America, regained his standing among the Indians, and put Muskogee's house in order.[49]

When Bowles considered Muskogee's future he saw a large area carved out of Spanish Florida and southwestern United States, now primarily inhabited by Indians but soon to be settled by a stream of whites coming there with his approval. Muskogee would be either a British protectorate or an outright British colony, and it would be civilized by the whites and by the Indians who in time would adopt the white man's ways. Printing was a characteristic of civilization, and William did not want Muskogee to lag behind in this area; he expected to have his own printer for official documents and even a newspaper. He described Muskogee's promising future and influenced a young printer, John Owen, to come to Muskogee. Owen apparently had published one of Reeves most ultra-conservative works indicating that the King was superior to the House of Commons; the youthful printer ran into trouble with the courts and found it convenient to leave the country.[50]

A diversified group was drawn to Bowles in London, but unfortunately many who were attracted to him were as penniless as the Director General. They looked to Muskogee either because it offered the prospect of thousands of Indian souls ripe for salvation, because of profits to be made from a commerce in furs and naval stores, because it offered those who had suffered from an American or European revolution a chance to recoup their fortunes, or because of a chance for glory and adventure. Assorted continental exiles wrote Bowles, offering their services and expecting to be reimbursed with large land grants.[51] Captain Baynton, a Loyalist comrade-at-arms at Pensacola and author of Bowles's biography published in 1791, took an apartment nearby in London, offered his advice and possibly his services.[52] Miscellaneous other soldiers, some Loyalists living in London, as well as sailors Bowles had recently encountered on British ships at Sierra Leone and in the St. Helena convoy, wrote and visited William and offered encouragement. Speculators in western lands, hard hit by the recent drop in land values, wondered if through Bowles's influence their holdings might be sold for a satisfactory price.[53] For the present few of Bowles's well-wishers were willing to actively throw in their lot with Muskogee's future, but should Britain resolve on a direct attack on Florida and Louisiana and should the Director General be successful upon returning to Florida, his admirers might not be so reticent.

During the seven months Bowles was in England he renewed old acquaintances and made many new ones. He was constantly in touch with Reeves and his large circle of friends, many of whom, like John Gifford, editor of the *Anti-Jacobin Review and Magazine,* William Windham, and John Bowles, a political pamphleteer, were outspoken leaders against republicanism at home and abroad. John Bowles was probably William's cousin, and they may have met when William first came to London. Unfortunately there is no account of the relationship between John and Cousin Eastajoca.[54] Other friends of Reeves were George Browne and his family. Browne, a steadfast admirer of William, outdid himself when learning of Bowles's return: "An English Bard, alas! he can no more, bids thee thrice welcome to Britannia's Shore; To sing thy praises fain wou'd I aspire, whom all the good and all the great admire. . . ."[55] Though Bowles realized that Browne was not likely to become poet laureate, William was flattered by being the subject of the poem, and this attention was another reason he so frequently visited this family. Browne was pinched financially but soon obtained a minor post in the North American customs service which provided a livelihood and, unfortunately, leisure to pen further lines. The Browne children were captivated by the tall stranger in queer dress, with flashing eyes and a quick smile, ever ready to charm them for hours. Browne's young daughter, about to return to school, was heartbroken at the prospect of not seeing her idol—"I love you so much."[56]

Professionally and socially Pearson, whom William had first met in 1790 and who recently had nursed him back to health, was one of Bowles's most intimate companions. The doctor had a varied circle of acquaintances, including outstanding scientists, English nobility (he was personal physician to the Duke of York's household), and leading figures of the London stage. Pearson's good friend was John Philip Kemble, long-time controversial manager of Drury Lane and member of a distinguished family numbering many actors and actresses. It was inevitable that Bowles, interested in the theater and ever priding himself an actor, should be drawn to Pearson's theatrical friends; and it proved both exciting and flattering to go to Drury Lane and see Kemble act and later to chat with him. Perhaps it was no more than coincidence that *The Revenge*, which had not been acted since Bowles was last in London, was again performed, with Kemble as Zanga.[57] Bowles was in his element and, dressed as an Indian, mingled perfectly in the company of actors and actresses.

Hannah Brand, a playwright and actress, proud of her classical knowledge though belittled because of her provincial Norwich accent, was one of many in the theatrical world enchanted by the Creek chief's manners and accounts of Indian life. Lest he draw too close to nature she stocked his trunk with mathematical treatises and works of Homer, Aristotle, Locke, and Demosthenes, which he appreciated most of all. She also included original verses for both of Bowles's wives, miscellaneous gifts for his daughter and son, and "a Norwich shawl for the venerable princess," whoever this Indian matriarch characterized by Bowles might be.[58]

The elderly Lord George Townshend, member of a politically powerful family, formerly Wolfe's second-in-command at Quebec and later lord lieutenant of Ireland, currently sitting in the House of Lords, was another admirer. He had met Bowles in London on his first visit, enjoyed his company, and was interested in Muskogee's future. Returning from London to his family seat at Rainham in Norfolk, he encouraged Bowles to come up for a visit. Business interruptions and confusion about whether part of the royal family was coming to Rainham caused delay. It was not until the year's end that Townshend wrote that the princess definitely was not coming after all and that Bowles was welcome anytime—"if you like shooting bring your gun." There is no record of what Bowles did at Rainham or any certain proof he made the visit. But there were good reasons to cultivate Townshend's friendship, and Bowles would have been a fool not to accept the invitation—besides, he liked shooting.[59]

Bowles frequently saw Dunmore when the irritable Scottish lord came to London to straighten out his tangled accounts and to try to obtain new employment. "I hope *Eastajoca* has not forgot his promise of dining with Lady Augustus Frederick [Dunmore's daughter married to the King's son] today . . . and I hope he will be dressed as Eastajoca ought to be; a word to the wise from his friend."[60] Though Dunmore introduced Bowles to prominent royalty and nobility, the Earl himself had lost much of his political influence and was of limited assistance in soliciting governmental support for Muskogee.

During his second London visit William was not the sensation he had been eight years before: there was no retinue of Creek and Cherokee chiefs and, with foreign soldiers of fortune numerous in London because of the war, he was not as much in the public eye. In 1790 he had always appeared dressed as a chief, and though during the past six years he had lost almost all of his native costume, this was still his usual attire after he made necessary arrangements with a London tailor. It can be safely assumed that William rather than the tailor provided feathers for the turban. Again his portrait was painted and, if it could be located, would shed light not only on his costume but also on the physical effect of his lengthy Spanish confinement and his recent illness. It was Reeves who engaged Thomas Phillips, with a studio in Leicester Square, to make this painting, apparently a good one, though it was not completed before William left.[61] Phillips was a rising artist, a student at the Royal Academy, soon to make his mark as a portait painter. It would have given William immense satisfaction to know that the hands wielding the brush would soon paint leading English nobility, men of letters, and even Napoleon.[62] Michael Flanagan, who met Bowles aboard the *Isis* near Sierra Leone and was now in London, regularly stopped by Phillips' studio to advise about the finishing touches. And Flanagan vowed, were it not for his wife and child, he would follow Bowles to Florida.[63]

William was growing impatient to return to America, partly because he felt the international situation dictated that he be there, partly because he wanted to see his Creek friends and family, partly because he was short of money and could not afford a longer fling at London society, and partly because he had no future anywhere else. There were countless last-minute details, many of which concerned Bowles's finances. Reeves worked indefatigably to extract money from the government and tried to placate Osborne, owner of the Hotel at Adelphi, where Bowles had run up a sizable bill.[64] Dr. Pearson, who had cared for Bowles when he arrived in England, insisted that his bill could be satisfied when the Director General returned with his American fortune. In the meantime, a statement that Pearson had attended William when dangerously ill would help the doctor when settling accounts with the government.[65] Bowles bid *adieu* to Pearson, Reeves, the Brownes, Townshend, and his many other friends and proceeded to Portsmouth. Sailing from here was the quickest way to reach Florida and, equally important, was the least expensive.

VII

Indomitable Eastajoca

IN EARLY February William went to Portsmouth and secured lodgings in the Crown Inn near the waterfront. A West Indian convoy was assembling, and Reeves and Brickwood had used their influence to obtain Bowles passage to America on the warship *Atlas*. It took time for all the vessels to arrive, for the stores to be loaded, and unfavorable weather resulted in additional delay. Bowles remained at the Crown Inn almost a month, busy buying a few high-priced delicacies to improve the routine fare on the long voyage and supervising the loading of his baggage, which fortunately was more extensive now than when he sailed to the Philippines with only one pair of trousers.[1] He had leisure to inspect the ancient port, to stroll upon the ramparts and view the bustling harbor thronged with ships, or to wander through the fortified town which smelled of fish and much else and was crowded by loud talking sailors, male hawkers selling food, hardware, and trinkets, and females vending other wares.[2] Letters from his London friends reached him at Portsmouth: Flanagan informing William that his portrait was almost complete;[3] Mrs. Browne urging that he watch out for his health;[4] William Sabatier, his father's friend he had not seen since 1790 in Halifax, now in England and volunteering sage personal and political advice;[5] and Hannah Brand checking to insure that the classics and presents for Bowles's Indian family were safely packed in his trunk.[6]

Just before leaving England Bowles wrote a final letter to the Duke of Portland, re-emphasizing that his southern Indians were eager to serve George III; that under his leadership they alone were more than a match for the several hundred Spanish soldiers scattered throughout Florida; but that should France and the United States, in addition to Spain, oppose him—as appeared probable—then British aid would be indispensable. Bowles asked Reeves to deliver the letter personally and to be vigilant in Muskogee's behalf: "You must be our ambassador and manage our affairs." At every opportunity, Bowles urged, recommend an expedition against Florida and Louisiana and hint to the American minister that a Muskogee alliance might be mutually advantageous. "Remember me to [my friends]; the wind is fair and we shall soon sail."[7]

Though Bowles shared in the apprehension over the possible appearance of an enemy fleet, the convoy made a safe, relatively quick voyage of only a month to the West Indies. Barbados, the most windward of all the Lesser Antilles, was the first stop, and William, like the rest of the passengers, eagerly bought fruit from the almost naked natives who swarmed alongside the *Atlas* in their small boats. He unloaded his baggage and at once made his way through Bridgetown's narrow, crooked streets, on into the countryside through cane fields and pasture, until he arrived at the Pilgrim, the residence of Governor George Rickets. At Reeves's insistence, the home government had written Rickets of Bowles's imminent arrival and ordered him to show the Creek leader every courtesy. Because of this letter and Bowles's engaging manner, William immediately won the Governor's confidence and admiration. William, put up in the Pilgrim, located on an elevation over a mile from town, was introduced to the island's leading notables: the sociability of "Governor Rickets and gentlemen of this island is . . . beyond description."[8]

His charm and letter of introduction aside, William felt there was a more important reason why Rickets should court his favor. In wartime all West Indian islands were vulnerable; any moment an enemy fleet might appear on the horizon; and wartime disruption of commerce could cause genuine suffering. Producing sugar and other staples and buying manufactures, horses, lumber, and even food from abroad, Barbados was no more self-sufficient than other West Indian Islands. Bowles knew that Barbados obtained foodstuffs and barrel staves from the United States, though it was probably illegal, and that French warships had interfered with this commerce. He suggested to the Governor that neutral Muskogee would be less vulnerable to French harassment: she easily could meet the needs of Barbados, and within six months her vessels would be here dotting Bridgetown's harbor. His reception at Barbados and news from Reeves that all opposition and difficulty was at an end made Bowles more optimistic than ever. Even so, he urged Reeves to make doubly sure that there was no legal impediment to Muskogee's vessels' freely entering major West Indian ports and to lay the groundwork for a commercial treaty soon to be negotiated by an official Creek ambassador.[9]

Because the Governor was unable to secure passage directly to Florida, Bowles remained at the Pilgrim, except when he rode over to neighboring plantations to spend a few days, for almost two months. The only solution to the transportation impasse was that he first go to Jamaica, centrally located and the Caribbean's foremost commercial center, and from there sail to Florida. At Bowles's request, Rickets provided letters of introduction to the Earl of Balcarres, Jamaica's governor, and to Hyde Parker, commander-in-chief of the naval forces stationed at the island, informing them of the Director General's dilemma and of his importance to British interests in America. At the same time Bowles accepted a berth on the frigate *Arab* while Rickets paid most of William's Barbados expenses, assuming Portland "with his usual goodness will uphold this payment."[10] With some reluctance Bowles left the Pilgrim's comforts but assured Rickets that before the year was out fully laden Muskogee vessels would be riding anchor at Bridgetown and promised to relay copies of dispatches to Whitehall through Barbados.

Arriving at Jamaica in June, 1799, Bowles found the island the scene of great bustle comparable to the activity he had witnessed here as a provincial ensign twenty years before during the American Revolution. The West Indies were a major theater of the present war, and the Jamaica station was Britain's most important naval base. Numerous warships and privateers were sent out from here against the enemy, while, in spite of the war, contraband trade flourished. Recently a British expedition from Jamaica had attempted to conquer Haiti, but tropical sickness and native opposition forced it to withdraw. Bowles brushed elbows in Kingston with French royalist refugees who counted themselves lucky if they escaped with their lives. He heard rumors of every description at Kingston: reports that there would be a new expedition against Haiti or that Jamaican maroons would rise again, that Louisiana and Florida had been ceded to France and Napoleon's troops were expected imminently, and that the United States and Britain had made a formal alliance.[11] He made his way with fanfare from the docks through the crowded city and presented his letters of introduction to Governor Balcarres. The Governor was attracted to the buoyant Indian and especially to his proposal that Muskogee could furnish timber and foodstuffs so necessary for the planters, French refugees, and soldiers here. Florida's economy naturally complemented that of the West Indian islands, a fact also appreciated by Napoleon.[12]

There were equally important reasons why Balcarres was hospitable. Bowles apparently had some sort of understanding with the ministry and could be useful in either an Anglo-American or a British attack on Florida and Louisiana. Bowles contended that Muskogee also could be a haven for French royalist refugees; they could leave Jamaica and no longer would be a financial drain on the British government. There was abundant land; the Indians had granted him an extensive tract along the coast; and French refugee planters might resume their careers here where there was fertile land and where they would be safe from republican fanaticism. The Director General was eager to have French colonists "of sound principles" and was willing to grant each family head one hundred acres and fifty more for each additional person.[13] Exiled French Catholic priests looked to Muskogee and were tempted by the potential harvest of pagan souls or by the prospect of ministering to the new French immigrants. Muskogee's liberal government, according to the Director General, tolerated all religions and the priests could come and take up land on equal terms with anyone else.[14] But the French priests along with the rest of the refugees were not willing to commit themselves until Bowles's claims to be the leader of an independent Muskogee were actually realized. An exception was the youthful Captain Neuville, who had served with the British forces at Haiti and who became William's aide-de-camp.[15]

Bowles chafed at the delay which kept him in Kingston for two months, but he kept occupied and was constantly in the company of "gay and delightful" Hyde Parker; of Governor Balcarres, who was frequently sick and taking mercury "doing penance for past sins" and who would be remembered primarily for his dirty fingernails by Lady Nugent, wife of Balcarres' successor; of General Churchill, second in command of the Kingston regiment of foot; or of Frenchmen and local merchants.[16] William had leisure to drive about the shore of the bay, to go over to the nearby capital at Spanish Town, and to visit Balcarres and Parker at their rural residences between Spanish Town and Kingston. At Jamaica he acquired twenty-five barrels of powder and thirty boxes of bullets. There is some question exactly who provided them, but there are almost conclusive indications that it was Balcarres, Parker, or possibly a merchant who was attracted by Muskogee's food, timber, and furs and by the prospect of increasing contraband trade with nearby Spanish possessions and who had been assured the government would reimburse him for the munitions.[17] Hugh Ferguson, a young relative of one of these merchants, a friend of Neuville, currently an humble clerk, was introduced to Bowles and induced to become Muskogee's collector of customs and subsequently the Director General's secretary. Ferguson, as he closed his ledger book to seek adventure in Muskogee, fancied himself another Robert Clive,

who earlier in India had quit his career as a clerk for the East India
Company and had won fame as a soldier.[18]

The reception at Kingston had been stimulating and, with Hyde
Parker finding Bowles passage on the sloop *Fox,* he prepared for the
final stage of his journey. Because Balcarres had been so agreeable and
had paid William's expenses, because Jamaica was much closer to
Florida than Barbados, and because Dunmore was no longer in Nassau
and there was concern that the new Bahamian governor was allied
with Dunmore's political enemies, Bowles made arrangements to send
his dispatches to Whitehall through Kingston. He was anxious to
return directly to Florida, but the *Fox,* ordered to deliver a detachment of artillery to the Bahamas, would have to stop at Nassau en
route. Bowles, after supervising loading of his baggage, which by now
was quite bulky, set sail on the *Fox* with Ferguson, Neuville, and two
French carpenters.[19]

Bowles had misgivings about going to Nassau at this time. He still
had friends there, above all Miller, but there was reason to believe
that the new governor, William Dowdeswell, even though he had been
instructed by Whitehall to assist Bowles, was a friend of Panton, Leslie,
and Forbes and that William would not be warmly received.[20] This
could alarm Neuville, Ferguson, and other potential followers who
might come to Muskogee, because all along Bowles had led them to
believe that he had a definite, though unofficial, understanding with
the British government. But for better or worse the *Fox* was bound
for Nassau, first sailing into the Windward Channel between Cuba
and Haiti, close enough to the latter for Bowles to hear Toussaint
l'Ouverture's artillery firing on Môle St. Nicolas, recently evacuated by
Britain and now desperately defended by the Negro general's political
rivals. After threading its way through the many uninhabited Bahama
Islands, the *Fox* at last approached New Providence. The island's low
silhouette, Nassau's buildings hugging the northern shore which
Bowles had first seen in 1783, was a familiar sight.[21] As the *Fox* slowly
entered the harbor, Bowles could see that the town had not changed
radically. It was a little larger, and with the war there were more
privateers about. Impressive new Fort Charlotte at the western end
of town was almost complete, and the governor's mansion, Government House, still commanded a marvelous view—but gone was its
former occupant.

Governor Dowdeswell, Leslie's friend, did not offer Bowles and his
retinue lodging and, in contrast to the governors of Barbados and
Jamaica, was no more cordial than officially necessary. Since Rickets,

Balcarres, and Parker all had helped Bowles to return to Muskogee and since he had instructions from Whitehall, Dowdeswell felt obliged to be civil, to formally receive the Director General at Government House, and even to pay some of William's expenses. This he did and no more.[22] Fortunately Miller, still on the council though with little political influence, was here, anxious to see Bowles and to hear first hand accounts of his adventures. The merchant was equally eager to work out details about establishing Brickwood's sawmill and about making another attempt on Panton's monopoly. Thomas Forbes, a member of Panton, Leslie, and Company, was here too, closely observing how many followers Bowles had, trying to ferret out what was in the mysterious barrels and chests aboard the *Fox* and discrediting William at every opportunity. Assuming Leslie's partisan London reports to Forbes were reliable, Bowles was out of favor and the ministry finally was aware of what a charlatan it was encouraging. Forbes was quick to pass these accounts along to Dowdeswell.[23] Yet, at almost the same time, Reeves was assuring Bowles that all opposition had been swept aside and that success was at hand. Only Bowles's conduct in Florida and future international developments would determine whether Leslie or Reeves was correct.

The closer Bowles approached Florida after leaving England the more accurately he was able to ascertain the state of affairs on the mainland. There had been many changes since his departure. McGillivray was dead, and although assorted half-breeds and whites claimed to be his successor, there was no recognized Creek leader. The Pinckney Treaty had been signed in 1795, and its effects were far-reaching: Americans freely trafficked at New Orleans, and Spain, though she took several years, abandoned her posts north of the thirty-first parallel. The Americans were relentlessly advancing on the southern frontier, and the Indians were more alarmed than ever about their hunting lands. For the first time since regaining the Floridas Spain had almost no influence north of the thirty-first parallel. The Creeks, living both north and south of this parallel, were dismayed by Spanish concessions in the Pinckney Treaty and did not recognize its provisions—unless there was no alternative. The Creeks were the best organized and, with the possible exception of the Choctaws, the most numerous of the southern Indians. They had long felt American pressure on the fringes of their hunting lands, but they still controlled the bulk of their territory. They were resolved that this would continue in the future.

One of the cardinal provisions of the Pinckney Treaty was that Spain agree to the thirty-first parallel as West Florida's boundary. But exactly where was this parallel? It was necessary to survey it jointly and to mark it so that Americans and Spaniards would not violate each other's territory and so, as stipulated in the treaty, each nation could supervise and restrain the Indians on its side of the line. The experienced American civil engineer, Andrew Ellicott, had been ordered to co-operate with his Spanish counterpart in making the survey. But it was not until 1798 when the Spaniards finally relinquished Natchez—north of the thirty-first parallel—that Ellicott was able to proceed down the Mississippi and begin his work.[24] Bowles had been watching attentively the Spanish-American dispute over Natchez and the subsequent reports that Ellicott finally was making headway on his survey.

The changing international picture was of even more interest. Four nations—the United States, Britain, France, and Spain—were concerned with the fate of Florida and Louisiana. Bowles wondered whether Spain could retain her freedom of action and not become a French satellite and whether Spanish authority, weak though it was, would continue in these provinces. Or would Spain cede them to France, or had she already done so, and were Napoleon's veterans on the way here? If current rumors could be believed, French troops were just over the horizon.

One of his most immediate concerns was to discover whether the United States was really going to war with France. The undeclared naval war had been going on for many months, and there was Federalist pressure for a formal break. But President Adams had just sent new commissioners to France to try once again to reach an honorable settlement. If the United States did not patch up her differences with France, would a common foe draw the United States and Britain closer together? This still seemed probable; there were signs that an Anglo-American alliance was imminent. Bowles and many others in reading the newspapers questioned why else the British General Thomas Maitland had gone to Philadelphia. Was he there just to work out details of Anglo-American commerce to Toussaint's newly independent Haiti, or would the Anglo-American accord be more far-reaching?[25]

All of these considerations were running through William's mind at Nassau. He had to discover if French troops actually were bound for Florida, whether there would be close Anglo-American co-operation in which Muskogee would be a junior partner to combat the Franco-Spanish alliance, and whether he should continue to make friendly overtures to the United States. It might be expedient to do so, but, because of American designs on the Old Southwest, it would be difficult for Muskogee to make any agreement with authorities at Philadelphia. The thirty-first parallel was one of several problems. It bisected Creek lands and either Bowles would have to recognize its validity or the United States would have to de-emphasize its significance. Both were possible, but neither was likely; as always, Bowles wanted to rely on the Creeks and other southern Indians and on whites who would settle in Muskogee, all of whom would be supported exclusively by Britain. Eventually he would have to come to terms with the United States, but after his white and Indian followers had expelled Spain from Florida the Pickney Treaty would be void, and he could negotiate anew from a position of strength.

But all Bowles's schemes and hopes would count for little unless he established himself as the prominent leader among the Creeks and neighboring Indians. Florida was just over the horizon, and he was anxious to return. So was Captain James Wooldridge, the *Fox's* commander. He had orders to take Bowles to the mainland and to complete his cruise; delay might see his crew almost completely disappear. Most of them had been impressed and, given the opportunity, especially the Americans, would like to merge into the island's population or sign aboard a merchant ship.[26] After bidding farewell to Miller and other New Providence friends, Bowles, Ferguson, Neuville, and the two carpenters boarded the *Fox* for the final stage of their journey. At the same time Forbes, when he was not telling Dowdeswell what a scoundrel Bowles was, wrote Panton in Pensacola details of the visit and that the demagogue was now returning to his "palace" on some fine river in Florida. There was never any doubt that he was returning to the Chattahoochee near the heart of the Lower Creek-Seminole country where he had left his supporters and Indian family in 1792, where his following was the strongest, and where some of these Indians had granted him a vast tract of land.[27]

Because of contrary winds and currents the passage around the Florida peninsula was a slow one; occasionally the mainland was visible, and for William it was a welcome sight. As the *Fox* approached Apalachee Bay Bowles, who had a fair knowledge of navigation and knew these waters well, pointed out landmarks and helped guide Captain Wooldridge to the Apalachicola River—the ultimate destination. Possibly in the distance he saw the mouth of the St. Marks River, and unquestionably he wondered what plans the Spaniards at the fort upstream and the employees of Panton's store had made for his reception. West of the St. Marks River were several low, sandy islands— Dog Island off the mouth of the Ochlockonee River followed by elongated St. Georges Island off the Apalachicola River's mouth.

In the vicinity of these islands the *Fox* ran into a furious storm, and all hands were busy at the pumps, reducing sail, or helping at the wheel; still the *Fox* took water and was blown perilously close to shore. In this crisis Bowles and the Captain bickered about how to save the ship. Wooldridge had his way and, as later charged by Bowles, through incompetence ran the *Fox* aground on the eastern end of St. Georges Island ineptly trying to reach the sanctuary of St. Georges Sound. In a last-ditch attempt to save the ship Wooldridge ordered stores and baggage heaved overboard. With dismay Bowles saw that part of his belongings were the first to go, and this did not further endear him to the Captain. The storm raged unabated, covering the island with up to two feet of water, but finally Bowles, working furiously along with the passengers and crew, helped transfer everyone and part of the cargo safely ashore. Bad weather continued for two more days, and the *Fox* broke up and sank off the tip of St. Georges Island, now christened Fox Point. The Director General's triumphant return to the Creeks had fizzled.[28]

There was no choice at first but to seek crude shelter and to wait for the storm to subside; later there would be time to figure out a way for the *Fox's* crew to return to Jamaica and for Eastajoca to go inland to his Indian friends and family. Fortunately a nearby ship came to Bowles's aid. Andrew Ellicott, United States commissioner to survey the thirty-first parallel boundary, was the most distinguished passenger aboard. He and his Spanish companions had been working their way eastward from the Mississippi River, meeting increased native hostility as they proceeded. The Indians distrusted surveyors, especially those running the new boundary, and were not reassured when Ellicott told them they would not be deprived of their lawful property.[29] The Creeks, hardly ever enthusiastic about treaties negotiated with the whites, were thoroughly unhappy with the Pinckney Treaty which divided Creek lands without their consent. Lower Creeks and Seminoles attacked Ellicott and his Spanish and American party near the mouth of the Flint River, forcing them to flee down the swollen Apalachicola in their small schooner. Soon Bowles asserted that, because of his well-known hostility to the Pinckney Treaty which arbitrarily divided Muskogee's lands, news of his imminent arrival prompted the Indians to drive Ellicott away. The surveyor, however, would have encountered Indian resistance whether Bowles appeared or not.[30]

Bowles in his plight was forced to appeal to Ellicott who had problems enough of his own but was relatively better off than William: "although we may differ in politics, yet as gentlemen we may associate, and be friends."[31] Wooldridge assured Ellicott that the Director General had no armed force and that he sincerely wanted to negotiate American-Muskogee differences.[32] For political and humanitarian reasons and sheer curiosity Ellicott, leaving his schooner damaged by the Indians behind for repairs, sailed over to nearby St. Georges Island in an open boat and furnished much-needed provisions to the waterlogged survivors. Contrary winds forced Ellicott to remain on the island for over a week, and he had lengthy conversations with Bowles, " a man of enterprise, and address, added to considerable talents."[33] William sanctimoniously recounted how he had been unjustly imprisoned by the Spaniards, how they unsuccessfully had urged him to lead the Indians against the United States, how the 1795 treaty ignored Creek rights, and how he was going to take Fort St. Marks and Panton's store if the garrison and Panton's employees did not withdraw immediately. Ellicott was not bored during his stay on St. Georges Island. But, in spite of Bowles's overtures for American-Muskogee co-operation, he urged the United States at all costs to oppose Bowles, who was a talented, ambitious individual posing a threat to American interest. With better weather and charts furnished by William, the American commissioner sailed around the Florida peninsula and ultimately reached Philadelphia, confirming reports that the Creek agitator was on the scene and that Indian hostility had prevented completing the boundary survey.[34]

As soon as Ellicott left, Bowles obtained a pirogue and, accompanied by a reluctant Wooldridge, paddled up the Apalachicola River, informing the Creeks and Seminoles strung out in their villages along the river that after seven years Eastajoca had returned home. He issued a call for a general council to meet at Wekiva on the Chattahoochee River six miles above the boundary to discuss how best to deal with the Spaniards and Americans. At Perryman's William was joined by his half-breed wife, Mary, and by his half-grown son, William, whom he had not seen since he was an infant.[35] After sixteen days Wooldridge returned to Fox Point on St. Georges Island, bringing welcome food to Neuville, Ferguson, and the other survivors; they were not overly impressed by the various Indian villages, each with several hundred irregularly spaced, bark-covered houses.

One of the main reasons why Creeks and Seminoles from both sides of the line agreed to assemble at Wekiva was disposition of the rum and munitions Bowles told them he had salvaged from the *Fox.* Ten out of twenty-five barrels of powder, ten of thirty boxes of bullets, and several kegs of rum had been saved. He wrote Wooldridge to guard the salvaged munitions carefully and to send them upriver with the Indians as soon as possible. "I shall not rest easy until the powder is here and out of reach of the Spaniards . . . be firm and we will get out of this with glory."[36] Wooldridge had his doubts. Newly christened Fox Point on St. Georges Island marking the site of the wreck might commemorate him to posterity but would win no recommendation for promotion from Admiral Hyde Parker in Jamaica.

Relations between Bowles and Wooldridge became chilly. Wooldridge never appreciated the Indian chief, who, as far as Wooldridge was concerned, had commanded little more than a hogshead in Pensacola Bay, giving orders how to navigate the *Fox.* For the time being each was dependent on the other and could not afford the luxury of an open split. Wooldridge and the *Fox's* crew, living on the island in an improvised shelter made of wood and canvas, relied on Bowles for food, while in turn they guarded his salvaged munitions. Eventually some of the Indians paddled downstream, brought additional food for the survivors, and, most important of all, loaded the munitions aboard and carried them into the interior. William maintained he was too busy to come personally; instead Ferguson, Neuville, Wooldridge, and the rest should all come upriver.[37] This was the last thing Wooldridge, a professional officer in the Royal Navy who knew little about the southern Indians and cared less, intended. He stayed and finally a British privateer picked up him and the remaining crew members. Many of those who had been impressed had seized the opportunity earlier to escape and make their way to the Spanish outposts on the St. Johns River. Those who were Americans were careful to conceal this fact when they were in the Indian country.[38] Wooldridge eventually reached Jamaica and, because of charges of negligence concerning the *Fox's* wreck, had to face a court martial. He was acquitted in spite of Bowles's diatribes.[39]

William had not been exaggerating when he contended he was too busy at Wekiva to come down to St. Georges Island. Nothing was more important than re-establishing his prestige among the Indians, and he was pleased, despite his shipwreck, that Eastajoca still had friends among the Lower Creeks and Seminoles. He capitalized on the latent mistrust of Panton, Leslie, and Company, whose prices had not gone down any over the past seven years: though "higher than in peace time . . . Indians nevertheless will still find at the old stand [St. Marks] sufficient clothing," and the like—if they will guarantee the safety of the firm's property.[40] With Eastajoca on the scene no such assurance was forthcoming. Bowles charged, apparently with justification, that because of the present war and disgust over the Pinckney Treaty, Panton was considering pulling out of Florida altogether, leaving the Indians to shift for themselves; and he threatened that if the Scottish merchant did not leave and continued to stock the Spanish forts with powder, then the Director General would capture him and send him home in irons as a traitor.[41] Panton's departure, voluntary or not, could only be a blessing for the Indians, because Bowles and his merchant friends—with King George in the background—were ready to meet every want. Those munitions on St. Georges Island were an indication of what was to follow.

Bowles harangued the Indians at length about the grievances they had against Spain. He knew there were many warriors who remembered how Britain had lavished presents during the American Revolution and that the Spaniards had never been so liberal. He denounced Spain for being party to the Pinckney Treaty, which bisected Creek territory and opened the door to American land speculators: "We have not agreed either by word or act to surrender the sovereignty of our country, nor never thought of so doing."[42] And look what Spain had done to Eastajoca, chief spokesman of the Creeks, perfidiously violating a safe-conduct pass and keeping him imprisoned for years in various quarters of the globe. The Spaniards were as bad as Panton —it was hard to distinguish between them—and both had to go. Bowles's arguments playing up Indian discontent with Spain and Panton, his gifts of munitions and rum salvaged from the *Fox* coupled with promises of larger presents by Christmas or spring at the latest, and his report that George III soon was going to have important talks for the natives, all had their effect.[43] The important message that Bowles expected from the Crown was that a British expedition was bound for Florida and that the King wanted to make an alliance with the southern Indians. This was not wild talk. At this time Britain was seriously considering plans for an attack on Florida and Louisiana. Bowles must have heard about these preliminary plans while in London—indeed he must have contributed to them. There was no way of knowing that unforeseen events would divert this expedition from Florida to Egypt.[44] Impressed by what Bowles had to say the Indians assembled at Wekiva, representing the Seminoles and Lower Creeks, "with one voice reelect you Director of our nation; . . . we are reduced to poverty and have no hoes, axes, or powder; you may have your place of residence on this river as selected . . . depart no more . . . and communicate our talks to England."[45]

Bowles had been operating primarily in Spanish Florida, and it was the Spaniards who were most alarmed by his return. They had had plenty of warning about his escape and designs from the *Concepción's* captain, from British and American gazettes, from Panton

and Leslie, and from the *Fox's* crew that deserted St. Georges Island.
If for no other reasons than his violated safe-conduct pass and imprisonment, the Spaniards knew that Bowles was their inveterate
enemy and would stir up whatever mischief possible. Spanish armed
galleys patrolled from East Florida to Apalachicola Bay, unsuccessfully
trying to intercept the Director General; while Thomas Portell, the
St. Marks commandant, offered $4,500 for Bowles's head—a reward
Thomas Perryman, who had not forgotten their quarrel eight years
ago, intended to collect.[46] At Panton's nearby store, the storekeeper
John Forrester brought the cattle in close and reported to his superiors
that there were no furs here; only a little powder and ball. "I have
everything out of this *good* fellow's reach."[47] This was no accident.
The 1792 seizure had taught Panton a lesson, and it was only to
others that he underestimated and depreciated Bowles. Forrester, as
in 1792, could retire to the fort, but James Durouzeaux, a semi-
literate interpreter who lived among the Lower Creeks and served
the United States and Spain alike, had no such protection. He notified
Governor Folch that the Indians were agitated after Bowles's arrival
and that if troops were not sent promptly then he would join the
Governor in Pensacola.[48]

The United States was also uneasy about Bowles's return. He had
been responsible for preventing the 1790 boundary from being run,
and now it was in his interest to disrupt the Pinckney Treaty line.
The United States was determined it should be run at all costs lest
Spain, France, or Britain in some fashion try to reassert their authority
north of the thirty-first parallel. Bowles never respected either of the
Floridas' northern boundaries and always insisted that foreign powers
could not arbitrarily divide Muskogee's lands by the Pinckney Treaty
or any other. Bowles's dealings with the Indians on the American
side of the line could undermine the program of Benjamin Hawkins,
the Southern Indian agent, who was trying to civilize the natives and
to encourage them to grow and spin cotton, raise cattle, and adopt
the white man's laws. Humanitarian reasons aside, the primary reason
for this program of the national government was to arrange it so
that the Creeks would no longer need their extensive hunting lands
which in time could be made available for white settlement.[49] Under
ordinary conditions Bowles would support Hawkins' program, but now
he found it expedient to denounce the American agent and to sympathize with the Indians, many of whom were reluctant to abandon
their traditional way of life. One of the first decisions at Wekiva was
to demand that any American—or Spaniard—who was in Muskogee
territory must leave under pain of death. If an American remained

and was authorized by his government, this would be an automatic declaration of war.[50] The closer Bowles had gotten to Florida the less likely it seemed to him that Britain would effectively co-operate with the United States. New American commissioners were already in France trying to end the undeclared naval war. They had been sent by President Adams, titular head of the Federalist party. Bowles realized that if this anti-French party was bent on an accommodation with France, there was no hope for an Anglo-American combination against Spanish (French?) Florida. Should the United States desire a reasonable settlement with the Creeks and should it want to negotiate a new treaty to replace those of 1790 and 1795, then American commissioners could come to Bowles; if not, any American caught in Creek territory was liable to the death penalty, with Hawkins heading the list: "Mr. Hawkins is the man, who if he is not gone, must go immediately, as he is a dangerous man and will cause some mischief . . . by staying."[51] It was the belligerent proclamations coming out of Wekiva that prompted the Tennessee congressman, William C. C. Claiborne, to propose that the House establish a commission to investigate anyone stirring up the Indians on American soil;[52] others in Philadelphia wondered if Bowles's appearance in Florida, accompanied by other suspicious movements, signaled a revival of the Blount conspiracy.[53]

All along Bowles's preference had been to establish an Indian state which would be a British protectorate, would keep France off the American mainland, and which the United States could accept or not. He never lost hope that Britain and the Indians could control Florida and Louisiana, and more than ever he stressed reasons why Britain should acquire these provinces. His timely letters kept Reeves informed about how frightened the Spaniards were since his arrival in Florida —in Pensacola they temporarily left the town to seek refuge in the nearby fort—how his followers had forced Ellicott to flee and stop running the boundary line, how the Creeks had re-elected him director general, and how, at a moment's notice, his Indian army was prepared to march against St. Marks and Pensacola. He urged Reeves to convey all this information to Home Secretary Portland and again advise the ministry that Muskogee is "at the service of Britain . . . and awaits orders." The government also should be made aware that, because of the loss of the *Fox*, there was a critical shortage of munitions among the Indians. Moreover, Reeves was to find out what had happened to John Owen, the printer who apparently had left England but had not reached Muskogee. His press, publishing to the world Muskogee's proclamations, important state papers, and details about the base treatment accorded Eastajoca during his imprisonment, would be more effective than scores of warriors.[54]

The British government now as in the past was divided about Bowles primarily because of confusion over what to do with Florida. The Earl of Liverpool, president of the Board of Trade, had doubts about allowing Panton to ship munitions to this province in wartime where they might end up in Spanish hands.[55] Replacing Panton with Bowles would solve this problem. But there were also peace rumors, and at the same time Portland wondered if the West Indian governors had not already gone too far in subsidizing Bowles.[56] In spite of talk of peace, there were other cabinet members who felt the concessions demanded by France would be too great and instead insisted on an aggressive campaign against the enemy. Henry Dundas, secretary of war, was one who wanted to seize key American ports to keep them out of French hands and to expand British commerce. New Orleans had a high priority.[57] Robert Liston, the British minister at Philadelphia, naturally was thoroughly confused about Bowles's relationship to Whitehall. He assured the United States that the British government had not sent Bowles to Florida with any sort of commission but privately assumed otherwise.[58] Bowles's future connections with the British government, however, depended on international developments and his achievements in Florida.

The re-elected Director General of Muskogee had little control over international affairs, but it was another matter whether or not he succeeded in Florida. His promises and impressive bearing already had won over a large number of Lower Creeks and Seminoles, and those whites or half-breeds who, like William Grey or John Galphin, had co-operated with him a decade ago, were still in the Indian country and ready, with some reservations, to follow their leader. His white followers, however, were not as numerous as he would like, and he was never swamped by offers of settlers wanting to become Muskogee citizens and to acquire one hundred or more acres of land. And if Ferguson and Neuville were examples, he was losing influence among those whites who already had accompanied him. The *Fox's* wreck and the prolonged stay and hand-to-mouth existence on St. Georges Island had been unpleasant experiences, and both men wondered if they should have left Jamaica. Captain Neuville began asking his chief a number of searching questions; foremost was, where was the Muskogee army? Bowles, who was in the interior furiously organizing the Indians and scraping up food for the *Fox's* survivors, was exasperated: "this country is hard . . . not like Arabian nights . . . men don't go to sleep on a dunghill and wake up in an Emperial Bed in a palace."[59]

Bowles maintained that he had not deceived Neuville, that the Captain would soon get his chance to command, but that he could return to Jamaica if he wished. Neuville was too young and full of adventure and had come too far to turn back now, but in the future he had more sense than to take the Director General's every statement at face value.

Hugh Ferguson, Bowles's secretary, also was having second thoughts. At the Indian village of Thackwithla Chattahoochee he began quarreling about his salary—a mere dollar a day—about the paltry gold half-joes William had advanced him in Nassau, and about who owned furniture salvaged from the *Fox*. Ferguson had sold a mahogany table to nearby Indians, a transaction not appreciated by William since he maintained the table was his. "Make Ben [Perryman] return the table . . . if not you will suffer the penalty of law in this country."[60] Ferguson truculently defended his innocence and insisted Wooldridge had given him the "old Table." "I do not rightly comprehend what you intended your washerwoman should tell me this morning. . . . As to anything insulting I prefer thinking that the girl has added it for her own amusement . . . for indeed it is only becoming her."[61] In the end Ferguson gave in and decided to remain in Florida, though during the fall and winter while cutting firewood and building log huts, look though he might, he was never able to catch a glimpse of the palace his leader had described while they were still in Jamaica.

The huts near the forks of the Apalachicola River which Ferguson —along with Bowles and the Indians—were building were warehouses for Muskogee's free port to replace those deserted and subsequently burned by the Spaniards eight years before on the Ochlockonee. William knew it was mandatory to open a commerce with New Providence or elsewhere in the West Indies. Because of the uncertainty and agitation, Panton was unwilling to risk wares among the Seminole and Lower Creek towns, and Bowles had promised to fill this vacuum. He began to establish those free ports or their equivalent which were supposed to have been opened in 1791. Though Bowles wanted "to see the Creek flag flying in all harbors and respected by the world at large," he was obliged to look primarily to Miller in Nassau who still was eager to break Panton's monopoly.[62] Miller was careful to keep the ministry informed about "the abundance of deer skins, furs, rice, corn, etc." to be had cheaply in Florida, about how the Indians craved British manufactures, and about why Britain, for both commercial and political reasons, should take over the Floridas. Since shipwreck cost Bowles part of his store of munitions, Miller maintained private merchants and the government should take prompt measures to sustain him.[63] William, for his part, was encouraging merchants from the Bahamas or anywhere else to come and trade with him: Muskogee's duties were moderate and potential profits high. He hinted that under his guidance Indians would be willing to make handsome land grants. Before Bowles had been in Florida many months an occasional Nassau vessel appeared to exchange merchandise for deerskins.[64]

It was apparent to Bowles that Spain was the chief obstacle to Muskogee's free commerce. She had put a price on his head; her galleys patrolled the coasts, and Fort St. Marks in the heart of Seminole-Lower Creek territory was always a menace. To facilitate commerce and to pave the way for expelling Spain from the Floridas and Louisiana, Bowles had to capture the fort. This was his prime objective—no secret to Reeves and Portland in London, British governors in the West Indies, or to Panton and the Spaniards. Captain Neuville was gratified that this objective would at last allow him to put his military talents to use, and Secretary Ferguson was heartened that there were more ambitious things at hand than chopping wood.

VIII

Revenge

HAVING WON over many Indians, in spite of his shipwreck and loss of supplies, confident of the backing of Nassau merchants and eventual open recognition by Whitehall, Bowles was more encouraged than he had been in a long time. Tedious months of delay and imprisonment in Spanish cells, lengthy voyages aboard British and Spanish ships, protracted negotiations in London and the West Indies—all were at an end. The time for action was at hand. The Old World and the New were unsettled, and there were London statesmen and merchants who considered Spanish America ripe for revolt and ready to become allied with and dependent on Britain. William was determined that when Whitehall ministers looked at Spanish America they would not be so bedazzled by the gold and silver of Mexico and Peru as to overlook the strategic location and resources of the Floridas and Louisiana. Muskogee must be included in the ministers' grand sweep of America. Bowles knew that if he captured St. Marks and other Florida posts, Britain would be quicker to openly encourage and subsidize him and to make expulsion of the Spaniards from Muskogee the initial step in dislodging them from all Spanish America.

Whether Muskogee prospered depended to a considerable extent on his own achievements. Well aware of this, he was busy in the interior, sometimes supervising building warehouses near the forks of the Apalachicola River, sometimes ascending the Chattahoochee River to Coweta exhorting the Lower and Upper Creeks to join him; at one point he went to Tampa to arrange for it to become one of his free ports. Though he did not approve of the Pinckney Treaty, he could not ignore it, and partly because of the boundary line established by this treaty he moved his family and established his headquarters at the largest and most important Seminole village of Miccosukee, thirty miles north of St. Marks on Lake Miccosukee, which was below the thirty-first parallel. Protected by the powerful chief Kinache, Bowles made this village, which stretched out for over two miles along the lake, Muskogee's unofficial capital. Kinache, almost the same age as William, disliked and distrusted the Spaniards and was the leader of the Indians who had chased Ellicott and his Spanish companions away when they tried to survey the boundary near the Apalachicola River. Though later circumstances over which he had no control would force Kinache temporarily to disavow some of Bowles's policies, this chief was always one of William's closest friends and warmest supporters. From Miccosukee William wrote his Nassau friends to send munitions and trading goods, to obtain a gunboat for the Muskogee navy, and to inquire about his printer, John Owen. Since Muskogee still had no official printer or newspaper, there was no alternative for the time being but to see if Miller could not get the Indian state's proclamations published in the *Bahama Gazette*. This paper, formerly closely identified with Panton and the Old Settler faction, had a new editor, and early in 1800 Muskogee's pronouncements ordering Americans and Spaniards away, establishing free ports, and welcoming royalist exiles were printed—although they were set in small type.[1] These notices contributed to speculation and apprehension both in the Bahamas and on the mainland. Forbes assured everyone that they were of no consequence; others were convinced that Hawkins had been run out of Creek territory or even had been assassinated; the Georgia governor wondered if the St. Marys settlers, many of whom were Loyalists and who had a long tradition of intriguing against the Spaniards, would be seduced by Bowles; while Governor Sevier in Tennessee was alarmed enough to urge doubling the state's militia.[2]

In spite of Forbes's, Panton's and Leslie's insistence that Bowles had an insignificant Indian following and that he was deemed a freebooter at Whitehall, the Spaniards always assumed that Britain was behind Bowles's return and realized he posed a serious threat. The paramount concern was how to lay hands on him. Spanish control of the Floridas and Louisiana was based primarily on minuscule garrisons bound together by the Spanish navy. Dominion over the interior depended on Indian allies, and at this time they were hard to find among the Seminoles and Lower Creeks. An excellent indication was the ineffectiveness of the $4,500 reward offered for Bowles, dead or alive. It was improbable that the tiny St. Marks garrison would risk marching any distance into hostile territory to seize the Director General.

There was one feasible alternative. Spain had a good navy—the third best afloat—and though none of her ships-of-the-line was stationed in Louisiana and Florida, there were available approximately a half-dozen light-draft galleys valuable in patrolling the Mississippi River and Gulf Coast inlets. Governor Marqués Casa Calvo at New Orleans sent Captain Manuel Garcia with three of these galleys and one hundred troops to patrol the Florida coastline and cut Bowles's communications and, if the chance presented itself, to capture him. Garcia knew that Bowles was likely to be found on the lower Apalachicola or Ochlockonee rivers and, using friendly Indians as scouts and loading his men into pirogues, tried to seize the intruder.

Aware that Garcia was after him, Bowles usually kept a jump ahead of the Spaniard. But in the vicinity of the mouth of the Flint River Bowles became careless and overconfident; Garcia discovered William's camp and attacked in the middle of the night. Startled and enraged, William fled half-clothed into the night, visions of prisons in Havana, Spain, and the Philippines spurring him on. Informed that, for the time being, Bowles did not have many followers with him, Garcia relentlessly pursued his quarry for over two days in the adjoining woods, capturing a trunk full of his belongings, some munitions, and two white subordinates, one of whom was Captain Neuville. Secretary Ferguson escaped, though hiding during the night almost completely submerged in a stream proved a disagreeable experience. Mary was not so fortunate. She was detained, deprived of almost all her belongings, and then freed, and she soon was able to rejoin Eastajoca. William, who knew the terrain and had the best reason of all for fleeing, escaped, even though he lost his trunk containing his turban, assorted clothing, books, and papers.[3] Hannah Brand would have been dismayed to learn that her classics were destined to adorn a Spanish bookshelf. Bowles's captured letters better clarified his unofficial relationship with Britain and his present intentions and confirmed what the Spaniards had known or suspected all along.

Garbled accounts of the raid appeared in the newspapers, and some reported that not only Neuville but also Bowles had been caught. Leslie lost no time in seeing that copies of these articles were available at Whitehall.[4] Some Indians, one of whom was the Potato King on the Flint River, had second thoughts about supporting Eastajoca: though "I am your friend . . . we ar pore and your pore. In this condison we can't halp onanother . . . ." The Spaniards have blocked up this river, and "we don't know wher to get on bolet nor on load of powder nor nothing. . . ."[5]

Garcia's galleys had been a nuisance to Bowles: they hampered communications with New Providence and contributed to his near capture. But William had escaped, and it was not feasible to make an extended march into the interior after him or to imprison his Indian followers—assuming that were possible. Bowles was still at liberty and, despite the reticence of the Potato King, still had numerous supporters. All along it was assumed that Panton's St. Marks store and the nearby Spanish fort were the initial objectives. According to Bowles, the Scottish merchant had deceived the Indians, was not making available sufficient goods, was charging too high prices, and, by supplying the Spaniards munitions during wartime, was a traitor to his country. There was validity to these charges, at least in Indian minds, and scores followed Eastajoca in his descent on Panton's store. With only a handful of whites, Negroes, and Indians available for defense and since Garcia and his men, who earlier had been nearby at Fort St. Marks, had departed, resistance was out of the question, and once again Bowles, supremely confident, was master of the Scot's warehouse, though this time the loot was not so large.[6]

Several miles downstream lay Fort St. Marks, the next objective. Bowles was being urged to take the fort—not that it was necessary— by Joseph Hunter who was in Apalachee Bay with one or possibly more of his ships playing cat-and-mouse with Spanish galleys among the small islands, reefs, and sandbars. The fort, if captured, would afford a refuge and signal opening an extensive commerce with Nassau merchants. Because Hunter was running short of provisions, because bad weather was setting in, and because the galleys were becoming more aggressive, William became apprehensive as Hunter's pleas for him to act grew more urgent. Delay proved costly; one of the galleys caught up with Hunter, forcing him to run aground and flee into the countryside. A number of the crew made their way to Bowles's camp, and Hunter eventually reached Nassau in mid-May.[7]

Hunter, having spent some weeks in Florida, was not overly dismayed by his vessel's loss. Though apparently Bowles had not been able to confer with Hunter personally, Bowles had sent the merchant first-hand accounts that St. Marks was being besieged and was near capitulation. Shortly after the fall of Panton's store Bowles had moved his army down to the fort and, to dispel any doubt, a white seaman— probably one of Hunter's—carried Muskogee's declaration of war to the fort's commandant: "We pray God the great disposer of all things, who knows the wickedness of our enemies, who knows the justice of our Cause to favor our exertions . . . God save Muskogee."[8] The veteran Spanish commander, Thomas Portell, after the rough handling his interpreter recently had received at Miccosukee and after the capture of Panton's store, was not surprised. He had hoped that the reward of $4,500 would insure that there would be no necessity for a defense, but the increasing number of Indians concentrating at the fort proved him wrong. Portell was reassured by the triangular fort's stone walls, by the twelve cannon mounted on them, by the fact that it was exposed to a land attack on only one side and that two small gunboats mounting five cannon were anchored alongside the fort, and by the fact that Spanish galleys and troops, as soon as they were aware of the attack, would come to his aid. But the Commandant, try as he might, could never get out of his mind the idea of hundreds of savages swarming over the walls, carbines in their hands, scalping knives at their belts.

A handful of Indians in war paint appeared before the fort on April 9, and by mid-month the Director General and several hundred Seminoles, Lower Creeks, and even a few Upper Creeks arrived to begin the siege. By laying siege to the fort Bowles was going against tradition; but without artillery he had decided that the only way to make Portell yield was to starve him out. There had been only a few instances in the past where American Indians, even when led by whites, had sustained a prolonged siege against a white man's fort and had forced the defenders to surrender. The Indians approached the fort from all sides: across the St. Marks River from the east and the Wakulla River from the west, and especially on the northern side exposed to the land but protected by a moat. There were always war parties near the fort firing at any careless Spaniard, while the defenders in turn replied sporadically with rifles and artillery.[9]

Bowles, who had acquired experience in siege warfare during the Revolution at Pensacola, realized that it would be folly for the Indians to storm the fort. It did not alter the fact, however, that Portell and his 88-man garrison were prisoners. They could not leave the fort; in the open they would be greatly outnumbered and at the Indians' mercy. The Commandant's only recourse was to husband his supplies, to hope that reinforcements were on the way, and to put up a bold front, avowing that he and the garrison would defend "the honor and arms of his Catholic Majesty until spilling the last drop of our blood."[10]

As both Bowles and Portell knew, outside relief was the key. From the beginning the Commandant had sent out pleas for aid. The several galleys cruising in the vicinity of Apalachee Bay were the closest source of help. Some two hundred miles westward was Pensacola and, even further away, New Orleans, and it was not long before the governors of these posts were aware of the St. Marks attack. Though St. Augustine was as close as Pensacola, the difficulty of over-land assistance through hostile Seminole territory where Bowles had many sympathizers was unlikely. St. Marks was in West Florida, and Portell looked to his superiors in Pensacola or New Orleans or to the galleys in the Gulf. In the meantime all he could do was wait.

The siege continued day by day, week by week, a unique phe-nomenon in Indian warfare. It was both an indication of Indian resentment against Panton and Spain and a clue to the effectiveness of Eastajoca's leadership and his promise that George III was about to resume his role in Florida. Day and night there were alarms and bursts of firing; casualties were light, but Portell's men were becom-ing nervous and exhausted. An increased liquor ration did little to lessen the garrison's tension. The first sign of relief appeared on May 6, over three weeks after the beginning of the siege, with the arrival of a provision ship; but Bowles captured this vessel, and its provisions better enabled his Indian army to keep the field.[11] To William's sur-prise, less than two weeks later the Spaniards repeated their folly and sent another unescorted provision ship. This time it was the *Sheerwater,* belonging to Panton, and it is hard to account for his recklessness. He and Governor Folch probably did not realize the seriousness of the situation and reckoned that the *Sheerwater,* armed with two light cannon, would have no difficulty in reaching the fort. And with a good supply of trading goods on hand at St. Marks, the Spaniards might encourage Bowles's Indians to desert.

In retrospect it is obvious that the dispatch of the *Sheerwater* was a blunder. She sailed to Apalachee Bay, apparently not encountering any of the galleys, and then cautiously entered the St. Marks River. The captain knew that the fort had been under attack and he and a few crewmen went ashore some distance downstream to determine if it were safe to proceed. This was his first mistake. The *Sheerwater* had been observed, and shortly after the captain and his party stepped ashore they were captured. Next Bowles, who had been concealed on the riverbank and had directed the seizure of the captain, ac-companied by a half-dozen whites, paddled out to the anchored vessel and surprised and overpowered the remaining five crewmen, who offered no resistance even though they had two cannon.[12]

News of the *Sheerwater's* capture unnerved Portell. This provided Bowles supplies to sustain his Indians indefinitely; it now appeared that all the outside aid the Commandant was likely to get was ships whose cargo only aided the enemy; and above all this recent capture gave Bowles a new advantage—cannon. Even though the guns were small and there was confusion whether there were just the two mounted on the *Sheerwater* or additional ones in the hold, Bowles now had artillery and white subordinates who had a rough knowledge about their employment.[13] There was the possibility that a breach might be opened in the fort's wall and that hundreds of Indians might stream through. That these Indians now did not normally burn prisoners at the stake was of scant consolation; nor was Portell reassured that his cannon, more numerous and of superior caliber, probably could destroy an enemy battery before it did any damage. Foremost in his mind was the fact that he was two hundred miles from any Spanish post, that the only succor in over a month had been seized by Bowles, that he and his men were tired and edgy, that a numerous enemy effectively had sealed him off, and that this enemy now had artillery. During the siege the Indians frequently had taunted the Spaniards about what would happen when the fort was stormed, and the isolated garrison, though it tried, was never able to ignore these native threats.

Early in April at the siege's beginning Portell had been haughty, adamant that the fort would never capitulate, and disdained treating his opponents as equals or as representatives of the sovereign state of Muskogee. Five weeks later, food and ammunition partially depleted and the enemy still at the walls, the Commandant modified his approach. William was encouraged when he began receiving frequent notes from Portell, and though the Commandant insisted he would never surrender, these communications were respectfully worded so as not to injure the Director General's pride. Perhaps all along Eastajoca had been right and they should meet face to face and discuss their differences. Bowles made it plain that he would never again parley inside the fort, and Portell, reluctantly accepting guarantees for his safety, agreed to meet Bowles in the grove of pine trees immediately in front of the fort. There was no doubt in William's mind that the Commandant was negotiating from weakness.[14]

Bowles, confident that his strategy was about to succeed, began the personal interviews in mid-May immediately after the *Sheerwater's* capture, and diplomatic formalities aside, he was interested in only one topic: would the Commandant surrender? Eastajoca threatened that if he did not his Indians would soon be inside the fort, and in the heat of battle he could not guarantee the garrison's safety. This spector always had been a nagging fear for the Commandant, who was over sixty years old and allegedly asserted he was not going to end his career in this isolated Spanish post. What should he do? There was food and drinking water on hand, not fare that would delight a gourmet, but sufficient to provide for continued resistance. Only a few of the garrison were sick or wounded, whereas the overwhelming majority were fit and capable of defense. There was always the possibility that prior pleas for aid would bring some effective response from the cruising galleys or from Folch at Pensacola. But these pleas for all practical purposes had gone unanswered for over a month; the attackers had artillery which conceivably could cause a breach or at least prevent reinforcements from coming upstream; and in the future suppose there should be hard fighting in which the Indians suffered heavy losses and subsequently starvation forced the garrison to yield. In view of Indian insistence on revenge, would the garrison be allowed to surrender? All of these thoughts raced through Portell's mind as he conferred with Bowles, as he debated with his lieutenants, and as he anxiously looked over the stone walls to see if relief were coming upriver. But the only movement was from scores of Indians in war paint. His subordinates were divided: some urging continued resistance, others insisting present exigencies dictated surrender.

Portell was guided by the latter. There was a long list of reasons why the garrison should yield, and there is every indication that the Commandant personally suggested the majority. He decided to capitulate. Presumably Señora Portell, an "agreeable Spanish lady," who had been at the fort throughout the siege, readily concurred. The terms, which Bowles had outlined in their conferences, were simple: the garrison must leave within twenty-four hours on the two small vessels; the troops could retain their arms, though the fort's artillery must remain; books within the fort, either Spanish or Panton's, could be taken away; and the garrison could not serve against the Indians until after reaching Pensacola.[15] The latter provision was insignificant, because, from prior experience, Bowles knew that Spain would not honor any agreement with Muskogee. What the garrison did or did not do after evacuating the fort was unimportant. What was significant was that Bowles's Indians had maintained an effective siege for almost six weeks and had forced almost a hundred-man garrison, still with food and in good health and protected by stone walls, to surrender. It was a tribute to the Director General's resourcefulness, energy, and ability that he kept his Indian army in the field so long, and it was also testimony to Spain's fragile hold on Florida and to the caliber of her colonial officers. It was unthinkable that Cortez, Alvarado, or Pizarro would have taken such a step as Portell.

The formal surrender took place on May 19, and by the following day the Spaniards were gone. Portell sailed down to the Gulf where he encountered the galleys and could not understand why they had

not come to his aid, while the Spanish captains could not fathom
why the Commandant had decided to evacuate. Pensacola and New
Orleans superiors soon asked why they all had not joined forces and
retaken the fort. Portell could never explain satisfactorily why he had
given in to Indians having arms "sufficient only to open a breach in
the heart of a coward."[16]

But Bowles was in his glory. His view from the fort of the Spanish
garrison sailing away and Muskogee's banner flying overhead was re-
compense for past indignities, broken promises, imprisonment, and
delay. He expected that the fort's capture would be the initial spark
resulting in Spain's being expelled from the Floridas and Louisiana;
it would inspire those potential settlers in the West Indies, Georgia,
or elsewhere to come to Muskogee; and it would encourage Britain,
which he knew was considering a Florida expedition, to assist him
openly. And under the Muskogee flag it would be safer for merchants
to come and trade. During the past months Hunter had vessels hover-
ing off the coast. Soon after the surrender Bowles relayed the triumphant news to the merchant: "Come as fast as you can. . . . I have a
pilot to bring you in."[17] In addition to increased trade there was the
prospect that whites might flock to Muskogee in considerable numbers as settlers and that the Indians, who in the past had not listened
to Eastajoca, would change their minds. This is precisely what William was hoping when he wrote Tostanee Opoie, an influential
Lower Creek chief who lived well above the thirty-first parallel: "the
great ruler of the world knowing the justice of our cause has been
pleased to make the arms of Muskogee victorious . . . the fort surrendered and we did not lose a man . . . communicate the news to
everyone so all may rejoice . . . I shall be glad to see you."[18]

Florida and Louisiana governors were aghast when they learned
that the fort really was in Indian hands and began considering means
for its recapture, while dreading the effect at Whitehall. Both Miller
in Nassau and Reeves in London hoped this would spur the government into action and redoubled their attempts to have Britain send
an expedition against Spanish America. Reports of the Spanish disaster
circulated throughout the Indian country. Benjamin Hawkins at
Coweta was alarmed over the enthusiasm Bowles's triumph created
among the Creeks above the line and saw the possibility that his system of peacefully civilizing the Indians would be undone. With dismay he observed that "this news has been received here and below
with extravagant joy. All contemplate British times and British presents, and many have flocked down for that purpose."[19] The older
and more cautious chiefs were more concerned about the long-term

effects and did not go down to St. Marks. But the elders did not lead war parties. The Georgia governor, James Jackson, after hearing about the fall of St. Marks, wrote Hawkins that he was confident the experienced Indian agent, by his own efforts, could resolve the crisis—but he stood ready to rush 5,000 men into Creek territory if necessary.[20]

Supposedly to calm Jackson, Bowles, with tongue in cheek, wrote the Governor and told him how he had been re-elected Director General of Muskogee, how he had given strict orders that no one should molest a United States or Georgia citizen, and as a result how there had been more tranquility in the Indian country after his return than ever. Bowles avowed his sole objective was peace—"while a man by the name of Col. Hawkins tries to make disturbance between us . . . my generosity alone has prevented me from ordering him shot. . . . I hope that such a man will not have influence enough to involve us in a war with you."[21]

The fort's fall and possible aftereffects were studied in Philadelphia. American differences with France were on the verge of being patched up, and the prospect of an Anglo-American expedition against Spanish colonies was fading from view. The Federalist administration and the Republican one which followed no more wanted to see the Union Jack on the Gulf Coast than the tricolor. This is why Jefferson told Hawkins that if worse came to worse the United States would have to expel Bowles from the fort.[22] If the United States were not going to co-operate with Britain against Spanish colonies, then Bowles hoped frontiersmen might make arrangements with Whitehall on their own. There is no positive evidence that Bowles intrigued with Blount and his associates, but it is probably more than coincidence that Dr. Nicholas Romayne, Blount's fellow conspirator, arrived in London at the same time as the news of the fort's capture.[23] What Bowles had begun accomplishing was what Blount, Romayne, Chisholm, and others had been talking about for years; like Bowles, they did not want Britain to remain in the background in the South.

Spain more than anyone was worried about the effect of St. Marks' capture. It was no secret that she had a weak hold on Florida, but the surrender of this post to a horde of Indians advertised this fact to the world at large. Unless it were soon recaptured, there would be an open invitation for others to join the Director General or to imitate his feat elsewhere at Spanish expense. There was no question that Spain could easily recapture this insignificant post, but she had larger worries: at home there was mounting subservience to Bonaparte, of which the retrocession of Louisiana and possibly part of Florida was an example; and there was increasing unrest in her colonies. Britain, with whom Spain was at war, might try to capitalize on this unrest. In the broad picture St. Marks did not count for much, and Spain never considered sending a major expedition for its recovery. Both the Floridas and Louisiana were a drain on the exchequer, and except for limited aid from the Mexican viceroy, the officials in these provinces would have to make out with the forces on hand.[24] And after all, Bowles's followers, at least to date, were almost exclusively Indian, so the limited forces available in Florida and Louisiana should have no difficulty in retaking the fort.

Immediately local Spanish officials had considered a counterexpedition. There had been some—but not much—talk of one when the weak-willed Portell encountered the galleys in the Gulf of Mexico. But the Commandant had made his decision at St. Marks and saw no reason to alter it. He continued his voyage to Pensacola and informed his superior Folch about details of the fort's capture. For several reasons, including that it was expedient to have several leagues between him and his commander, Portell dictated his letter from Fort San Carlos de Barrancas at the entrance to Pensacola Bay.[25]

Hugh Ferguson also was in Pensacola, and if not urging an expedition against his former chief, was just as vehement as the Spaniards in reviling him. Ferguson had realized that Florida life would be hard, but the transition from the routine of a Jamaica clerk to the Florida wilds had been too much of a jolt. Initially there had been the *Fox's* shipwreck and the subsequent privation on St. Georges Island; this was followed by hard manual labor building huts and cutting firewood; then next came Garcia's expedition which captured Neuville and almost got Ferguson—he spent a night in the water and wandered about the woods lost for the next five days; and though he was at the St. Marks' siege, he did not alter his plans for quitting his superior at the first opportunity. Soon after Portell's departure Ferguson went on a fishing trip and never returned. He sighted one of Panton's vessels in the Gulf, surrendered himself, and secured passage to Pensacola where he babbled all about William's plans and forces. Of particular interest to the Spaniards was the fact that Bowles had barely a dozen white followers—a point not stressed by Portell—and though they had old, small-caliber cannon, there were not many who knew how to employ them.[26]

The disclosure of Bowles's relative weakness was the spark that Folch needed. As soon as he had heard about the fort's fall he had begun contemplating a counterstroke. There were available the galleys sent from New Orleans that had been used earlier against Bowles, and there was a force composed of regulars from New Orleans and miscellaneous able-bodied men at Pensacola. Theoretically the former St. Marks' garrison was available, but it had to stay to help guard Pensacola—and Folch could think of a better reason why they should be left behind. If Bowles did not have trained white subordinates to service his artillery effectively—and according to Ferguson he did not—there was no reason why Folch's force could not recapture the fort. The vessels assembled for the expedition included three galleys, two gunboats, and two schooners. Garcia, who had had previous experience in going after Bowles, commanded the ships; Pedro Olivier, who had been with Garcia when they almost captured Bowles, was in charge of the troops; and Folch assumed over-all command. With Panton wishing them well, the Governor sailed out of the harbor's narrow entrance eastward to Apalachee Bay, entered the St. Marks River, and cautiously began to approach the fort.[27]

Hostile eyes ashore observed Spanish progress; Eastajoca would not be surprised by Garcia's fleet a second time. Bowles, better than Ferguson, knew Muskogee's weakness and that the Spaniards were perfectly capable of retaking the fort. He also knew that the Spaniards had a knack for procrastination and assumed there would be time—more time than he was allowed—to strengthen Muskogee's defenses. William had not been idle and had encouraged Nassau merchants to furnish trading goods and armed privateers, and from them or anyone else had tried to acquire experienced artillerymen. A few whites, encouraged by Bowles's success, some of whom knew something about artillery, had come to the fort so that he had almost thirty assorted white followers when the Spanish expedition appeared. Several hundred Indians were still there, content with the stores acquired from Panton's warehouse, from within the fort, from New Providence merchants, and most recently from the Spaniards themselves. A Cuban merchant ship bound for New Orleans had stopped by St. Marks for water just before Folch arrived. At the first report of the vessel's approach Bowles had been quick-witted enough to substitute the Spanish banner for Muskogee's, and the ship captain did not discover his mistake until too late. The cargo strengthened Eastajoca's hold over the Indians, though it did not make his artillery any more effective.[28]

This is what Folch assumed as he neared the fort and demanded its surrender. He exchanged several notes under a flag of truce, and Bowles "accidently" fired on one of the ships carrying a white flag as it positioned itself dangerously close to the fort.[29] In the interchanges Bowles, appalled at seeing his recent success undone and desperately looking about for outside succor, requested time to assemble all the chiefs to discuss whether the fort should be given up; if not he threatened a stout defense.[30] But the decision as to whether the fort would surrender was not the Indians' to make, a circumstance recognized by both Folch and Bowles. The Director General had been stalling for time, and Folch, though he had procrastinated in the past, insisted on an answer. He assembled his lieutenants and reviewed last-minute details of the plan of attack: the three galleys, his most powerful ships, would take up positions on three sides of the fort. One would sail up the St. Marks River, another into the Wakulla, and the third, supported by the gunboats, would position itself near the rivers' intersection. The first two galleys would prevent escape, and all the ships would bombard the fort into submission. Or, if this plan failed, Olivier would be at hand to send his troops in through a breach.[31] The ships began to assume their positions and commenced the bombardment. At first one of the galleys went aground, and Bowles's artillery fire kept the Spaniards at bay. In time, however, the grounded galley got into action, and the Spanish fire intensified. William decided retreat was the only recourse, a decision hailed by the Indians. Before and during the bombardment Bowles transferred most of his supplies to several vessels anchored in the St. Marks River just above the fort, and on these vessels or afoot he and his followers made their escape, heading for Miccosukee. After an hour and a half it was all over: the Indian flag, a frown on the Muskogee sun, was lowered, and Spanish troops, with few casualties on either side, again were masters of St. Marks.[32]

Within the fort there was only rubble from the damaged stone walls, broken *aguardiente* bottles, and miscellaneous litter—the "arch villain" had gotten away. There were those who felt that Folch should not have waited until morning to approach the fort or have wasted time by negotiating but instead should have marched his troops overland during the night. Then he could have captured not only the fort but also the Director General.[33] With luck Folch hoped to seize his adversary anyway. Just how far up the St. Marks River could Bowles sail? He would have to stop at some not-too-distant point and transfer his supplies to packhorses. Folch expected to have Spanish forces on hand when this took place, and the galleys were admirably suited for such work. Light draft, powered by both sail and oars, they were at their best on rivers where neither current nor winds could inhibit their progress. A galley and smaller gunboat set out after Bowles, forced him to seek refuge in a nearby creek, and finally to abandon his poorly armed vessels and their cargo. The day after the fort's capture the victorious Spaniards returned with Bowles's bilander and three smaller vessels loaded with food and munitions and another trunk of William's correspondence.[34]

Later Folch and Panton, assisted by Ferguson, sifted through Bowles's letters. These, along with those earlier seized by Garcia, allowed the Spaniards to piece together more accurately Bowles's relationship with New Providence merchants and with Reeves and Whitehall and to discover in more detail who his Indian friends were. But these letters did not disclose anything that Folch basically did not know, and the numerous details about William's relationship with Hannah Brand, the Brownes, Pearson, about what purchases he made, and about who visited him in London and the West Indies are of infinitely more interest to the historian. The Spaniards would file and make copies of this correspondence and preserve it in their archives, and fortunately these archives proved more durable than Muskogee's. Later Bowles was not so accommodating; because of fear that his letters might again fall into Spanish hands and because of a scarcity of paper, he did not make many, or any, copies of his correspondence.[35]

He did not fret about his trunk's falling into Folch's hands. What was distressing was that he had lost St. Marks and valuable stores aboard his vessels. Apparently he had suffered a crushing defeat from which it would be difficult to recover. But, appearances were deceiving and all was not lost. He still had a large Indian following, was protected by the influential Kinache at Miccosukee, and the Spaniards exaggerated when they maintained the Director General retained his freedom by hiding out in a swamp.[36] The Seminoles and many of the Lower Creeks still had no dependable source of manufactures, and Eastajoca's promises, many of which recently had been fulfilled at the expense of Spain and Panton, still had their appeal. Folch, the galleys, and even part of the troops could not remain forever at St. Marks. Bowles was aware that the half-dozen or so galleys and regular troops stationed in Louisiana and Florida were always overtaxed, whether dealing with intruders like himself, protecting the Gulf ports from privateers, patrolling the Mississippi and lesser rivers to prevent contraband trade with the Americans or the British in Canada, or maintaining the precarious link between New Orleans and St. Louis. When Folch and the galleys withdrew, once again St. Marks would become an isolated Spanish citadel in hostile territory. Eastajoca had taken it once; he could do so again.

Regardless of how many times St. Marks changed hands or how many of the Director General's trunks the Spaniards captured, in Bowles's mind this was only preliminary maneuvering. With good reason he was convinced that the minute British troops and warships appeared in the Gulf, Florida would easily succumb; the basic decision was yet to be made at Whitehall rather than at Miccosukee. There were the usual reasons why Britain should openly intervene, and these, along with promises of continued support from Nassau merchants, buoyed Bowles's spirits. In the meantime he was planning another attack on St. Marks: "Let every man hold fast the name of Muskogee and not enter into the schemes of our enemies. . . . Consider that Muskogee is attacked by the Spanyards with intent to destroy it and that it is the duty of every man to defend it to the utmost of his abilities. . . . I for my part am ready to lead you. I study both night and day for the benefit of Muskogee."[37]

On the other hand Folch dared not risk sending his small force to Miccosukee where Eastajoca was surrounded by so many friendly Indians. Recognizing the impasse, each tried to win through negotiation an advantage not to be gained by force. Bowles proposed anew a Spanish-Muskogee alliance, which meant that Spain would have to recognize Muskogee on his terms, thereby extending Spanish influence far north of the present Florida boundary; for this reason the proposal should be kept secret from the United States.[38] Though Bowles did not stake his future on Spanish recognition, nothing could be lost by the interchange, and possibly Spain would offer to have the Director General and his Nassau friends replace Panton. Folch, for his part, had little to offer except that negotiations best could be carried out at St. Marks: "Your safety is guaranteed . . . you can believe me. I am the nephew of Miró who wrote me from Spain how agreeable your company had been on the long voyage."[39] But William would never be caught in the fort unless Muskogee's sun was waving over it.

Bowles, even though nothing came of the negotiations, had some basis for thinking the Spaniards might suggest his replacing Panton. The Scottish merchant felt Spain had sold him out in the Pinckney Treaty, was alarmed by rumors that France was going to take over the Floridas and Louisiana, resented the charges by fellow countrymen that he was stocking the Florida presidios with munitions in wartime, and at the same time had been approached by various Americans. His apprehension and dissatisfaction might become so great, or the reaction in London over his sending munitions to Florida so strong, or the appeals of the Americans so inviting, that he might suddenly desert the Spaniards as, with proper notice, he had every legal right to do. Because of his great influence over the southern Indians he had been approached by the Americans—probably Blount had tried to win his co-operation in 1796—and now Hawkins was showing him every courtesy, insisting that the United States would help him collect his large Indian debts in American territory and forwarding the latest intelligence about Bowles.[40] As always the Spaniards had their doubts about Panton, now they were greater than ever and they would like to replace him—but not with Bowles! Present disadvantages in dealing with Panton would be magnified many times should he be replaced by the Director General.

The threat that Bowles would draw the southern Indians into his orbit alarmed Hawkins and was reason enough for him to have a friendly correspondence with Panton. For the most part, since 1783 Americans had had no use for this Scottish Tory who had been arming and intriguing among the Indians. But by 1800 anti-Tory passions had subsided, and Bowles's menace drew the two together. If the Director were successful, it spelled the downfall of Hawkins' plans for civilizing the Indians and the overthrow of Panton. Agitation in Lower Creek villages on the Chattahoocheee River far above the thirty-first parallel forced Hawkins to withdraw from Coweta eastward to Ft. Wilkinson on the Oconee River. He encouraged the Indians, especially the Seminoles and Lower Creeks, to hold a general council and decide what measures should be taken against Bowles, and invitations—the broken days—for such a meeting were sent out twice to no avail.[41] The younger warriors, not enthusiastic about becoming sedentary farmers, were being supplied with munitions by Eastajoca, were elated by their success against St. Marks, and were eager to attack again once the galleys and some of the Spanish troops withdrew. This gave Hawkins another concern, because the Pinckney Treaty stipulated that the United States would restrain its Indians from atacking the Spaniards. What would the United States do if there were a formal Spanish request?[42] From the Indian standpoint following neither Hawkins nor Bowles was a satisfactory policy in the long run. Bowles, however, held out the prospect of a dependable source of manufactures not immediately accompanied by a hoard of settlers, and for the time being Hawkins was at a disadvantage. It was in his interest to co-operate with Panton, and in view of Bowles's hostile designs and of Spain's fragile hold on Florida, it was in Panton's interest to cultivate this friendship.

Florida was more agitated than ever in 1800. This was the year that Spain, in a supposedly secret treaty, ceded Louisiana and apparently much of West Florida to France, contributing to the venerable rumors that French troops were about to appear or that British regulars would get there first.[43] British troops sent to Florida undoubtedly would co-operate with those in Canada, who, according to reports, were ready to descend on Louisiana.[44] Whether British forces appeared in the Gulf of Mexico or not, Bowles, now that Folch and the galleys had withdrawn, was encouraging the Indians again to go against the fort and was entreating New Providence merchants to come to Muskogee's aid. Because Panton, in effect, had withdrawn from the Lower Creek-Seminole territory, here was a golden opportunity for these merchants. And Miller's and Hunter's vessels were supplying Muskogee with trading goods, while Nassau privateers harassed St. Marks' tenuous communication with the ouside world. Late in the summer Spain organized another expedition to go against the Director General. This small force, after leaving New Orleans, was blockaded at Mobile by Nassau privateers—apparently at Bowles's suggestion—and nothing came of this latest expedition.[45]

There was another question that Bowles knew was yet to be answered: what whites would rally around Muskogee's banner? Thousands of French royalists needed a home; could Muskogee yet provide a haven? Would Americans around Natchez, Mobile, and southern Georgia, many with British sympathies, throw in their lot with Muskogee, and would Georgians, who long had eyed Florida and unsuccessfully tried to take East Florida in 1795, co-operate with the Director General?[46]

Bowles always assumed that Muskogee eventually would be peopled by whites; whether they came from the British or French West Indies or the United States was of secondary importance. Never did large numbers flock to his Indian state, and as time passed William looked more and more to those who lived on either the Georgia or Florida side of the St. Marys River—a curious mixture, technically Spanish or United States citizens, frequently Loyalist in sentiment, and feeling no great attachment to Georgia, the United States, or Spain. Though these whites included all shades of the political and social spectrum, the one thing they had in common was a passion to acquire Florida lands, if possible without accompanying Spanish rule. This was evident in the abortive 1795 rebellion when Spanish outposts temporarily fell into rebel hands. In a short time, however, Spain retook them, crushed the rebellion, confiscated the lands of the ringleaders and imprisoned a few.[47] It was natural that these restless souls paid close attention to Bowles's activities—in many respects a replica of theirs in 1795—and it was even more natural that Bowles should look to them.

One of the first things he did after capturing St. Marks was to write Richard Lang, William Jones, and Dr. Reddington, persecuted leaders in the 1795 rebellion though still living on or near the St. Marys River, asking them to raise their forces again and promising that all would be liberally rewarded at Spain's expense.[48] If they could induce their friend, the influential General Clark of Georgia, to co-operate, so much the better. An offer to appropriate Spanish lands was always enticing, and Jones, Lang, and Reddington, who had followed Bowles's career since his first expedition in 1788, were interested. They were to raise an army, join Bowles, and much, or even all, of East Florida was the prize. Now, as for the past twelve years, there were always a few on the St. Marys quick to join Bowles, and had Spain not so quickly recaptured St. Marks, had Lang not gotten drunk and disclosed the whole scheme,[49] and had the Georgia governor not promptly issued a proclamation insisting that anyone who went with Bowles would be jailed,[50] William might have recruited a several hundred man army and, had his luck held, might have become master of a lot more than St. Marks.

Bowles thought that even after the fort's recapture, the St. Marys settlers, aware of how easily Spanish posts had fallen to them and Bowles, still might rally to the Muskogee banner. He visited the St. Marys River in the fall of 1800. Though an armed Nassau privateer with supplies and munitions was cruising about the river's mouth ready to co-operate, vigilant Georgia and Florida patrols made life unpleasant for William, captured a few of his followers of whom Lang was the most outstanding, and at one point forced Bowles and three Negro slaves to abandon their personal effects in a hurry and swim across the St. Marys River to safety.[51]

Bowles was not discouraged, and, whether writing letters from Miccosukee or making quick journeys up the Chattahoochee River and into East Florida, could not tell what fortune held in store. He only knew that fate had yet to cast her final throw.

IX

By Land and Sea

EARLY IN 1801 it was difficult to predict how Muskogee would fare. Bowles, disappointed by his reverses but confident of eventual success, could still count on an Indian following and was relatively safe at Miccosukee, even though it was only thirty miles from St. Marks. But there was no doubt in his mind that, unless he continued to furnish the Indians manufactures, Muskogee would melt away. Maintaining commercial ties with Nassau was essential and as always was a primary concern. Though Florida's peltry could not compare with that of Canada, individual merchants could make handsome profits from the southern fur trade. Miller, Joseph Hunter, and George Walker, excluded by the Spanish concession granted solely to Panton, Leslie, and Company, knew this and, coupled with the fact that they were not able to employ their vessels profitably as privateers, this is why they continued to encourage and subsidize William in spite of their ships' being captured. Miller was in financial difficulty and, with Dunmore's assistance, was in London trying to straighten out his accounts. Now it was especially Hunter and Walker in Nassau who, at William's suggestion, wrote flattering notes to influential chiefs, who offered to maintain a battery wherever a warehouse were constructed, and who sent ships to exploit this commerce. They procured just enough deerskins to whet their appetites.[1]

A friend, associate, and sometimes partner of Miller, Hunter, and Walker was John DeLacy. His background is obscure except that he was a Bahamian merchant in political opposition to Panton and Forbes. Like his partners, he wanted to reap profits from the southern fur trade at Panton, Leslie, and Company's expense. It was for this purpose that he sailed to Florida, making an extensive tour of the southern Indian territory, ranging from Tennessee to the Mississippi to Pensacola, everywhere gathering statistics on the potential trade and invariably talking with the scores of white or half-breed traders, most of whom were in Panton, Leslie, and Company's employ. These traders had to be won over if DeLacy expected to divert this commerce to himself and his friends. DeLacy aimed to take over all this commerce by establishing a store on the headwaters of the Chattahoochee, and after assuming the Lower Creek-Seminole trade, he expected to draw the Upper Creeks, Cherokees, Chickasaws, and Choctaws into his ambitious scheme. If this were achieved the total market for British manufactures, according to his estimates, would be almost four million dollars. Bowles, who must have encouraged DeLacy to come to Florida in the first place, figured prominently in his project, and it was natural that the merchant dropped by Miccosukee.[2]

In their lengthy conversations, it became apparent that there were two ways of taking over Panton, Leslie, and Company's trade. One was to assume that Britain would occupy Florida to keep out France, and Bowles maintained that, when this occurred, he would become the British Indian superintendent. Under these circumstances there would be no room for the "half-Spanish" Panton, Leslie, and Company and he would see to it that DeLacy and his friends could immediately move in. In view of the reports that France had acquired and would take over Louisiana and at least West Florida, such an eventuality was possible.[3]

Reports had been reaching Bowles at Miccosukee that there might be a general European peace. If Britain made peace with France and Spain and if Spain retained the Floridas, DeLacy could not expect to dominate the southern fur trade in the wake of a successful British expedition. An alternative—more appealing to DeLacy than to William—was, with Spanish consent, to replace Panton, Leslie, and Company. The differences and suspicions between Spain and this company could be played up, Eastajoca's authority over the southern Indians emphasized, and, if necessary, Governor Folch and other influential Spaniards could be bribed to bring about a Spanish-Muskogee treaty. DeLacy, to a greater extent than Bowles, was obsessed with profits to be made by the fur trade; whether this was accomplished under Spanish or British aegis was of secondary importance.[4]

But Bowles was not blind to profits from the fur trade and land speculation, and it is an open question what he would have done had Spain made him an attractive offer. All along he assumed, however, that Muskogee should be in the British sphere. After all, he had British citizenship and, in Spanish eyes, he was still a fugitive. During DeLacy's extended visit at Bowles's house, which was just outside Miccosukee where the Director General lived with his family and Negro slaves, the two became close friends and DeLacy grew attached to William's wife and son. At length Bowles and DeLacy decided on an immediate course of action. DeLacy, on his own or in conjunction with Miller, Hunter, and Walker, agreed to send trading goods, while Bowles was to insure that his Indians had skins available in exchange.[5] He suggested several places to transact the business, probably somewhere on the Apalachicola or Ochlockonee rivers, but possibly at Cedar Key, Tampa, or elsewhere. If the site were to be permanent, William wanted it fortified to make Spanish cruisers keep their distance, and he hoped that initial commercial ventures would become more extensive.

DeLacy returned to Nassau where he set about encouraging other merchants to underwrite Muskogee cargoes. Satisfactory arrangements were worked out but not with Miller, Hunter, and Walker. Miller was still in London, and the others had lost several of their vessels to Spanish galleys and were unwilling or unable to finance more.[6] For a while Bootle Johnson, John Ross, and others who earlier usually had been associated with Dunmore helped out.[7] DeLacy became Bowles's most important Nassau representative and link with the outside world, and it was usually his ships after late 1801 that reached Bowles with their welcome cargoes of trading goods.

These goods helped the anxious Bowles meet Indian needs and allowed him to retain a following. Minister Marqués de Casa Irujo at Philadelphia, after the news of the fort's recapture and Bowles's flight into the swamp, was prematurely relieved that the menace of this troublesome intruder had passed.[8] DeLacy's collaboration was an important reason why Irujo was proved wrong, or as Hawkins put it, "the mischief makers are afoot again."[9] St. Marks was not formally besieged, but Eastajoca made sure there were always war parties about hampering communications with the outside world and preying on careless hunting and wood cutting detachments. Through force or enticements Bowles prevailed on Negroes to leave their masters and join the Indians, something the blacks had been doing for centuries. Spanish citizens between St. Augustine and the St. Marys River, some of whom had been Loyalists or United States citizens, suffered most. Sometimes the slaves fled on their own initiative, though more frequently they were captured by war parties.

One of those who had lost his slaves was Francis Fatio, a Loyalist who after the Revolution remained in Florida, prospered, became a Spanish subject, and enjoyed the confidence of the authorities. He sent his son, Francis Fatio, Jr., to Miccosukee to arrange for the return of his Negroes. Fatio had many conversations with Bowles, and, after it was discovered they had been in the New York garrison together at the end of the Revolution, they reminisced at length. Bowles, however, refused to return the Negroes, and Fatio could only return and report to his father how the shabbily dressed plunderer was in distress and maintained at Kinache's expense. That the son had failed in his mission and that Bowles's Indians even took his horses must have distorted his report.[10]

The Seminoles had Negro blood in their veins, and with Bowles on the scene the percentage was increasing. Slaves that found their way to Miccosukee came from both the Spanish and the American sides of the line, and because of this Georgians, in this rare instance, could make common cause with their Spanish neighbors.[11] Occasionally the Spaniards ventured out of St. Marks to surprise Bowles when there were not many warriors about, but the Director General always was forewarned. The new commandant, though more aggressive than Portell, equally appreciated that St. Marks was isolated in hostile country and that a setback outside the fort would spell disaster. Normally he was content to remain in the fort, and hostile Indians lurking about reaffirmed the wisdom of this decision.[12]

Muskogee's most sensational and controversial exploits were not on land but on sea. In the past the Muskogee sun occasionally was seen at the mast of a merchant ship, but now such vessels were more numerous and more dangerous. Muskogee had a navy, not one to make Nelson tremble, but formidable enough to hamper Spanish commerce in the Gulf of Mexico. There were no ships-of-the-line, only privateers; nevertheless these swift, lightly armed vessels, hardly ever more than three in number, played havoc with solitary Spanish merchant ships. Privateer crews were of different nationalities: English, Spanish, Negro, even Indian, though invariably the captains were British with Nassau contacts and West Indian sailing experience. Many of them were friends of Miller, Hunter, Walker, Jones, and DeLacy, and each was attracted to Muskogee by the same thing—money. Muskogee's privateer commissions were more liberal than Britain's: the captain and crew kept two-thirds of the plunder while the state got only one-third.[13]

The Muskogee navy was elaborately organized. Captain Richard Powers of Nassau, commanding the *Muskogee Micco,* was in overall charge, and Captains James Ward and Gipson directed other privateers. There was an impressive air of legality, beginning with Bowles's formal declaration of war which warranted issuing privateer commissions, including in detail the manner in which the privateers were to conduct themselves on the high seas, providing admiralty courts for condemnation, and the all-important establishing of a procedure for the distribution of spoils.[14] Muskogee's navy functioned in an elementary fashion. Almost a dozen Spanish ships were brought into the Apalachicola River or elsewhere during 1801 and 1802, and with few exceptions all were condemned. Courts-martial were convened, with Powers as president and William McGirth as judge advocate, to maintain discipline among the polyglot Muskogee crews. One Spanish mariner was condemned for attempted desertion; Lieutenant Willoughby killed a fellow officer who was trying to encourage the Muskogee crew to desert, and the court not surprisingly absolved Willoughby of any wrong doing; the court, or Bowles and Powers on their own, warned of the consequences should anyone insult the flag of Muskogee or not rigorously comply with her maritime code.[15]

A few swift privateers can disrupt enemy shipping. A handful of Confederate cruisers would inflict enormous losses on the Northern merchant marine during the Civil War just as did the Muskogee privateers on Spanish merchant ships now. It was as difficult later for the United States navy to capture the *Alabama* and *Shenandoah* as it was for the Spanish navy to capture the *Muskogee Micco* and *Tostonoke* in 1802. Normally Powers brought his prizes into the Apalachicola River where, under the Director General's supervision, condemnation formally took place. Because of the many demands made on them, the Spanish galleys were constantly overtaxed. They had to patrol hundreds of miles of coast, but they could not sail too far into the Gulf where they would be at a disadvantage against larger enemy sailing ships flying the Muskogee or British flag. Always of concern was that if the galleys ventured too far afield or met with misfortune, St. Marks would be dangerously exposed. It had capitulated before because galleys did not come to the rescue, and with Bowles at Miccosukee, history could repeat itself. Solicitude for St. Marks restricted the galleys' movements and encouraged Muskogee privateers to come and go at will.

It appeared that Spanish galleys could sail into the Apalachicola River and cripple the Muskogee navy headquarters, but there were high bluffs upstream below the mouth of the Flint River where Bowles had placed artillery—at least the Spaniards were convinced this was true—and they refused to enter.[16] For this reason and because Spain had ceded Louisiana and apparently West Florida and was not inclined to reinforce these provinces, the Muskogee sun terrorized Gulf shipping for almost two years. Bowles's share of the captured prizes and of the goods sent by DeLacy provided William with a constant supply of manufactures and permitted him to retain his Indian following.

Had he not been able to do so his other pretensions would have counted for naught. Although overseeing Muskogee's navy and improvising stratagems for DeLacy's vessels to elude the Spaniards consumed most of William's time, he never lost sight of his ultimate objective—that Muskogee be taken under Britain's wing. To facilitate this he had to give Britain more precise information about the Indian state—its boundaries, the number of Indians, and its form of government. Bowles had been turning these matters over in his mind for years. And whatever its boundaries and whatever Indians were included, Muskogee had to have a capital. Around 1790 Bowles insisted it was Coweta, the head war town of the Lower Creeks on the Chattahoochee River, but after his return in 1799 when the Pinckney Treaty had gone into effect, he moved his capital further south closer to the Seminoles, first at Wekiva on the Chattahoochee and later at Miccosukee on Lake Miccosukee. But he was always able at any moment to move the seat of government, which was not embarrassed by cumbersome archives. Frequently Bowles, in visiting the Lower Creeks, crossed over to the American side of the line, causing Hawkins discomfort. Though the American Indian agent was more likely to be at Coweta than the Director General, in fact the area around here was a no man's land. It had been expedient for Bowles to maintain his capital at Coweta before because it was in the heart of the Lower Creek country and close by the Cherokees. But now Dragging Canoe, Wellbank, and a host of other Cherokee leaders were dead; William's headstrong Cherokee son had moved west of the Mississippi after 1794 with a small band of Chickamaugas; those remaining, abandoned by Spain after the Pinckney Treaty, were inclined to an accommodation with the United States; and after the Jay Treaty and Fallen Timbers they realized it was futile to look to the British in Canada or probably anywhere else. Earlier Bowles had drawn his main support from the Lower Creeks and Chickamauga Cherokees; now he relied primarily on the Seminoles and to a lesser extent on the Lower Creeks, most of whom lived in villages on or near the Chattahoochee, Apalachicola, Flint, and Ochlockonee rivers. There were many reasons why, after his return in 1799, Muskogee's capital, though at times it might vary a few miles, should always be among the Seminoles and south of the thirty-first parallel. As important as any was that Bowles would rather cope with opposition from weaker Spanish forces rather than those sent out by an increasingly powerful United States.

At Muskogee's capital Bowles constantly attempted to perfect the organization of his government, and since the state was threatened on all its boundaries, it was logical that the army and navy received most attention. Powers, though he had no exact title, was in effect the lord high admiral, while Captain Neuville headed the army. But the captain's brief acquaintance with Bowles had been disagreeable; he had been surprised and captured by Garcia's expedition, and subsequently was imprisoned. It is improbable that he ever met Cunningham, but had the opportunity arisen, the two would have had much in common to discuss. After Neuville's departure no figure emerged as Bowles's second in command. Dr. Reddington, a friend of Lang, Jones, and probably DeLacy, involved in the 1795 East Florida rebellion and with Bowles when he attempted to raise an army on the St. Marys in 1800, resided awhile at Miccosukee and, commissioned Muskogee's commissary of war, encouraged a few of his friends to join the Director General, but he himself sailed for Nassau after some months.[17] An assorted group of whites—or those who were almost white—always was on hand: William and Zachary McGirth, William Grey, Peter Shugert, John Hague, and William Harris, all of whom were experienced Indian traders; an occasional Spanish deserter; and those nondescript persons who found it convenient to be governed by Muskogee's lax laws instead of the more stringent ones of Britain, the United States, or Spain.[18]

William was always eager for other whites to be drawn to Muskogee and for them to come from a more stable element of society. Ever since 1799 he had tried to get a printer—that herald of frontier civilization—to join him. Owen, who when Bowles was in London had agreed to come, much to William's disgust got no further than Nassau. Here he decided his future would be more promising with the *Bahama Gazette*, which earlier under Wells had been violently anti-Bowles and Dunmore, but after Wells's death was in need of an editor. Though Owen stayed in Nassau with the *Bahama Gazette*, Bowles tried to buy his original type and presumably would have published the *Muskogee Sun* or its equivalent on his own.[19] Wellbank, whose brains had been bashed in with a "lightwood not" and who formerly had been James Rivington's apprentice at the *Royal Gazette* in New York during the Revolution, was sorely missed.

Bowles talked much about the necessity of an official printer for a newspaper, official proclamations, and the new national constitution. As always he insisted that Muskogee should have a constitution. He had asked Dunmore's advice about details, and now he solicited assistance from Reeves, Miller, and DeLacy. Bowles envisioned a frame of government appropriate for the Indians and for the many white immigrants, and one with adequate safeguards against Jacobinism. Since he was constantly in the field—or swamp according to his detractors —against the Spaniards, Bowles reported to his friends that he had been too busy to complete his constitution, but with luck it would soon be ready. The Director General, as he visualized Muskogee's future, always saw an independent state, dominated and eventually colonized and exploited by whites, in close relationship with and dependent on Britain: "there is room here for many people to make handsome fortunes."[20]

The Indians, who already had adopted part of the white man's civilization, would have to complete the process. A considerable number of the Creeks, perhaps ten per cent, probably more, had Caucasian blood in their veins, and the percentage was far higher if one considered only the chiefs and leaders. Bowles assumed that with even more intermarriage between the two races, with increased white immigration, and with the Indians' accepting more and more of the white man's ways, in time the natives would disappear as a separate group. This was a more practical, and certainly a more humane policy, than that soon to be relentlessly pushed by the United States—removal of the Indians to west of the Mississippi River. Even if William had available some region where he could relocate the southern Indians, such a course was unthinkable. His roots among the Indians were too deep, his appreciation of their courage and dignity was too great, and his affection for his wife and children too strong to ever consider eventually removing the Indians to any other region.

Muskogee's boundaries were still vague; William seldom discussed them in detail—he preferred not to. Unless American frontiersmen co-operated, still a possibility, it was improbable that any of Muskogee would be on the American side of the line, though Eastajoca never elaborated on this point to his Indian friends. Whatever the boundaries, the future Muskogee, a state which eventually would have features of the white man's civilization rather than those of the Indians, was never far from Bowles's mind. Only this could explain his request, written from Miccosukee where he was surrounded by a handful of whites, a mestizo family, and scores of others ranging from halfbreed to pure Indian or Negro, requesting that Chelsea pensioners be sent to man Muskogee's grammar schools. In the meanwhile he expected to survey ten square miles for a university.[21]

In addition to preparing a national constitution—and even one for the proposed university—and to commanding the army and the navy, the enterprising Director General also conducted Muskogee's foreign relations. Spain was foremost in his mind. Miccosukee and St. Marks were only thirty miles apart, and there were frequent contacts: sometimes Bowles's Indians prowled around the fort, maintaining an ineffective siege; on other occasions the Spaniards sallied forth in a vain attempt to capture him. Diplomatic negotiations continued throughout. William, pressured by DeLacy, still proposed a Spanish-Muskogee alliance whereby he and DeLacy would replace Panton, Leslie, and Company; the Spaniards, declining to negotiate at Miccosukee, continued to attempt to entice him into the fort, to try to win over Kinache and undermine Eastajoca's Indian influence, and especially to strive to seal Bowles off from outside contact.[22] If Hawkins could help contain the Director General so much the better.

It was inevitable that Spain and the United States would work in concert against William's intrigues. Spain normally did not have much use for the United States, but Bowles's running loose at will was embarrassing. This is why Panton and Spanish officials had co-operated with Hawkins and is why the Spanish minister, Carlos Martínez de Irujo dined with Secretary of State James Madison and Secretary of War Henry Dearborn in Washington discussing joint measures against the troublemaker.[23] Both Madison and Dearborn knew that Bowles's headquarters was at Miccosukee and assumed, at least in public, that the Director General confined himself to the Spanish side of the line. Assuredly, if he entered American territory, Hawkins would have seized him.[24] But Bowles, with many Lower Creek friends, crossed the line at will, and Hawkins, on his own, was not able to capture the Director General in Indian territory. "The chiefs who listened to Bowles's promises of abundant and cheap goods are now naked and hungry and without ammunition . . . they blame me for their suffering but it is Bowles's fault. During the ferment I must remain in their midst."[25] What he meant by "their midst" was either at the Creek Agency at Fort Wilkinson or at Natchez on the Mississippi with only occasional visits to the interior. Whether his authority here was greater than Eastajoca's depended on the exact time and place. Hawkins tried to discredit Bowles, who allegedly had only a handful of followers "more attentive to frolicking than fighting,"[26] and attempted to lure Panton's successors away from Spain by encouraging a large Indian land cession on American soil in payment for debts.[27] The Indian agent logically assumed that unless Britain came to Bowles's aid, the adventurer's designs would be frustrated. In the meantime the Florida hubbub was having ill effects above the line. It was really the Spaniards who were to blame. Hawkins secretly proposed to his superiors a plan that would put an end to Bowles;

that it would spell the downfall of the Spanish regime in Florida was also certain.[28]

Bowles realized that his salvation depended on British intervention: "I have said so much on this subject to British ministers, I am reluctant to say more." In reality he was never finished with any subject, and he stressed all the old arguments, denounced Hawkins and James Wilkinson who he said were in Spanish pay—a statement that was half true—and hoped Whitehall would not allow the United States, any more than France, to acquire Louisiana and part of Florida.[29] Both Miller and Reeves were in London and tried to prod the ministry into action. There were those in the government who agreed with Bowles, Miller, and Reeves, who wanted an aggressive campaign against France and Spain, and were unwilling to make sweeping concessions in the current peace negotiations—but they were in a minority. Miller had a special reason for being in London and urging the government to countenance Bowles. In the past, either in co-operation with Dunmore or after the Governor's recall, Miller had advanced large sums to William, and these funds, both Miller and Dunmore maintained, had been employed in the government's interest and should be reimbursed by the exchequer. Their pleas had been unsuccessful to date, and these and other losses had Miller on the verge of bankruptcy.[30] His distress was the reason DeLacy had replaced him in Nassau. Bowles's British enemies were just as vocal in justifying Panton, Leslie, and Company's conduct, in insisting that Miller's claim not be paid, and in vilifying William. In Nassau, Forbes, who had superseded Panton, was prompt to inform the new governor that Bowles was a thief and a rogue, though he did not unnecessarily "want to prepossess your mind against him,"[31] a phrase which could stand as the understatement of the year.

Though William had received only three European papers since returning to Florida, he had sufficient contact with the outside world to know that either France might take over Louisiana and Florida or that there might be a general peace, or both. For Britain to make peace was no more in Muskogee's interest now than in 1790, and he eagerly scrutinized every shred of evidence indicating Britain was taking a firm stand against the First Consul and was preparing an expedition to counter his American designs. During the winter of 1801-1802 Bowles was disturbed by the peace rumors but took heart at the mounting evidence that Napoleon, after a decade of French procrastination and frustration, was seriously attempting to resurrect France's New World empire, primarily at Spanish expense. Haiti,

Louisiana, and West Florida probably would be the nucleus, and there was no limit to what other territories might be added. William assumed Britain would be forced to intervene to counter Napoleon and was determined to leave no doubt at Whitehall or the world at large that Muskogee stood ready to help oppose France. A year and a half after St. Marks' recapture, in which there had been half-hearted thrusts, counterstrokes, and dabbling at negotiation, the Director General, with every resource at his command, again took the offensive. Powers and the Muskogee marine harried the Spaniards as never before, bringing in four prizes in December alone.[32] Large parties of Indians descended on the area surrounding St. Augustine, bringing off sixty Negroes and other booty, forcing a small group of New Englanders, who wanted to colonize sixty miles south of St. Augustine, to abandon their settlement and thereby alarming all the whites so that they sought refuge in the capital.[33] DeLacy in Nassau struggled to insure that supplies regularly reached Eastajoca, at the same time bombarding the ministry with the customary reasons why it should intervene.

The Director General, radiating confidence, remained about Miccosukee, using to best advantage the munitions supplied by DeLacy and Powers and, arousing Indian distrust of Panton, Leslie, and Company and the Spaniards, prepared to take the field with a vengeance against St. Marks. By mid-January Bowles, a dozen or so whites, and almost five hundred Indians surrounded the fort. "We did not come here to contest with you in writing but to besiege the fort."[34] Muskogee's flag had flown over St. Marks once; it would again. His objective was the same as in 1800—to starve the fort into submission. But now the obstacles were compounded; the spiritless Portell, replaced by Jacob Dubreuil, was no longer in command, and in addition two galleys were stationed alongside the fort. Bowles realized his limitations. "I am now besieging Ft. San Marcos and request ammunition and six to eight battering cannon. With one company of artillery and five hundred light troops, I can deliver Pensacola, Mobile, and New Orleans . . . also send me a few frigates. . . . Make this known to His Majesties Ministers and forward supplies to Tampa."[35]

The Indians, including Lower Creeks from the American side of the line, maintained the siege during January, February, and into March, and Eastajoca expected that once again he would stand victorious atop the fort's stone walls. This time, because of the determination of the new commandant, the presence of the two galleys, and the relatively prompt dispatch from New Orleans of a hundred men and three additional galleys, the siege was not as effective.[36] Without suitable

artillery Bowles could make no impression on the fort, and this time the
Spaniards did not inadvertently come to his aid by dispatching unescorted supply vessels. He could always hope that Powers, DeLacy,
or the British government would furnish the necessary artillery, or that
there would be threats to Spanish colonies elsewhere and the galleys
and part of the troops would have to withdraw. Optimistic that one
or more of these would come about, William continued making a
supreme effort on both land and sea.

His hopes remained high during January and February, but by
March they were dashed. With the advantage of hindsight it is obvious,
and even Bowles may have sensed, that fate had made her final play—
Britain had made peace with France and Spain at Amiens.[37] DeLacy,
hearing the news in March, knew well what it meant for Muskogee
and lost no time writing William, telling him of the dismal state of
affairs at Nassau: "I have seen a paragraph of the Duke of Portland's
letter . . . to the Governor of this place with respect to you and the
nation . . . peace is become absolutely necessary to you. . . . I shall
dispatch a small vessel from hence to the Havannah . . . with letters
to the Captain General . . . offering to become a mediator on their
[Spanish] part to you."[38] Portland's dispatch told of the Amiens settlement, of which a by-product was that Britain severed all connection,
official or unofficial, with Muskogee. It meant that Bowles would get
no battering cannon or anything else and that the Indian state would
be on its own to come to terms with the Spaniards. The peace brought
to the forefront the status of Muskogee's navy. For the first time since
the early 1790's all the major powers were at peace. In a period of
universal peace would Muskogee seamen, sailing for a non-recognized
Indian state apparently in no way dependent on Britain, be considered
legitimate privateer crewmen or outright pirates?

Dismayed, William saw his dreams falling apart on every side.
DeLacy hoped something could still be salvaged. Negotiations that
would lead to his and Bowles's replacing Forbes, accompanied by
appropriate bribes, had to begin right away. Because of the sudden
change of events, DeLacy decided to sail to Florida and confer with
the Director General. So he boarded the *Favorita*, a ship which had
made numerous successful runs between Nassau and Florida and which
was now loaded with Indian goods and a few cannon, and set sail
for Muskogee. The siege was still underway, but Spain had sent reinforcements and had almost every Louisiana and Florida galley on the
scene. This DeLacy found out to his grief. Two galleys spied the
Favorita anchored off Dog Island between the Apalachicola and
Ochlockonee rivers and attacked swiftly. DeLacy was the real prize,

though the Spaniards were delighted that the munitions and cannon never reached the Director General.[39] Through gross neglect DeLacy allowed the Spaniards to capture his correspondence outlining in detail his proposed commercial undertaking with Bowles and the present status of negotiations with Whitehall and Spain.

An inventory was made of the *Favorita's* cargo disclosing assorted interesting items: new uniforms for Bowles and Kinache; various trunks of clothes, one of which belonged to Thomas Bowles; and two original letters of William Blount.[40] Thomas Bowles is a common name. Did this trunk belong to an insignificant crewman aboard the *Favorita,* or did it belong to William's younger brother? John Bowles had come to Florida in 1792; was Thomas trying the same thing a decade later? If so, was he a passenger aboard the *Favorita* or already with William? Unfortunately little is known about the trunk and nothing about the owner. Equally tantalizing are Blount's two original letters in DeLacy's correspondence. Blount had been expelled from the Senate in 1796, subsequently had been elected speaker of the Tennessee state senate, and in 1800 had died. Obviously his letters were not recent and probably had been written around 1799-1800 when DeLacy was in or near Tennessee. They may have been routine letters—it is unthinkable that Blount would again commit the folly of his letter to James Carey which had exposed the Senator's earlier conspiracy—but it is also true that there were many indications of a revival of the Blount conspiracy around 1800. It is significant that Blount wrote DeLacy even about the most routine matters.

DeLacy, Bowles's most prominent Nassau champion, had been captured and soon was en route to Pensacola and New Orleans, all the time trying to expain away his incriminating correspondence and moving farther and farther away from the Director General. Indeed most of Bowles's supporters had their backs to the wall and were faring badly. Adam Montgomery, who accompanied DeLacy and was to have become William's new secretary, was captured and never even saw his chief.[41] In Nassau all Bowles's friends were "cut up or shamefully deserted." Robert Hunt, long-time member of the governor's council, "is broke of all his offices . . . Miller is in England and his affairs there considerably embarrassed . . . Hunter also is in England and is said arrested for debt . . . supposedly he and Walker dissolved partnership. . . . Old Mr. Sterling still stands true but can do little,"[42] and "poor old Middleton is in jail for debt."[43] Dunmore and Miller were fighting to save their financial necks in London; the wealthy Brickwood was not inclined to venture more capital in Muskogee; Reeves was now the King's Printer, and he, Windham, and others denounced the

Amiens concessions and urged an aggressive campaign, with little immediate effect.

Both Spain and the United States took heart at the peace and stepped up co-operation and countermeasures to bring about the Director General's downfall. One argument used, a telling one, was that Bowles was deserted by Britain, that whatever promises he had made about being a British superintendent or agent, if they had not been false all along, certainly were now, and that because he was abandoned by Britain and because of the Spanish blockade, he could no longer supply the Indians. If they were to have powder and ball for the hunt and not starve, they had better get into the good graces of Hawkins at the American Creek agency or of the Spaniards at St. Marks. In the ensuing months large numbers did, and for the first time since Bowles's return Hawkins was not embarrassed by the Creeks' flocking down to Florida or with the fear that the Director General's talks would carry much weight on the American side of the line. The Spaniards, increasing their presents, redoubled efforts to make peace with the Seminoles and for the first time enjoyed a measure of success. Spain and Forbes maintained that only they could conduct a dependable trade, that they had no designs on Indian lands, and that abundant presents awaited if the Indians would come to St. Marks. In August, 1802, twenty-two principal chiefs, the most important of whom was Kinache, representing a majority of the Seminoles, came to terms with the Spaniards. A major provision was that the Indians would have nothing to do with Bowles, and it was hoped some would be inspired to collect the reward that had been offered for his capture when he returned to Florida. The peace was far more popular with Spain than with the Indians; some accepted it in good faith, most were apathetic, while a sizable minority was not even represented at St. Marks.[44]

To Kinache Bowles had been the symbol of the period during the American Revolution when Britain had been in Florida lavishly distributing presents and had not threatened Indian territory to the extent that Americans did later. By regaining the Floridas in 1783, Spain was responsible for the British exodus and subsequent Indian distress. Kinache came to St. Marks because he had little choice. DeLacy was captured; no one was rushing to take his place, and supplies from Spanish prizes now were hard to come by. For the time being Spain and Forbes held the key to the indispensable Indian trade, a fact that even Kinache could not ignore. He had come to terms with Spain for the same reasons as the Chickamaugas after Bowles's departure in 1792.

Contributing to Spain's success and Bowles's cheerless situation was

the downfall of the Muskogee navy. Its heyday had been the winter
of 1801-1802, but the navy went into a decline after the Treaty of
Amiens. The Muskogee sun was not completely swept from the seas
however, and Bowles's vessels with their multicolored crews still preyed
on Spanish shipping in the Gulf, taking prizes and allegedly committing unspeakable atrocities on the captured crews. After the peace of
Amiens, Spaniards in distant Mérida in Yucatán were perturbed that
privateers manned by English crews, though flying the Muskogee
banner, still stifled the port's commerce.[45] Since there was peace Spain
could better deal with those Englishmen sailing for Muskogee, and
warships, outfitted at Mérida, Havana, and in Florida, helped curb
Powers and his lieutenants.

The fact that Bowles's privateers were still at large after the Peace
of Amiens was an important reason for the demise of the Indian state.
The distinction between privateer and pirate frequently was a thin one
in the West Indies, and Spain from the beginning considered Muskogee
seamen pirates. At first she was reluctant to prosecute them to the
full extent of the law because Bowles always had a few Spanish
prisoners and he, or until the recent peace, Britain, might retaliate.
What effectively swept the Muskogee marine off the seas was that the
Nassau government also began to treat Bowles's sailors as pirates—in
some cases an apt description because bowlegged Captain Gipson, in
an excess of zeal, had made prize of a British ship.[46] That Bowles's own
government had turned against him, with justification in Gipson's case,
was the greatest blow yet. Because of Gipson's imprudence, because at
first Britain made a determined effort to maintain the peace and not
to antagonize Spain unnecessarily, and because John Halkett, the new
Bahama governor, was Bowles's enemy, British cruisers helped the
Spaniards track down Muskogee privateers. Whenever any of the
crews reached Nassau they were immediately arrested and tried for
piracy.[47]

Halkett, who had taken office in 1801, was a friend of Forbes and
of the heirs of the New Settler faction. He maintained it was absurd
that the British government even remotely could have been behind
Bowles. The best way to restore harmony to the Bahamas and Florida
was to rid them of "the remaining dregs of Lord Dunmore's junto."[48]
The Governor was trying to deny Miller his council seat should he
return and in the meantime urged the exchequer not to reimburse
Miller for his past reckless expenditures. There had been peace in
these parts, alleged the Governor, until Miller and his crew brought
Bowles back in 1799 to set up in Florida a "piebald government . . .
propped up by issuing mock commissions and holding sham courts . . .

[supported] by white American, British, and Spanish outlaws."[49] With Halkett at Government House it is not surprising that almost a dozen Muskogee mariners were tried for piracy and a handful executed. Powers himself was arrested and was fearful that his neck might be stretched,[50] while Gipson's bowlegged knees furiously knocked in the relative safety of Savannah. Halkett energetically co-operated with Spaniards and Americans alike in trying to bring other pirates to justice.[51] It was as obvious to the Spaniards as to the Bahamians that Halkett was no Dunmore. Panton had died and had been buried at sea off the Berry Islands early in 1801 at the time when Bowles was creating maximum turbulence. The political change in Nassau and the imprisonments and executions for piracy must have made the Scot rest easier in his watery grave. His partners, Forbes, Leslie, and John Innerarity, were alive, however, and their vengeance sweet.

The impact of the Peace of Amiens on Muskogee was one of the worst setbacks in Bowles's career. The Director General was always an optimist or at least outwardly so, and there were still a few dim rays piercing the pall of gloom. For awhile he got a trickle of supplies through Powers and Gipson and in the spring and summer was usually in their company. There were always some Seminoles William could count on, and Kinache, even though he had succumbed to Spanish entreaties, was still Bowles's friend and entertained him occasionally at Miccosukee.[52] He also hoped that Britain would soon become dissatisfied with the Amiens concessions and with the aggressive peacetime policies of Napoleon, one of which was taking over Louisiana and part or all of Florida. Perhaps Britain at long last might realize she was going to have to send an expedition to the New World to fight Napoleon. This is exactly what Windham, fearful that France would become master of two worlds, was recommending: "It is really a point on which may hinge the fate of the world [and] great use may be had of the Indian chief Bowley."[53]

William, more cut off from the outside world than ever, did not know what Windham was suggesting or, until much later, the exact state of European diplomacy. At first after the Peace of Amiens Bowles remained with Powers and Gipson about the Apalachicola and Ochlockonee rivers and usually could be found in Miccosukee. But eventually the privateer captains left never to reappear, and after the Seminoles signed their treaty with Spain and because of Miccosukee's proximity to St. Marks, it was not safe to remain at the capital for any length of time. William had to move about frequently; his following shrank; and by the fall he was forced to abandon the area which had been Muskogee's headquarters since 1799. With his wife Mary, little Billy, and only one Negro servant, he wandered about, gradually making his way toward the east coast, careful never to approach any Spanish settlement.[54] His objective was to restore contact and commercial intercourse with the outside world, and he headed for the southern Florida peninsula, which was frequented by Bahamian wreckers and turtlers. By the end of October he was at Biscayne Key anxiously inquiring about all his Nassau friends, but few remained save "old Mr. Sterling." From here or elsewhere on the deserted Atlantic coast Bowles wanted to resume the skin trade with Nassau, though first he had to know exactly how Muskogee's vessels would be received in New Providence. It had always been a question of interpretation whether his ships would be legally admitted by customs, and with Halkett, who had paid scant heed to Bowles's protests about the condemnation of a Muskogee privateer, in Government House it was obvious what that interpretation would be.[55] Only in the Philippines had William been more dejected.

X

Death of the Director General

WILLIAM, tired and discouraged, ranged throughout Florida's interior during the winter of 1802-1803, vainly trying to re-establish commercial relations with Nassau and, by playing up native differences with Spain and the United States, seeking to restore his position among the Indians. Amid conferences with small groups of Seminoles, caring for his wife and son, and moving about to avoid surprise by the Spaniards, there were periods of inactivity and time for reflection. He reviewed his life's four, short, melodramatic decades, beginning with a pleasant childhood in frontier Maryland cut short by the American Revolution, followed by an extreme oscillation of his fortunes. Though they were at a low ebb now, surely fate, as in the past, would again smile on him.

He had several alternatives. One that had occurred to him off and on during the past was to return to Maryland. Twenty years had dulled anti-Tory passions, and many who had not been so outspoken in time resumed their careers unmolested. This happened to Philip Barton Key, who had been with the Maryland Loyalists at Pensacola and who shortly after the Revolution returned to Maryland, served with distinction in the state and national legislatures, and was not blamed for his "youthful indiscretion"; his nephew would write the "Star Spangled Banner."[1] Bowles's family had moved over into Washington County, and though Thomas soon died, his widow remarried and her children by her first and second husbands became respected members of the community. John, who had tried unsuccessfully to join his brother in Florida in 1792, returned home and eventually held local political offices and also served in the state legislature.[2] Thomas, Junior, who may have come to Florida for a brief spell, James, and probably some of William's other brothers were active in politics.[3] It was not many years after the Revolution before Eleanor Bowles's sons were entrenched in the local squirearchy. It is conceivable that, even after an absence of twenty-five years, William might have returned home and attempted to carve out a new career as a planter.

The main reason he had not returned to his family immediately after the Revolution was that he had fought for George III; now he feared that the United States would prosecute him for his post-revolutionary activities once he set foot on American soil. It was no secret that the government would like to, and recently General James Wilkinson assured Spain that Bowles would be put away for a year if the opportunity presented itself[4]—but on what charge? Precisely what law had he violated, and did the national government, or Georgia, or the Indians themselves have jurisdiction in the Creek country? Several years later Aaron Burr ran afoul of the law because of his expedition down the Mississippi, yet eventually the courts freed him. William had a better legal chance than Burr. He considered returning to his native Maryland, but he could never bring himself to take the final step.

With his Florida prospects dim, another possibility was to return to England, where he had influential friends and family connections and where twice in the past he had been lionized during his visits. If he went, however, he would be returning in defeat, would have little influence at Whitehall, and would be subject to violent criticism and ridicule in the press. There was the danger in Britain, as in the United States, that he might be imprisoned either for commissioning Muskogee privateers or for debt. The Bahamas were another place in the British Empire where William had friends and might seek refuge, but, with Halkett at Government House, William never gave this a serious thought.

He had spent most of his adult life among the Indians; his wife and children were here; and William divorced from the Indians would fade into obscurity. For better or worse his fortunes were bound to those of the southern Indians, and he could still hope. Now as always capricious international developments were responsible for his plight. If he had learned anything during his lifetime it was that change was the norm; this had been true during the American and French revolutions and was continuing with Napoleon. Those circumstances that were responsible for his present distress might be altered overnight: Britain might be forced to send an expedition to America to keep Louisiana and Florida out of French hands. Whether Napoleon would keep Louisiana, sell it to the United States, or restore it to Spain was still in doubt. Though Britain would not fight to keep New Orleans out of American hands, there was still the question of East and West

Florida. Had they been ceded to France and would Napoleon in turn sell them to the United States, or would he restore them to Spain? Should France or Spain retain the Floridas it was possible that a British expedition would yet appear. Recently Spain had lost Trinidad and France various sugar islands; could British forces not take over Florida next? Spain was not reassured as British diplomats pressed for a clarification of Florida's status.[5] Negotiations at the Tuileries, Aranjuez, and Whitehall were foremost in William's mind as he wandered among the Seminoles.

He also pondered what Jefferson and his cabinet and Americans outside the government were thinking about Florida. A common American assumption was that eventually the Floridas would be incorporated into the United States. The outlet to the Gulf of the future states of Mississippi and Alabama, carved out of Georgia's western lands, was through thinly populated Florida. Americans had never concealed their designs on Florida, and some of these Americans were Bowles's friends. William, although he was not overly optimistic, considered it possible that the Americans, on their own or with their government's approval, might co-operate with the Indians to expel the Spaniards from Florida, temporarily resulting in an independent state. This state would probably gravitate toward the United States or possibly toward Britain. Eastajoca, with his influence over the Indians and his unremitting hostility toward the Spaniards, could play a role, and this was another reason to remain in Florida.

Committing his own destiny to that of Florida, he had to make the best of existing circumstances and to hold together as many of his white and Indian followers as possible. Few white men had been able to exert effective leadership over the Indians without at the same time supplying them with guns, powder, blankets, and such, and William's predicament—one that he could not immediately resolve—was where to obtain these trading goods. During the winter and spring of 1803 he received only a trickle from outside sources. He probably conserved a small quantity of munitions from the period when he was besieging St. Marks and when prizes were coming in regularly to Muskogee, and he traded a few deerskins to a Nassau merchant; for the most part, however, he had to rely on promises. Under existing circumstances he could only maintain prestige among the Indians by inflaming their distrust of Spain and the United States and by praying that Britain or someone would come to his aid before it was too late.

It was never difficult to set the Indians against the United States and Spain. There was a long tradition of native hostility toward the Spaniards dating back to the earliest days; the attacks on Fort St.

Marks were the most recent examples of anti-Spanish feelings. The Seminoles were not satisfied with the treaty signed at St. Marks and would have no moral qualms about breaking it. After the treaty went into effect Kinache, influenced by his traditional affection for Bowles, by his limited store of trading goods and promises of more, and by his denunciations of Spain and Panton, wavered between openly allying with Bowles and honoring the Spanish treaty.[6] The Seminoles were primarily concerned with Spain, whereas the Creeks proper were more interested in American policies. Hawkins was the symbol of American ambitions and would have encountered resistance whether Bowles was at Miccosukee or Manila: many warriors did not want to become civilized or to have Georgia's boundary extended westward to the Ocmulgee. They formed the opposition party, and Bowles intended to utilize them along with his Seminole friends.

By the spring of 1803 he was back at Miccosukee. James Vernon and a few other whites were with him and retained their faith in Muskogee. Whenever Bowles left Miccosukee to visit other Indian villages, he usually entrusted Mary and his son to Vernon's care. Eastajoca still maintained the fiction of Muskogee's sovereignty and sent out the broken days for a renewed assault on St. Marks. But the Muskogee navy was defunct; there was no indication that the Director General had any dependable source of munitions, and on every hand he was greeted with a negative response to his invitation to take the field against the fort.[7] He could do little more than talk, an art in which he was proficient in several languages, but he could not prod the Indians into taking up the hatchet. They willingly vented their grievances against Spain which were formally recorded in the Muskogee minutes,[8] and Thomas Perryman, William's enemy, a friend of Spain and of Hawkins, who had never been able to collect the reward, had his head knocked against a post when he incorrectly gauged the temper of some Seminoles.[9] For the time being, however, William had to bide his time among his Seminole family and friends and await future developments.

Of great importance was the Indian council in which delegates from the Upper and Lower Creeks, Seminoles, Cherokees, Chickasaws, and Choctaws would be represented. It was to be held in May at the Hickory Ground, a sacred meeting place in the heart of the Upper Creek country near present-day Montgomery, Alabama, where McGillivray's Scottish father formerly had his residence. Hawkins was anxious for the conference to take place and for months had been paving the way for the Indians to approve an extension of the Georgia boundary and the capture of Bowles. The Indian agent had become disturbed by reports that Bowles was still at large and was even planning to come to the Hickory Ground in person.[10]

These rumors were well founded, and it is interesting to speculate what prompted William to take this risk. Though the Hickory Ground was remote from any white settlement, a hundred miles north of the thirty-first parallel, it was well into American territory. He had never had a large following among the Upper Creeks, and there were even fewer friends among the Chickasaws and Choctaws. Presumably a few Cherokees still had a high regard for the Director General, and his picture may have still hung in a Chickamauga cabin. His enemies always had insisted that he was an imposter and a liar with no commission from the British government. These charges were only half true during the Nootka crisis and in 1799, because he had access to the ministry and had obtained limited encouragement. Bowles's detractors, still branding him a charlatan in 1803, were now closer to the mark. The British governor at Nassau treated the Muskogee banner with contempt; it was illegal for merchants there to trade with the Director General, although a few were able to; and Whitehall, certainly for the time being, had cast him aside. With all this opposition and the dangers involved, it is hard to see why he ventured to the Hickory Ground.

Having made his decision to stay among the Indians, it never crossed his mind to retire passively in an obscure Seminole village. He was a proven warrior and leader, could speak, with varying degrees of proficiency, three Indian dialects, and, having an Indian wife and children, had partially merged himself with the native psyche. Few knew the Indians better than Bowles, though Hawkins would not publicly admit it. Accompanied by Seminoles, of whom Kinache, who blamed the Spaniards for his brother's recent death, was the most prominent, Eastajoca resolved to go to the Hickory Ground and denounce Spain and the United States as only he could. He believed that there was a reasonable chance that the assembled Indians, urged to maintain their dignity and territorial integrity, would rally around their eloquent champion, elect him king of all the southern Indians, and place their fate in his trust. The pretense that he represented all the southern tribes was not new, just more far-fetched in 1803.[11]

But what would follow should his wildest dreams come true? The Indians, should they attempt to maintain their traditional way of life and to restrain the Americans, would have to be willing to use force. To do this Eastajoca had to furnish munitions, hardware, and clothing, and no one was more conscious than he of the fact that, at least for the moment, he could not make good promises to supply these trading goods in large quantities. William realized the odds were against him and that he was steering a delicate course. That Britain would soon resolve to take Florida and Louisiana was the one thing that would save him. By the spring of 1803, however, it was becoming more probable that the United States would purchase at least part of Louisiana (possibly including West Florida) and that Spain would retain the rest of Florida. Even if France sold Louisiana to the United States—and it still was not an accomplished fact—Britain might want to take the Floridas anyway. An abrupt change in European diplomacy that would put a British expedition in the Gulf of Mexico would make William's bid to be elected king of the southern Indians not so preposterous. There was only a slim chance that this dream would come true—the reports that Redcoats were actually at St. Augustine and Tampa were quickly disproved—but Bowles was a gambler.[12] Besides, he would be accompanied by loyal Seminoles and should have little fear for his personal safety.

The Indians began to assemble at the Hickory Ground around mid-May. The Upper Creeks were the first to arrive, followed by delegations from the Lower Creeks and neighboring tribes, until they numbered over four hundred. An occasional white face could be spotted: traders in the employ of Hawkins or Panton, Leslie, and Company, of whom James Durouzeaux, the old Lower Creek trader and interpreter, was one of the more prominent, along with John Forbes, now head of Panton, Leslie, and Company, Hawkins, and Esteban Folch, son of the Pensacola governor. Forbes was there to negotiate a land cession from the Indians to satisfy an earlier debt, and both he and the young Folch expected to participate in Bowles's denouement. Indeed, this was the main reason that Folch was there. His instructions were precise—remove Bowles from the Indian country. Spain preferred that the Indians should seize him and turn him over to the Spanish or the Americans; if this was not possible then a leading chief should be encouraged to assassinate Bowles; and as a last resort the chiefs should order him out of the nation. But at any cost, Bowles must go.[13]

There had been much prior talk and negotiation about Spanish-American co-operation to capture Bowles, and this is one of the reasons Hawkins, Forbes, and Folch all were at the council. To dispel any rumors of American disagreement with Spain, Hawkins invited Forbes and Folch to lodge with him. Everyone was assembled except the Seminoles, and there were doubts whether they would attend. Finally runners brought word that "all the Mickassoky gang" were

approaching with Eastajoca at their head. Their entrance was digni-
fied but tension seethed below the surface. With little outward ceremony they were assigned to camp with the Cherokees ". . . now for
bella horrida bella!"[14]

The council could begin, and no one, least of all the whites, could
predict its outcome. Eastajoca, haughty and disdainful, proceeding
directly to the council square, alleged that Hawkins and Folch might
be "caught in their own trap." At every opportunity Eastajoca turned
viciously on Hawkins and the Americans, who were grabbing Indian
lands and emasculating the warriors. He insisted that only he, as Director General of the Creek Nation, was able to protect Creek interests
and that the other tribes would do well to draw under his wing. He
was a half-pay British officer, had always been countenanced by London, and without any hesitation maintained that he was still speaking
in behalf of George III. Folch, Hawkins, and Forbes, like Bowles,
white islands in a red sea, grew apprehensive and wondered if by
some freak the Director General might turn the tables.

As the deliberations continued they were reassured, and the plans
they had laid beforehand began to take effect. Hawkins, Jefferson,
and Secretary of War Henry Dearborn in the past had discussed
measures to put Bowles out of the way and had wrestled with the involved issue of exactly what law he had violated. The individual
states apparently had no jurisdiction over him, and he was not a
traitor; on exactly what federal statute could the government base its
case? Bowles easily could be brought to trial in the United States, but
whether he would be convicted was another matter. But there were
no legal entanglements for Spain. Bowles was an escaped prisoner,
had insulted the Spanish flag on land and sea, and could be imprisoned indefinitely should the Spaniards lay hands on him. Hawkins
had been ordered to secure Bowles and place him in such a position
that he could not bother the United States ever again. Both Hawkins
and Dearborn concurred that the most expeditious course was to
insure that the meddler ended up in Spanish hands.[15]

Indian grievances that Bowles accentuated were genuine, and his
talks made an impression. But if the Indians adopted a hard line
toward the United States and Spain they would need a new white
father; was George III ready to assume that role? If so, where was
the commission to his deputy? Eastajoca could produce no docu-
ment, especially in the company of Forbes and Hawkins, that would
imply that Britain was coming to the Indians' aid, and with France's
failure in Haiti and the probable sale of New Orleans and adjoining
territory to the United States there was no sign that a British expedi-

tion was coming to the Gulf of Mexico.[16] Had one appeared, Bowles could have gotten by without any documents. But in May, 1803, he stood alone, abandoned by Britain, confronting the unrelenting hostility of Hawkins, Forbes, and Folch. The Indians had to trade with the whites, and the Director General's assurances that he could arrange this commerce had a hollow ring. In contrast to Bowles's promises, Forbes, and particularly Hawkins, had on hand an abundant supply of powder, guns, saddles, blankets, and tafia. This gave them an advantage which they used with effect. At one point William overheard the Singer, who had been with McGillivray at New York, whispering in Creek to the Cherokee interpreter, and the fragments William picked up made him turn white—though probably not so pale as Folch later maintained. Bowles knew he was taking a wild gamble but assumed that since he was accompanied by Seminoles and since he was in a white town no harm would come to him personally. What he overheard made him suspect he had erred, and secret negotiations continued behind the scene. With the approval of most of the council, a party of Upper Creeks—half-breeds at some time employed by Forbes and friends of the deceased McGillivray, including Sam Moniac, who had gone to New York with McGillivray, Charles Weatherford, Bob Walton, Mad Dog, and the Singer—headed by Forbes and Hawkins, marched boldly into Bowles's camp, seized the Director General, and placed him in handcuffs. The blacksmith sent by the United States to help civilize the Creeks provided tailor-made handcuffs, and Folch, who had accompanied Hawkins, personally helped secure them. The Seminoles, far from home, outnumbered and overawed by the other Indians, remained sullenly passive—"a general murmur, for the day only, ran through the chiefs in opposition."[17] It was all over. William, ever ready to rely on his wits and to gamble, had lost. Without a moment's delay a party of Upper Creeks began to escort him to Mobile, visions of the $4,500 reward spurring them on.[18]

Historians have been interested in this conference at the Hickory Ground, and some have criticized the role of the United States. It has been charged that the United States in capturing Bowles and handing him over to Spain was no more scrupulous of international law than Napoleon in arresting the Duc d'Enghien on German soil.[19] This comparison is valid only from the white man's viewpoint—and it was the Indians who actually captured Bowles. Though Hawkins had the handcuffs made and Folch helped slip them on, none of this could have happened without Indian approval. Hawkins always insisted he would take Bowles if the Indians did not, yet federal marshals and troops were conspicuous by their absence. The Hickory Ground was near the center of Indian territory and the Creeks and, to a lesser extent, the other tribes, retained much of their independence. The council at the Hickory Ground was an Indian one and the ultimate decision to imprison Bowles and hand him over to the Spaniards was a native one. This is not to deny that Hawkins, Forbes, and Folch put great pressure on the Indians to reach this decision, for earlier these three were well aware that the issue was in doubt and that in some fashion Bowles might have dramatically turned the tables. From the standpoint of the Indians, who for the moment considered it judicious to ally with the United States and Spain rather than with Bowles, who could produce no British commission, his seizure was justified. These Indians regarded themselves as sovereign; they were not a party to the Pinckney or any other treaty dividing their lands; and, if they wanted to heed Hawkins' and Forbes's advice, they had a perfect right to do so.

Regardless of the legality, William was in irons and was entrusted to Indians for delivery to Mobile. Closely guarded by Moniac, Weatherford, and other Upper Creeks, he made his way down the Alabama River in a pirogue. For once he was silent, his mind almost numb. Occasionally there were flashes of the tension at the Hickory Ground and of Hawkins' confidently striding into the Seminole camp; again his mind wandered to happier days in Frederick, London, and Nassau; at times he gazed ashore at the clusters of Indians gathered to see the shackled prisoner pass; although he knew they would not starve, he fretted over who would care for Mary and his son; always in his mind's background, despite the hot Alabama sun, were recollections of the clammy solitude of a Spanish cell. At night, the prisoner and his guards stopped at one of the many Indian villages or camped in the open.

Four days out they were downstream from present-day Selma and, after eating supper, bedded down on an island in the middle of the river. The Indians, overconfident, made the mistake of being careless and during the night William freed himself, silently crept down to the river, stole a pirogue, and escaped. It is not clear whether Hawkins' blacksmith had chosen the wrong profession or whether William had been bound merely with rope and had cut or gnawed through his bonds. In any case there was no sign of him in camp the next morning—only the abandoned pirogue on the opposite shore which in his haste he had neglected to hide. The Indians, shamed that their prisoner had escaped and fearful that they would not be rewarded at Mobile, in a flash were on his trail. The pirogue led to his tracks and soon William once again was in their clutches.[20] It is a mystery why Bowles, an excellent woodsman and in the prime of life, did not elude his captors; perhaps he only cut the ropes binding him but was still hampered by the handcuffs. Firmly rebound and closely guarded, the dejected Bowles continued his voyage down the Alabama River, and there was no future opportunity to escape. The Spanish governor and Panton, Leslie, and Company employees, on hand to greet him at Mobile and to reward the Indians, were as overjoyed that the strategy at the Hickory Ground had succeeded as they were anxious to get their prisoner out of Florida. Six soldiers assigned as his guard escorted him aboard a ship bound for New Orleans. In the Louisiana capital, agitated by rumors concerning cession to the United States, it was the same story all over again; without delay Bowles boarded the *Aguila* bound for Havana.[21]

News of Bowles's capture, spreading rapidly, usually was greeted with satisfaction. Hawkins, pleased that this blackguard had been dispatched so smoothly, assumed that the design of civilizing the Indians and of putting their excess hunting lands to the plow could proceed peacefully. The Indian agent, who detested Bowles and had received many insults from him, nevertheless had a certain professional respect for the Director General and was mystified by his recent actions. "It was inconceivable to me that Bowles, who understood a good deal of the Indian language, had been here formerly and routed General McGillivray, should not have been able to make the necessary distinction between the past and the present. . . . Yet he goes on reacting his former part of the Director General, until he was apprehended in the midst of his guards, and adherents and at the eve in imagination of being a king of the four nations, and quits the stage in irons."[22] Bowles, no less than Hawkins, was aware that there had been a profound change among the Indians and that it was dangerous to come to the Hickory Ground. But had a British expedition arrived in the Gulf, then Bowles might have dropped in on the Mobile governor under different circumstances, and Hawkins would be open to charges of misjudging affairs.

As events turned out, Hawkins and his Washington superiors had every reason to be elated. France had just sold Louisiana, which according to the American interpretation included West Florida, and Spain's days in East Florida seemed to be numbered. All the United States had to do in order to acquire the Floridas was to be patient and be available when Spain's grasp began to slip.[23] Bowles was gone, "safely deposited in Moro Castle," and though some of the Lower Creeks and Seminoles resented his capture and were reluctant to comply with the terms of the Treaty of Fort Wilkinson that ceded additional lands, the Upper Creeks supported Hawkins and the treaty, "and in the end they will have their way."

The Spaniards, who did not agree that the United States inevitably would take over the Floridas, nevertheless were overjoyed at Bowles's capture. Foremost was Jacobo Dubreuil at St. Marks: "With the most uncommon satisfaction I have heard [the news]" from Thomas Perryman, and the picture was further brightened when Perryman and the Indians brought Vernon, one of William's few remaining white followers, to the fort. Subsequently this Indian brought in two Spaniards Bowles had taken prisoner. Perryman had never forgotten the quarrel with Bowles and the recent head knocking and, except that he felt the Spaniards were ungenerous in rewarding him, finally was obtaining complete satisfaction.[24] For the first time since 1799 a St. Marks commander could sleep easily and not worry whether tomorrow the Indians again would be outside the walls. Neither the Spaniards in Florida nor those anywhere else had any real inkling of the misfortunes that soon would befall the mother country and her American colonies. Putting Bowles out of the way was just another indication that she was determined to keep the Floridas, and, who could tell, maybe before it was too late Napoleon would return Louisiana.

The Treaty of Amiens, Napoleon's failure in re-establishing his American empire, American annexation of Louisiana and possibly West Florida, the demise of the Old Settler faction in the Bahamas, and Bowles's recent capture, all had been mortal blows for Muskogee. That there seemed to be no future for a Director General of the Creek Nation was uppermost in William's mind as the *Aguila* sailed toward Havana in mid-June. During his career he visited Havana three times: first as a paroled youthful ensign in a provincial regiment; again in 1792 unsuccessfully trying to negotiate a treaty; and once more in 1803. The formidable Morro, grey and somber on the promontory guarding the harbor's entrance, had not changed. With little ceremony the guard escorted him through the city, over the fort's drawbridge, and down to his cell. The familiar sound of the key turning in the lock was as if there had been no interruption during the past five years.

At the same time that William was being incarcerated in the Morro, Alexander Stephens, a friend of Miller, was bringing out a new edition of Bowles's life. Two reasons for doing this were to encourage Whitehall to reimburse Miller for the sums he had advanced Bowles and also to spur the government to adopt a more aggressive policy in America. As his manuscript was going to press, Stephens heard of

Bowles's imprisonment and added a prophetic postscript: "The fate of this man depends on the Floridas . . . if Spain cedes them to the United States it will be of little consequence what happens to Bowles. . . . Otherwise he will be immersed in the dungeons of the Morro or be sent a slave to the mines."[25]

Little is known of Bowles once he passed through the fort's massive entrance. Always closely guarded, more than likely in chains, he enjoyed few liberties; the smell of salt water and the waterfront, the sound of waves crashing against the solid base of the fort, and occasional glimpses of blue sky were his only contacts with the outside world. He may well have recalled the words of Zanga as from the battlements of a Spanish fort overlooking the sea he meditated on his plight: "Whether first nature, or long want of peace, had wrought my mind to this I cannot tell; but horrors now are not displeasing to me: I like this rocking of the battlements. Rage on ye winds, burst, clouds, and waters roar! You bear a just resemblance of my fortune, and suit the gloomy habit of my soul."[26] The wheel of fortune had made almost a complete circle. Spanish officials were amassing evidence for William's trial, yet at best his sentence merely would change the place of his imprisonment.

Another prisoner awaiting trial at the Morro was a brief acquaintance—the hapless Portell. Spanish justice, sometimes sure, was never swift, and since 1800 Spain had been gathering evidence against the former St. Marks commandant, his subordinates who agreed to the capitulation, and the commanders of the galleys who passively remained in the Gulf. Though Portell was not treated as rigorously as Bowles, it was ironic that both were simultaneously in the Morro, one for taking St. Marks, the other for surrendering it, both being tried by the same power. It was not until 1805 that Spain reached a decision in Portell's case; he was dismissed, while his subordinates and the galley commanders received lesser penalties.[27]

Though it was no consolation as time monotonously ticked by, many of those who in the past had been identified with Muskogee were not faring much better than their leader. Miller was still in London unsuccessfully badgering the government to reimburse him for sums advanced to Bowles, while Halkett and Forbes were busy trying to insure that Miller, should he dare return to the Bahamas, would never resume his seat on the council.[28] All of Bowles's Nassau friends were politically ruined, some were imprisoned for debt. As William whiled away the hours in his cell, former Muskogee mariners were ruing the day they ever walked the deck under the Muskogee sun. Those assorted whites who had been with Bowles at Miccosukee either fell into

Spanish hands, secretly returned to the United States, or faded into obscurity among the Indians. The natives themselves, making the best arrangements possible with Spain and the United States, in spite of grumblings among the Lower Creeks and Seminoles, were relatively passive. But even in 1803 there were few Indians who at some time did not mull over the logic of Eastajoca's recent denunciations of the Spaniards and Americans; and in the period immediately preceding the disastrous Creek defeat at Horseshoe Bend in 1814, many Indians would regret that they had allowed Eastajoca to be taken from their midst.

Using Portell's case, in which it took five years before a judgment was handed down, as a yardstick, William could expect a decision in 1808; but he never found out what it was. He died on December 23, 1805, in the military hospital.[29] Circumstances surrounding his death are obscure. Public reports claimed that the Spaniards had chained him in a dungeon deprived of light and air and had systematically starved him to death or that William on his own refused to eat, wasting away to a mere skeleton, and finally died.[30] The exact cause of his death probably never will be known. Perhaps the disease contracted in the Philippines followed him to Havana and eventually took its toll. Perhaps the Spaniards did deliberately mistreat him— they definitely reduced his food allowance[31]—and pushed him into the grave. Syphilis was partly responsible for McGillivray's early death; one wonders, when in the past William requested mercurial ointment for a friend, who the friend was.[32] The possibility that he deliberately took his life cannot be completely discounted. The privations of his youth, the periodic Spanish imprisonments, and the present dismal routine and lack of hope may have snapped his reason. Accounts that Bowles charged the Spaniards with persecuting him and with trying to poison him and that he refused to eat anything for many days before his death may have been true.

Whatever the exact cause of death, the published reports that Bowles existed only on oranges for forty days before finally dying of starvation must have made Eleanor Bowles moan. She, of course, had been remarried for many years, was surrounded by numerous progeny in Washington County, and probably had not seen William since he was thirteen. John, and Thomas who may have gone to Florida briefly, were close by and respected members of the community. But this did not help much, and she could only think of the happiness when as a young girl many years ago she had married Thomas Bowles, of how bright the future appeared, and of the joy over their firstborn—a son. Now he was dead, and there had been no one there to comfort him in his last hours or to place flowers on his grave. Nor did she even know where his grave was. Though Eleanor Bowles had much to be thankful for and many other children to fret over, the light that was extinguished in the Morro saddened the rest of her days.

William had two families; only the one in Maryland was white. It is frustrating enough trying to trace his Frederick County relations, yet the difficulties are compounded when one moves to the Indian country. He was here for over twenty years, during which period he had no less than two wives, one a Chickamauga, the other a Lower Creek, and by them he had at least two children, probably more. His Chickamauga son, refusing to come to terms with the advancing Americans, went west of the Mississippi where he became a famous chief, a friend of Sam Houston, and eventually lost his life fighting the Americans in Texas. Chief Perryman's daughter, Mary, was William's other wife. She and "little Billy" had been with William almost constantly since his return in 1799. Mary and Eleanor Bowles never met, but it is safe to assume that their reactions and grief were similar when they heard accounts of William's death early in 1806. "Little Billy" grew up among the Seminoles and became chief of Paynes Town. Like Kinache, he was a leader in opposing American troops when they invaded the Floridas during and immediately after the War of 1812. William, ever priding himself a warrior, had he lived would have had reason to be proud of his sons.[33]

Bowles, Director General of the Creek Nation, who had kept the Southeast in turmoil for almost two decades, was gone, his dreams unfulfilled. Despite much talk and publicity to the contrary, he never expected to establish and maintain an independent Indian state for any length of time. Though he was a chief, had an Indian family, and knew the native customs and language, he was aware that Muskogee, if it aspired to nothing more than an Indian state, was doomed to extinction. Establishing Muskogee's sovereignty was merely the first step toward bringing certain territory directly or indirectly under Britain's dominion. He knew that the Floridas and the lower Mississippi Valley might be linked to Canada, with Britain taking over in North America where France left off, or that the Floridas and New Orleans by themselves might be brought into the British orbit. From Drake's day down to Napoleon's, Britain had contemplated taking over key Spanish-American ports so as to monopolize New World trade. Off and on Britain considered these plans throughout Bowles's career, and the year after his death thousands of British regulars, led by the future Duke of Wellington and Miranda, were poised in southern English ports to strike at Spanish America. Florida and even Louisiana might well have been secondary objectives. Upheavals in Spain diverted this expedition to the Iberian Peninsula, but it is an example of the hope that inspired Bowles to go to the Hickory Ground and that sustained him in Florida throughout his career.[34]

The contingency that Bowles pinned his hopes to in 1803 eventually occurred in 1814 when a powerful British expedition directed against Louisiana and part of Florida appeared in the Gulf. Once again runners spread the news among the Creek and Seminole towns that George III would take them under his protection, liberally supply them with guns and powder, and protect them from the Americans. Many of these Indians, one of whom was Bowles's son, disenchanted with the prospect of becoming farmers and relinquishing even more of their hunting lands, readily enlisted in the British cause.[35] One can not but suspect that had Bowles been on the scene during this period the southern Indians would have co-operated more effectively with Tecumseh, who was trying to organize a general western Indian confederation against the Americans, that the Creeks when they took the warpath would have been more united and made Andrew Jackson's victory at Horseshoe Bend dearer, and that throughout Indian co-operation with the British would have been more beneficial. One must also wonder what would have happened if Bowles were still alive and if it were Jackson rather than the British who was disastrously routed at New Orleans. At this point a British Gulf Coast colony might have come into being in which future historians would rank Bowles as a founding father.

Bowles's contemporary, Miranda, had vainly tried to wrest American colonies from Spain and in the end also died in a Spanish prison. But much of what Miranda strove for during his lifetime eventually was achieved and posterity honored him as "el precursor." Since the United States acquired the Floridas and Louisiana, even after death Bowles was not so fortunate. Throughout there is much similarity between Bowles's and Miranda's careers, and on several occasions they were in the same place: in opposite camps at Pensacola in 1781 and in London urging an attack on Spanish America during the Nootka crisis and again in 1798. But curiously there is no indication that they ever met or in any way co-operated.[36]

Bowles was one of the most colorful and controversial figures to cross the stage of the Old Southwest. Gregarious, versatile, a natural leader, evoking either admiration and friendship or bitter denunciation, destiny had thrown him into the Indian country, and, utilizing his talents to the fullest, he played out the game until the end. Though Spain's American empire was on the verge of crumbling, it was not immediately apparent during his lifetime. Spain still was a respectable opponent, and it would have been far better if he had been killed leading a war party or defending St. Marks to the last. With his wide-spread interests, his love of conversation and flair for the dramatic, at home in a London drawing room or an Indian village, always considering himself a warrior-soldier, fate was not kind to let him rot away in isolation at the prime of life.

Notes

ABBREVIATIONS

Acct.	Account
Add. MSS	British Museum: Additional Manuscripts
AGI	Archivo General de Indias, Seville
AGN	Archivo General de la Nación, Mexico
AGS	Archivo General de Simancas
AHN	Archivo Histórico Nacional, Madrid
AHR	*American Historical Review*
ANC	Archivo Nacional de Cuba, Havana
ASP, IA	*American State Papers, Indian Affairs*
CO	Colonial Office
DAB	*Dictionary of American Biography*
DNB	*Dictionary of National Biography*
EF	East Florida Papers
ETHSP	*East Tennessee Historical Society Publications*
FHQ	*Florida Historical Quarterly*
FO	Foreign Office
GDAH	Georgia Department of Archives and History
GHQ	*Georgia Historical Quarterly*
Hist. MSS Com.	Great Britain, Historical Manuscripts Commission
JSH	*Journal of Southern History*
LC	Library of Congress
leg.	legajo
MVHR	*Mississippi Valley Historical Review*
NA	National Archives, Washington
NCHR	*North Carolina Historical Review*
núm.	número
PRO	Public Record Office, London
WMQ	*William and Mary Quarterly*

CHAPTER 1

1. The best accounts of colonial Frederick Town are in John T. Scharf, *History of Western Maryland. Being a History of Frederick, Montgomery, Carroll, Washington, Allegany, and Garrett Counties from the Earliest Period to the Present Day* . . . (Philadelphia, 1882), I; and Thomas J. C. Williams, *History of Frederick County, Maryland, from the Earliest Settlements to the Beginning of the War Between the States* (Frederick, 1910), I.

2. Douglas Southall Freeman, *George Washington, A Biography* (New York, 1948-1957), II, pp. 28ff.

3. *Gentleman's Magazine*, XXXVII (April, 1767), p. 192; *ibid.*, LXIII (June, 1793), p. 581; Henry R.

Plomer, George H. Bushnell, and Ernest R. McC. Dix, *A Dictionary of the Printers and Booksellers Who Were at Work in England, Scotland, and Ireland from 1726 to 1775* (Oxford, 1932), pp. 31-32. Thomas M. Farquhar, *The History of the Bowles Family* . . . (Philadelphia, 1907), pp. 141-142, erroneously states that William's father, Thomas, and Carington were brothers.

4. Maryland Land Office, Annapolis, Md., Liber JK#T, JK#U; BC and GS 14, 15, 16, 18, 25, 27, 29, 33, 35, 36, 37.

5. Scharf, *History of Western Maryland*, I, pp. 433, 480; Bennett Allen to Governor Sharpe, Frederick Town, June 6, 1768, in William H. Browne, Clayton C. Hall, Bernard C. Steiner, eds., *Archives of Maryland* (Baltimore, 1883——), XIV, p. 502.

6. Sources for William's family are Farquhar, *Bowles Family*, p. 142; documents on "Bowles Establishment," Md. Land Off., Liber JK#U and JK#T; and Thomas Bowles's will, Sept. 7, 1787, Courthouse, Washington County, Md., Liber A. Farquhar errs in the name of one of Thomas' daughters and does not recognize that Thomas died in 1787 and that soon afterward his widow, Eleanor, married Samuel Bowles. Thomas' and Eleanor's children apparently numbered twelve, and Samuel and Eleanor had at least two daughters and a son and possibly another son named Thomas.

7. Thomas Bowles's deposition, Dec. 9, 1766, in Browne, *et al., Archives of Maryland*, XXXII, pp. 171-172.

8. (7th ed.; London, 1787) ; the book went through numerous editions.

9. Bowles to Estevan Miró, *Mississippi*, May 26, 1792, in Miró to Conde de Aranda, Cádiz, June 19, 1792, LC, Spanish transcripts, AGS, estado, leg. 6916.

10. Meeting of the Inhabitants of Frederick County at the Court House, Nov. 18, 1774, *American Archives: Fourth Series. Containing a Documentary History of the English Colonies in North America, from the King's Message to Parliament, of March 7, 1774, to the Declaration of Independence by the United States,* ed. Peter Force (Washington, 1837-1846), I, p. 986.

11. Scharf, *History of Western Maryland*, I, 137, 143; Williams, *Frederick County*, I, p. 97.

12. Documents on "Bowles Establishment," Md. Land Off., Liber JK#U.

13. Md. Land Off., Ledger and Journal, Commission for Confiscated British Property, pp. 202, 221.

14. The best account of the military significance of the Loyalists is Paul H. Smith, *Loyalists and Redcoats: A Study in British Revolutionary Policy* (Chapel Hill, 1964).

15. Paul L. Ford, ed., *Orderly Book of the "Maryland Loyalist Regiment," June 18th, 1778, to October 12th, 1778* . . . (Brooklyn, 1891), pp. 6-9; Esther M. Dole, *Maryland During the American Revolution* (Baltimore, 1941), p. 212.

16. John Almon's *Remembrancer*, VI (1778), pp. 209-210; Thomas Jones, *History of New York During the Revolutionary War, and of the Leading Events in the Other Colonies at That Period,* ed. Edward F. DeLancey (New York, 1879), I, pp. 241-251.

17. John R. Alden, *The American Revolution, 1775-1783* (New York, 1954), pp. 201-203; William S. Stryker, *The Battle of Monmouth* (Princeton, 1927), pp. 27ff.

18. Ford, *Orderly Book,* pp.13-27; General Clinton to George Germain, New York, July 5, 1778, Almon's *Remembrancer,* VI (1778), pp. 347ff.

19. Ford, *Orderly Book,* p. 30.

20. *Ibid.,* pp. 37-108; Jones, *History of New York,* I, pp. 287ff.

21. Hugh Gordon to Edward Winslow, Pensacola, March 20, 1779, in William O. Raymond, ed., *Winslow Papers, A. D. 1776-1826* (St. John, 1901), pp. 45-46.

22. *Ibid.*

23. For a description of Kingston and Jamaica see Maria Nugent, *Lady*

Nugent's Journal, Jamaica One Hundred and Thirty-eight Years Ago, ed. Frank Cundall (London, 1939) ; and Robert Renny, *An History of Jamaica . . .* (London, 1807).

24. Gordon to Winslow, March 20, 1779, in Raymond, *Winslow Papers,* pp. 45-46.

25. Monthly Returns of His Majesty's Provincial Corps of Pennsylvania and Maryland Loyalists, West Florida, April, 1779, LC, Public Archives of Canada, Series C, Vol. 1907, photostat; Benjamin Baynton, *Authentic Memoirs of William Augustus Bowles, Esquire, Ambassador from the United Nations of Creeks and Cherokees, to the Court of London* (London, 1791), pp. 4ff.

26. John Campbell to Clinton, July 12, 1780, in Great Britain, Hist. MSS Com., *Report on American Manuscripts in the Royal Institution of Great Britain* (London, 1904-1909), II, p. 154.

27. Baynton, *Authentic Memoirs,* pp. 12-13.

28. Details of Pensacola during the Revolution are in Cecil Johnson, *British West Florida, 1763-1783* (New Haven, 1943), pp. 200ff.

29. Baynton, *Authentic Memoirs,* p. 16.

30. *Ibid.,* p. 22. Information about Bowles's Indian family by necessity is based on fragmentary comments made by Bowles or his contemporaries and by information supplied by Miss Theda Wammack, director, The Creek Indian Memorial Association. See also Albert Woldert, "The Last of the Cherokees in Texas, and the Life and Death of Chief Bowles," *Chronicles of Oklahoma,* I (June, 1923), pp. 179ff. All of the evidence, though frequently vague and skimpy, supports the above account.

31. Benjamin Hawkins, *A Sketch of the Creek Country, in 1798 and 99* (Savannah, 1848), p. 73.

32. John W. Caughey, *Bernardo de Gálvez in Louisiana, 1776-1783* (Berkeley, 1934), pp. 149ff.

33. *Ibid.,* p. 207.

34. John Campbell to Clinton, Pensacola, Jan. 7, 1781, Hist. MSS Com., *Report on Am. MSS,* II, p. 234; Baynton, *Authentic Memoirs,* pp. 29ff.

35. Baynton, *Authentic Memoirs,* pp. 36-38.

36. "A Journal of the Siege of Pensacola, West Florida, 1781," in Francisco de Miranda, *Archivo del General Miranda* (Caracas, 1929-1950), I, p. 182; Albert W. Haarman, "The Spanish Conquest of British West Florida, 1779-1781," *FHQ,* XXXIX (Oct., 1960), pp. 12ff.

37. Donald E. Worcester, ed. and trans., "Miranda's Diary of the Siege of Pensacola, 1781," *FHQ,* XXIX (Jan., 1951), p. 191.

38. Ford, *Orderly Book,* p. 12; New York *Royal Gazette,* July 7, 1781.

39. William S. Robertson, *The Life of Miranda* (Chapel Hill, 1929), I, p. 22.

40. Frederick Mackenzie, *Diary of Frederick Mackenzie, Giving a Daily Narrative of His Military Service as an Officer of the Regiment of Royal Welch Fusilers during the Years 1775-1781 in Massachusetts, Rhode Island and New York* (Cambridge, 1930), II, p. 566.

41. Monthly Returns, Aug. 20, 1781 - June 24, 1783, LC, Public Archives of Canada, Series C, Vol. 1905.

42. New York *Royal Gazette,* Jan. - May, 1782. The best published account of the New York theater during the Revolution is George C. D. Odell, *Annals of the New York Stage* (New York, 1927-1945), I, pp. 185ff.

43. New York *Royal Gazette,* Feb. 13, 1782; E. Alfred Jones, "The Real Author of the 'Authentic Memoirs of William Augustus Bowles,' " *Maryland Historical Magazine,* XVIII (Dec., 1923), p. 307; Edward Young, *The Revenge; A Tragedy* in John Bell, ed., *British Theater* (London, 1791-1802), XXI.

44. Baynton, *Authentic Memoirs,* pp. 36ff.

45. Bowles to Miró, May 26, 1792, LC, Spanish transcripts, AGS, estado, leg. 6916. Unfortunately there are no details about this duel.

CHAPTER II

1. Wilbur C. Abbott, *New York in the American Revolution* (New York, 1929), pp. 260ff; Thomas J. Wertenbaker, *Father Knickerbocker Rebels: New York City During the Revolution* (New York, 1948), pp. 248ff.

2. Abbott, *New York in Revolution*, pp. 269-270.

3. Journal of Capt. P. Kennedy, St. John, Oct. 10, 1783, in Raymond, *Winslow Papers;* Guy Carleton to General H. E. Fox, New York, Oct. 21, 1783, in Hist. MSS Com., *Report on Am. MSS,* IV, p. 420.

4. Wilbur H. Siebert, "The Loyalists in West Florida and the Natchez District," *MVHR,* II (March, 1916), p. 482.

5. New York *Royal Gazette,* July-Oct., 1783; the Frenchman, LeClerc de Milfort, who lived among the Creeks and whose memoirs, however, are not reliable regarding details about Bowles, positively asserts that William left New York for the Bahamas in the company of a troupe of actors. LeClerc de Milfort, *Memoir; or, A Quick Glance at My Various Travels and My Sojourn in the Creek Nation,* ed. and trans. Ben C. McCary (Kennesaw, Ga., 1959), p. 74.

6. The most recent and best over-all account of the Bahamas is Michael Craton, *A History of the Bahamas* (London, 1962).

7. Johann D. Schoepf, *Travels in the Confederation, 1783-1784,* ed. and trans. Alfred J. Morrison (Philadelphia, 1911), II, pp. 279ff.

8. Statement of the number of inhabitants . . . of Bahamas, Nassau, Nov. 1, 1785, PRO, Chatham Papers, CCCXLVIII.

9. Thelma Peters, "The Loyalist Migration from East Florida to the Bahama Islands," *FHQ,* XXXX (Oct., 1961), pp. 137-138.

10. The best printed account of contemporary political conditions is in William Wylly, *A Short Account of the Bahama Islands, Their Climate, Productions, etc. . . .* (London, 1789); further details for the years 1784-1786 are in PRO, CO 23/25.

11. Baynton, *Authentic Memoirs,* pp. 45-47; Peters, "Loyalist Migration," p. 137.

12. Philip M. Hamer, "The British in Canada and the Southern Indians, 1790-1794," *ETHSP,* II (1930), pp. 107ff; J. Leitch Wright, Jr., "British Designs on the Old Southwest: Foreign Intrigue on the Florida Frontier, 1783-1803," *FHQ,* XLIV (April, 1966), pp. 265ff.

13. Baynton, *Authentic Memoirs,* p. 41. Though Baynton's details are not always accurate, he asserts that Bowles visited his father in Maryland.

14. Benjamin Hawkins to James Burgess, Kasihta, Nov. 27, 1797, in Hawkins, *Sketch of the Creek Country,* p. 11.

15. Bowles's testimony, New Providence, April 9, 1788, PRO, CO 23/27.

16. Alexander Stephens, ed., *The Life of General W. A. Bowles, A Native of America — Born of English Parents in Frederick County, Maryland, in the Year 1764* (London, 1803), pp. 15-16.

17. Thomas P. Abernethy, *The South in the New Nation, 1789-1819* (Baton Rouge, 1961), pp. 74ff.

18. Accounts of the Creeks are in Hawkins, *Sketch of the Creek Country;* John R. Swanton, *Early History of the Creek Indians and Their Neighbors* (Washington, 1922); Edwin C. McReynolds, *The Seminoles* (Norman, 1957); and Emma Lila Fundaburk, ed., *Southeastern Indians: Life Portraits; A Catalog of Pictures, 1564 - 1860* (Luverne, 1958). For McGillivray see John W. Caughey, *McGillivray of the Creeks* (Norman, 1959).

19. Arthur P. Whitaker, ed. and trans.,

Documents Relating to the Commercial Policy of Spain in the Floridas, with Incidental Reference to Louisiana (DeLand, 1931), pp. xxvii ff.

20. *Ibid.*, pp. xxx ff. Spain's economic plight was not unique in Florida. After the Revolution there were similar conditions in the Missouri Valley, on the Mosquito Shore, and elsewhere, and Spain was forced to grant concessions like those which Panton held in Florida to other British merchants.

21. Arthur P. Whitaker, "Alexander McGillivray, 1783-1789," *NCHR*, V (April, 1928), pp. 198ff.

22. Lydia Parrish Papers, pp. 404ff., University of Florida Library, Gainesville; John Brown to George Elliott, New Providence, June 10, 1787, PRO, CO 23/27.

23. Unfortunately there is no biography of Dunmore; there are brief accounts by Louise P. Kellogg in the *DAB* and J. M. Rigg in the *DNB*.

24. Representations of Bowles and Creek-Cherokee chiefs to George III, London, Jan. 3, 1791, PRO, FO 4/9; a detailed account of Britain's commercial policy is Frances Armytage, *The Free Port System in the British West Indies; A Study in Commercial Policy, 1766-1822* (London, 1953).

25. Hamer, "British in Canada and Southern Indians," pp. 107ff.

26. *Gazette of the State of Georgia*, Nov. 15, 1787.

27. "An Account of the Present Situation of Affairs in the Bahama Islands," PRO, CO 23/28.

28. *Ibid.*

29. Bowles's expenses, Jan. 5, 1788-Oct. 7, 1789, PRO, CO 23/31; Lawrence Kinnaird, "International Rivalry in the Creek Country, Part I, The Ascendancy of Alexander McGillivray, 1783-1789," *FHQ*, X (Oct., 1931), 69.

30. The standard monograph about McGillivray with valuable documents is Caughey, *McGillivray;* a more objective appraisal of the Indian leader is in the articles by Arthur P. Whitaker, "McGillivray, 1783-1789"; and "Alexander McGillivray, 1789-1793," *NCHR*, V (July, 1928), pp. 289-309.

31. Declaración de Tomás Miller, Pensacola, Aug. 11, 1788, AGI, Cuba, leg. 1394; declaración de Enrique Snell, Pensacola, Aug. 6, 1788, AGI, Cuba, leg. 1394.

32. McGillivray to Arturo O'Neill, Little Tallassie, Aug. 12, 1788, AGI, Cuba, leg. 201; McGillivray to Miró, Sept. 20, 1788, AGI, Cuba, leg. 2361.

33. Declarations by Hugh McDonald, John Lovern, Moses Duir, *et al.*, St. Augustine, Nov. 21, 1788, LC, ANC, Fla., leg. 1, expediente 24, núm. 2, Cuban transcript; memorial of William Panton, John Leslie, and Thomas Forbes to William Grenville, London, June 19, 1789, PRO, CO 23/29.

34. Declaraciones referentes a Guillermo Bowles, AGI, Cuba, leg. 1395; testimony of Abraham Belleny, Nassau, March 2, 1789, *Bahama Gazette*, Aug. 15, 1789.

35. McGillivray denied to the Spaniards that he requested Bowles to enlist mercenaries but later in New York confirmed Bowles's assertion to a Canadian agent. George Beckwith's memorandum, in Lord Dorchester to Grenville, Quebec, Sept. 25, 1790, PRO, CO 42/69.

36. Declaraciones referentes a Guillermo Bowles, AGI, Cuba, leg. 1395.

37. Declarations by Hugh McDonald . . . , LC, ANC, Fla., leg. 1, expediente 24, núm. 2, Cuban transcript.

38. Zéspedes to José de Ezpeleta, St. Augustine, Dec. 2, 1788, AGI, Cuba, leg. 1395; Conde de Floridablanca to Antonio Valdes, Aranjuez, May 9, 1789, LC, Spanish transcripts, AHN, estado, leg. 3887, expediente 1, doc. 157.

39. Miró to McGillivray, New Orleans, Dec. 13, 1788, AGI, Cuba, leg. 201.

40. McGillivray to Leslie, Little Tallassie, Feb. 8, 1789, LC, EF, 114J9.

41. Panton to Zéspedes, Apalachee, Jan. 8, 1788, LC, EF, 116L9.
42. Phineas Bond to Duke of Leeds, Philadelphia, Dec. 28, 1789, PRO, FO 4/7; McGillivray to Panton, Little Tallassie, Oct. 8, 1789, in Caughey, *McGillivray*, pp. 251-254.
43. McGillivray to Miró, Little Tallassie, Feb. 1, 1789, in Duvon C. and Roberta Corbitt, eds. and trans., "Papers from the Spanish Archives Relating to Tennessee and the Old Southwest," *ETHSP*, XIX (1947), pp. 82-83.

44. McGillivray to Leslie, Little Tallassie, Nov. 20, 1788, LC, EF, 114J9.
45. Thomas Forbes to John Wells, Nassau, Aug. 20, 1789, *Bahama Gazette,* Aug. 15-22, 1789; Stephen Haven to John Wells, Nassau, Aug. 20, 1789, *ibid.*
46. Charge to Grand Jury of Bahama Islands, Feb. 24, 1789, AGI, Cuba, leg. 1395.
47. *Lucayan Herald and Weekly Advertiser,* Aug. 19, 1789, PRO, CO 23/30.

CHAPTER III

1. McGillivray to O'Neill, Little Tallassie, June 20, 1787, AGI, Cuba, leg. 200.
2. Meeting of chiefs of Six Nations, Shawnees, Delawares, and Cherokee deputies to speak for western and southern Indians, Niagara, Oct. 2, 1783, PRO, CO 42/15; Speech of United Indian Nation, near mouth of Detroit River, Nov. 28 and Dec. 18, 1786, PRO, CO 42/50.
3. The most recent treatment of the Cherokees is Grace S. Woodward, *The Cherokees* (Norman, 1963); not as detailed but in many respects more valuable is Robert S. Cotterill, *The Southern Indians; The Story of the Civilized Tribes before Removal* (Norman, 1954), pp. 3ff.
4. Cherokee petition to George III, Kasihta, Lower Creeks, May 7, 1789, PRO, CO 42/68.
5. John P. Brown, *Old Frontiers; The Story of the Cherokee Indians from Earliest Times to the Date of Their Removal to the West, 1838* (Kingsport, 1938), p. 3.
6. Creek Petition to George III, Coweta, May 6, 1789, PRO, FO 4/7; Cherokee Petition to George III, May 6, 1789, PRO, FO 4/7.
7. David Craig to William Blount, Knoxville, March 15, 1792, *ASP, IA,* I, pp. 264-265.
8. Bowles to Lord Dorchester, July 7, 1790, PRO, CO 42/68.
9. Memorial of Panton, Leslie, and

Forbes, June 19, 1789, PRO, CO 23/29.
10. Lord Dunmore to Grenville, Nassau, March 1, 1790, PRO, CO 23/30.
11. George Beckwith's memorandum, in Dorchester to Grenville, Quebec, Sept. 25, 1790, PRO, CO 42/69; Caleb Swan, "Position and State of Manner and Arts in the Creek, or Muscogee Nation in 1791," in Henry R. Schoolcraft, *Information Respecting the History, Condition and Prospects of the Indian Tribes of the United States . . .* (Philadelphia, 1851-1857), V, p. 276.
12. Petition of Creeks and Cherokees to George III, Coweta, March, 1789, PRO, CO 42/87; Thomas Dalton to Lord Sydney, London, May 30, 1789, PRO, CO 42/87; Dalton to Grenville, London, June 8, 1789, PRO, CO 42/87.
13. John G. Simcoe to Alured Clarke, Navy Hall, July 29, 1793, in Ernest A. Cruikshank, ed., *The Correspondence of Lieut. Governor John Graves Simcoe, with Allied Documents relating to His Administration of the Government of Upper Canada* (Toronto, 1923-1926), I, pp. 392-393.
14. Thomas Forbes to Wells, Nassau, Aug. 20, 1789, *Bahama Gazette,* Aug. 15-22, 1789; Stephen Haven to Wells, Nassau, Aug. 20, 1789, *ibid.;* testimony by Abraham Belleny, Nassau, March 2, 1789, *ibid.*

15. Bowles's testimony, New Providence, Aug. 15, 1789, *Lucayan Royal Herald and Weekly Advertiser*, Aug. 19, 1789, PRO, CO 23/30.

16. Bowles to Floridablanca, Nassau, Aug. 30, 1789, PRO, CO 23/15; Bowles to Manuel de Zéspedes, Nassau, Aug. 30, 1789, PRO, CO 23/15.

17. Dalton to Evan Nepean, New York, Aug. 3, 1790, in Frederick J. Turner, ed., "English Policy toward America in 1790-1791," *AHR*, VII (July, 1902), p. 721.

18. Documents in PRO, FO 72/17 reveal how the Nootka crisis developed. The best published account is William R. Manning, *The Nootka Sound Controversy. Annual Report of the American Historical Association for the Year 1904* (Washington, 1905).

19. Bowles to British government, 1790(?), copy, AGI, Cuba, leg. 203.

20. Nepean to Wylly, Whitehall, Sept. 17, 1789, PRO, CO 24/14.

21. Bowles to Dorchester, Quebec, July 16, 1790, PRO, CO 42/68.

22. William Sabatier to Bowles, Westminister, Feb. 25, 1799, AGI, Cuba, leg. 212B.

23. Bowles to Dorchester, July 16, 1790, PRO, CO 42/68; John Parr to Grenville, Halifax, Sept. 20, 1790, PRO, CO 217/62.

24. Unsigned letter in Dorchester to Grenville, Quebec, July 26, 1790, PRO, CO 42/68.

25. Bowles to Dorchester, Quebec, July 7, 1790, PRO, CO 42/68.

26. "Observations on Colony of Kentucky," in Dorchester to Sydney, Aug. 27, 1789, PRO, CO 42/65.

27. Grenville to Dorchester, Whitehall, Oct. 20, 1789, PRO, CO 42/65.

28. Winthrop Sargent to St. Clair, Ft. Steuben, Aug. 17, 1790, in Clarence E. Carter, ed., *The Territorial Papers of the United States* (Washington, 1934——), II, p. 301.

29. Simcoe to Clarke, July 29, 1793, in Cruikshank, *Correspondence of Simcoe,* I, pp. 392-393.

30. Dorchester to Grenville, Montreal, July 26, 1790, PRO, CO 42/68.

31. *Ibid.;* Bowles to Parr, Halifax, Sept. 20, 1790, PRO, CO 217/62.

32. Memorial of John Connolly, Quebec, Nov. 17, 1794, PRO, CO 42/102.

33. *Ibid.;* Beckwith's memo in Dorchester to Crown, Quebec, Sept. 25, 1790, PRO, CO 42/69; Julian P. Boyd in *Number 7, Alexander Hamilton's Secret Attempts to Control American Foreign Policy, with Supporting Documents* (Princeton, 1964), pp. 3ff., makes it clear that Beckwith was a secret and unofficial agent, that he was negotiating with Hamilton rather than the American government, and that Hamilton misrepresented Beckwith's conversations.

34. Caughey, *McGillvray,* pp. 40ff.

35. Carlos Howard to McGillivray, Philadelphia, July 18, 1790, AGI, Cuba, leg. 182.

36. Beckwith's memo, Sept. 25, 1790, PRO, CO 42/69.

37. *Ibid.*

38. American-Creek Treaty, New York, Aug. 7, 1790, in Charles J. Kappler, ed., *Indian Affairs, Laws and Treaties...* (Washington, 1903—), II, pp. 25-28, contains only the public articles. The secret articles providing for McGillivray's pension and commission and for the United States' trading with the Indians in case of an Anglo-Spanish war, are summarized in Whitaker, "McGillivray, 1789-1793," pp. 298-299. Whitaker had the secret provisions verified from the original treaty in the State Department.

39. Count of Revilla Gigedo to Floridablanca, Mexico City, Feb. 28, 1791, AGN, correspondencia de los virreyes, segunda serie, tomo 30.

40. Bowles to Parr, Halifax, Sept. 20, 1790, PRO, CO 217/62; Parr to Nepean, Sept. 22, 1790, PRO, CO 217/62; Richard Hughes to Grenville, *Adamant,* Sept. 22, 1790, PRO, CO 217/62.

41. For a detailed treatment of the Nootka crisis, see Manning, *Nootka Sound Controversy.*

42. London *Daily Advertiser,* Oct. 30, 1790.

43. Thomas Inglis(?) to Biddulph(?) and Co., Portsmouth, Nov. 9, 1790, PRO, FO 4/8.

44. *Bahama Gazette,* Jan. 11-14, 1791.

45. Grenville to Dorchester, Whitehall, Oct. 5, 1790, PRO, CO 42/68.

46. Allen's negotiations with British authorities either in Canada or in London during 1791 and the preceding years can be followed in PRO, CO 42. See also Alfred L. Burt, *The United States, Great Britain and British North America from the Revolution to the Establishment of Peace after the War of 1812* (New Haven, 1940), p. 70.

47. Robertson, *Miranda,* I, pp. 94ff.

48. London *Daily Advertiser,* Nov. 4, 1790.

49. Marqués del Campo to Miró, London, Dec. 14, 1790, AGS, estado, leg. 2618.

50. David Humphreys to Jefferson, London, Nov. 2, 1790, in Frank L. Humphreys, *Life and Times of David Humphreys, Soldier-Statesman-Poet, Belov'd of Washington* (New York, 1917), II, pp. 56-57.

51. *Bahama Gazette,* April 22-26, 1791.

52. London *Daily Advertiser,* Feb. 9, 1791.

53. Autos seguidos contra el aventurero inglés Guillermo Bowles, July 8, 1793, LC, Spanish transcripts, AHN, consejo, leg. 21,067; George Townshend to Bowles, Rainham, Oct. 30, 1798, AGI, Cuba, leg. 216A.

54. George Pearson was one of the foremost British chemists and medical doctors, a pioneer as an early advocate of vaccination, a correspondent and eventually a violent critic of Edward Jenner, and a close friend of the famous actor John Philip Kemble.

55. William Lewis, *Commercium Philosophico-Technicum; or, the Philosophical Commerce of Arts; Designed as an Attempt to Improve Arts, Trades, and Manufactures* (London, 1763) was a standard treatise on metallurgy, the manufacture of glass and porcelain, and the making of paint and ink.

56. Bowles to John Reeves, Manila, Jan. 18, 1797, Add. MSS 37,876.

57. Jones, "Real Author," pp. 302-308.

58. Baynton, *Authentic Memoirs;* J. Y. to Baynton, Charing Cross, Nov. 10, 1790, AGI, Cuba, leg. 203.

59. Milfort, *Memoir,* p. 77.

60. Bowles to Grenville, Osborn's Hotel, Adelphi, Dec. 15, 1790, PRO, FO 4/8.

61. Thomas Bowles's will, Sept. 7, 1787, Courthouse, Washington County, Md., Liber A.

62. Bowles to Greenville, Dec. 15, 1790, PRO, FO 4/8.

63. Throughout Bowles's career, his ambition was to establish a nominally independent Indian state in the Southeast. He expected that his state would have close ties with Britain and might eventually become a British colony. Bowles called his state the combined Creek-Cherokee nations, the Creek Nation, or Muskogee, and as time passed he used the latter two titles almost exclusively. The Muskogee language family includes most of the southern Indians—Creeks, Chicksaws, Choctaws, Seminoles, though not the Cherokees. For Bowles the term Muskogee and Creek were almost synonymous. Normally when he referred to Muskogee he meant the Creeks and their close kin, the Seminoles, though while he was in London in 1790-1791 he was also including the Cherokees. Muskogee's boundaries were flexible and at a minimum included the territory inhabited by the Lower Creeks and Seminoles; the extreme limits took in almost all of the Southeast east of the Mississippi River including Cherokee territory. Bowles encouraged white settlers to come to Muskogee and expected it would develop into a civilized state recognized by all nations. Though he made progress in organizing an army and navy, in framing a constitution, in developing an educational system, and in establishing a land office, no major power un-

equivocally recognized Muskogee. The Creeks, Cherokees, Seminoles and other southern Indians, however, whether they considered themselves part of Muskogee or not, always regarded themselves as independent.

64. Representations of Bowles and Creek-Cherokee chiefs to George III, Jan. 3, 1791, PRO, FO 4/9.

65. London *Daily Advertiser,* March 17, 1791.

66. Campo to Floridablanca, London, April 15, 1791, LC, Spanish transcripts, AHN, estado, leg. 3889 bis, expediente 10, núm. 3, photostat; memorial of Bowles and Creek-Cherokee chiefs, London, March 25, 1791, *ibid.*

67. Bowles to Grenville, Adelphi, Jan. 7, 1791, AGI, Cuba, leg. 2372; *ibid.,* Jan. 25, 1791, PRO, FO 4/9.

68. Grenville to Dorchester, Whitehall, March 7, 1791, PRO, CO 42/73.

69. London *Daily Advertiser,* March 30, 1791.

CHAPTER IV

1. London *Daily Advertiser,* April 3, 1791.

2. Bowles to ?, Nassau, June 11, 1791, PRO, CO 23/15.

3. Dunmore to Grenville, Nassau, June 8, 1791, PRO, CO 23/31.

4. *Ibid.,* June 9, 1791, PRO, CO 23/31.

5. Bowles to Grenville, New Providence, July 22, 1791, PRO, CO 23/31; Henry Dundas' memorandum, Sept. 26, 1791, PRO CO 23/31.

6. *Bahama Gazette,* Aug. 2-5, 1791.

7. A variation of this flag was a rectangle, divided in the middle, with a diagonal cross in the center of one side and a sun with human features in the center of the other; LC, Spanish transcripts, AHN, estado, leg. 3889 bis, expediente 10, núm. 51 and 52, photostat. Additional details are in Lyle N. McAlister, "William Augustus Bowles and the State of Muskogee," *FHQ,* XXXX (April, 1962), pp. 323-324. It is possible that the first Muskogee flag was made in London before Bowles returned to Nassau.

8. Bowles to Grenville, New Providence, July 22, 1791, PRO, CO 23/31.

9. Beckwith to Dorchester?, Philadelphia, Dec. 2, 1791, Turner, "English Policy toward America," pp. 734-735.

10. McGillivray to Panton, Little Tallassie, Oct. 28, 1791, AGI, Cuba, leg. 2362.

11. Report of Mr. Middleton, *Bahama Gazette,* Dec. 16-20, 1791; Bowles to Dunmore, Camp Apalachee, Feb. 6, 1792, PRO, CO 23/31.

12. Middleton report, *Bahama Gazette,* Dec. 16-20, 1791; Wylly, *Short Account of the Bahamas,* p. 8, says 1788 population was about 9,300; Craton, *History of Bahamas,* p. 166, claims population in 1789 was 11,300. A large percentage of either of these numbers was Negro slaves.

13. McGillivray to Panton, Oct. 28, 1791, AGI, Cuba, leg. 2362; Beckwith to Dorchester?, Dec. 2, 1791, Turner, "English Policy toward America," pp. 734-735.

14. Knox to St. Clair, War Dept., Dec. 2, 1791, *ASP, IA,* I, p. 184.

15. Knox to McGillivray, Feb. 17, 1792, *ibid.,* p. 246.

16. Milfort, *Memoir,* p. 92.

17. Dunmore to Dundas, Nassau, Dec. 19, 1791, PRO, CO 23/31.

18. Campo to Floridablanca, London, April 15, 1791, LC, Spanish transcripts, AHN, estado, leg. 3889 bis, expediente 10, photostat.

19. Extract of a letter from St. Augustine to a gentleman in Savannah, *Georgia Gazette,* Sept. 15, 1791; Luis de las Casas to Juan de Araoz, Havana, Sept. 26, 1791, LC, Spanish transcripts, AHN, estado, leg. 3889 bis, expediente 10, photostat; extract from McQueen's diary, 1791, in Walter C. Hartridge, ed., *The Letters of Don Juan McQueen to His Family, Written from Spanish East Florida, 1791-1807* (Columbia, 1943), pp. 13-14.

20. Las Casas to Conde de Campo de Alange, Havana, Feb. 8, 1792, LC, Spanish transcripts, AHN, consejo, leg. 21,067.

21. Bowles to O'Neill, Coweta, Dec. 4, 1791, LC, Spanish transcripts, AHN, estado, leg. 3889 bis, expediente 10, photostat.

22. Spanish arguments in 1791-1792 over whether to continue Panton's monopoly are in AGS, estado, leg. 2618.

23. Proclamation, General William A. Bowles, Director of Affairs, Creek Nation, Usachees, Oct. 26, 1791, LC, Personal Misc., Acct. 6662.

24. Bowles to Joseph Ellicott, Usachees, Dec. 12, 1791, LC, Personal Misc., Acct. 5643.

25. George Hammond to Jefferson, Philadelphia, Dec. 14, 1791, PRO, FO 115/1; Hammond to Grenville, Philadelphia, Dec. 19, 1791, PRO, FO 115/1.

26. Grenville to Hammond, Whitehall, Jan. 3, 1792, PRO, FO 115/1.

27. Extract of a letter dated near Cho'ta, Feb 1, 1792, in William P. Palmer, Sherwin McRae, Raleigh E. Colston, et al., eds., Calendar of Virginia State Papers and Other Manuscripts . . . (Richmond, 1875-1892), V, pp. 480-481.

28. Craig to Blount, March 15, 1792, ASP, IA, I, pp. 264-265.

29. Simcoe to Dundas, London, Aug. 12, 1791, in Cruikshank, Correspondence of Simcoe, I, p. 50.

30. Declaration of William Cunningham, New Orleans, April 11, 1792, AGI, Cuba, leg. 152A.

31. Charles Stevenson to Simcoe, New York, Feb. 7, 1792, in Cruikshank, Correspondence of Simcoe, I, p. 110.

32. Bowles to Dunmore, Camp Apalachee, Feb. 6, 1792, PRO, CO 23/31.

33. Cunningham's deposition, New Orleans, April 2, 1792, LC, Spanish transcripts, AHN, consejo, leg. 21,067.

34. Testimony of John Hambly, St. Augustine, Jan. 26, 1791, LC, Spanish transcripts, AHN, consejo, leg. 21,067; deposition of Edward Forrester, Ft. St. Marks, Feb. 28, 1792, AGI, Cuba, leg. 2371; the best published account with supporting documents is Lawrence Kinnaird, "The Significance of William Augustus Bowles' Seizure of Panton's Apalachee Store in 1792," FHQ, IX (Jan., 1931), pp. 156ff. Estimates of Panton's loss varied. To the Spaniards Panton insisted that it exceeded fifteen thousand dollars, while to his partner he estimated it to be only ten thousand dollars. Panton to Carondelet, Pensacola, LC, Cuban transcripts, April 12, 1792, ANC, Fla., leg. 1, expediente 5; Panton to Forbes, Pensacola, April 28, 1800, Greenslade Papers, University of Florida Library.

35. McGillivray to Panton, Little Tallassie, March 12, 1792, LC, ANC, Fla., leg. 1, expediente 5, núm. 18b, Cuban transcript.

36. Francisco Xavier Guessy to Gov. of East Fla., San Marcos de Apalachee, Jan.(?), 1792, LC, Spanish transcripts, AHN, consejo, leg. 21,067.

37. Leslie to Panton, Ft. St. Marks, Jan. 30, 1792, AGI, Cuba, leg. 203.

38. Panton to McGillivray, Pensacola, Feb. 9, 1792, AGI, Cuba, leg. 203.

39. Diary of Joseph de Hevia, 1792, LC, Spanish transcripts, AHN, consejo, leg. 21,067.

40. Bowles to Commandant of San Marcos, Jan. 4, 1792, LC, Spanish transcripts, AHN, consejo, leg. 21,067; Bowles to (?), Camp Apalachee, Jan. 31, 1792, AGI, Cuba, leg. 205.

41. Diary of Hevia, 1792, LC, Spanish transcripts, AHN, consejo, leg. 21,067.

42. Deposition of Cunningham, April 2, 1792, LC, Spanish transcripts, AHN, consejo, leg. 21,067; Leslie to Panton, Jan. 30, 1792, AGI, Cuba, leg. 203; deposition of Forrester, Feb. 28, 1792, AGI, Cuba, leg. 2371.

43. Leslie to Panton, Apalachee, March 9, 1792, LC, ANC, Fla., leg. 1, expediente 5, núm. 18, Cuban transcript.

44. Bowles to Capt. on board the ves-

sel that may arrive at Ochlockonee, St. Marks, Feb. 29, 1792, AGI, Cuba, leg. 2371; Hevia to Bowles, *Galga,* Feb. 22, 1792, LC, Spanish transcripts, AHN, consejo, leg. 21,067.

45. Leslie to Panton, March 9, 1792, LC, ANC, Fla., leg. 1, expediente 5, núm. 18, Cuban transcript.
46. *Ibid.*
47. John Bowles to William A. Bowles, New Providence, April 21, 1792, AGI, Cuba, leg. 205.

48. *Ibid.*
49. Milfort arrived with almost four hundred Indians at the Flint River but dismissed most of them, allegedly because of economy, before proceeding to the Ochlockonee. Panton to Carondelet, Pensacola, April 12, 1792, LC, ANC, Fla., leg. 1, expediente 5, núm. 24, Cuban transcript.
50. Leslie to Panton, March 9, 1792, LC, ANC, Fla., leg. 1, expediente 5, núm. 18, Cuban transcript.

CHAPTER V

1. Carondelet to Floridablanca, New Orleans, March 22, 1792, LC, Spanish transcripts, AHN, consejo, leg. 21,067.
2. Arthur P. Whitaker, *The Spanish American Frontier: 1783-1795; The Westward Movement and the Spanish Retreat in the Mississippi Valley* (Boston, 1927), pp. 163-164.
3. Bowles to Carondelet, New Orleans, March 13, 1792, AGI, Cuba, leg. 2371.
4. *Ibid.,* March 14, 1792, AGI, Cuba, leg. 2371.
5. Panton to Carondelet, Pensacola, March 17, 1792, LC, ANC, Fla., leg. 1, expediente 5, núm. 19, Cuban transcript.
6. Carondelet to Panton, New Orleans, March 24, 1792, AGI, Cuba, leg. 214.
7. Panton to Carondelet, Pensacola, April 12, 1792, LC, ANC, Fla., leg. 1, expediente 5, núm. 24, Cuban transcript.
8. *Ibid.,* April 16, 1792, núm. 27.
9. McGillivray to Carondelet, Little Tallassie, April 10, 1792, AGI, Cuba, leg. 204.
10. Cunningham's deposition, April 2, 1792, LC, Spanish transcript, AHN, consejo, leg. 21,067.
11. Wellbank to Bowles, Camp near Ochlockonee, March 6, 1792, in Wellbank to Carondelet, March 8, 1792, AGI, Cuba, leg. 152A.
12. Las Casas to Floridablanca, Havana, April 21, 1792, LC, Spanish transcripts, AHN, consejo, leg. 21,067.

13. *Ibid.;* Bowles to Las Casas, April 14, 1792, LC, Spanish transcripts, AHN, consejo, leg. 21,067.
14. Las Casas to Floridablanca, April 21, 1792, LC, Spanish transcripts, AHN, consejo, leg. 21,067.
15. Las Casas to Campo de Alange, Havana, March 28, 1792, LC, Spanish transcripts, AHN, consejo, leg. 21,067.
16. Miró to José Pontalba, May 27, 1792, in Caroline M. Burson, *The Stewardship of Don Esteban Miró, 1782-1792* (New Orleans, 1940), p. 31.
17. Bowles to Miró, May 26, 1792, LC, Spanish transcripts, AGS, estado leg. 6916.
18. Stephens, *Life of Bowles,* p. 28.
19. Wellbank to Dunmore, Usachees, June 18, 1792, PRO, CO 23/31.
20. Wellbank to Miller, Usachees, June 10, 1792, PRO, CO 23/31.
21. Dunmore to Dundas, Nassau, Aug. 28, 1792, PRO, CO 23/31; Las Casas to Juan Nepomuceno de Quesada, Havana, June 27, 1792, LC, EF, 2B; Dunmore's commission to Philatouchy, Bahamas, Feb. 5, 1793, LC, EF, 114J9.
22. Carondelet to Aranda, New Orleans, August 20, 1792, LC, Spanish transcripts, AHN, estado, leg. 3898, apartado 3, núm. 11, photostat; McGillivray to Panton, Little Tallassie, Nov. 28, 1792, AGI, Cuba, leg. 204.
23. Dunmore to Dundas, Nassau, July 20, 1793, PRO, CO 23/32; addi-

tional details are in AGI, Cuba, leg. 152A.

24. Dunmore to Dundas, Nassau, Aug. 28, 1792, PRO, CO 23/31; Jacob Townshend to Blount, Estanoula, Feb. 15, 1793, *ASP, IA,* I, p. 439.

25. James Seagrove to Washington, Rock Landing, July 5, 1792, *ASP, IA,* I, p. 305; Seagrove to McGillivray, St. Marys, Oct. 8, 1792, *ASP, IA,* I, p. 314.

26. Washington to Jefferson, Mount Vernon, Aug. 23, 1792, in John C. Fitzpatrick, ed., *The Writings of George Washington from the Original Manuscript Sources, 1745-1799* (Washington, 1931-1944), XXXII, p. 130.

27. Washington to David Stuart, Philadelphia, July 9, 1792, *ibid,* p. 85.

28. McGillivray to Seagrove, Little Tallassie, May 18, 1792, *ASP, IA,* I, p. 302.

29. Burson, *Miró,* p. 31.

30. Bowles to Floridablanca, *Mississippi,* June 18, 1792, LC, Spanish transcripts, AHN, consejo, leg. 21,067; Bowles to Aranda, Cádiz, July 28, 1792, LC, Spanish transcripts, AHN, consejo, leg. 21,067.

31. El secretario del consejo de Indias, Madrid, Sept. 22, 1792, LC, Spanish transcripts, AHN, estado, leg. 3889 bis, expediente 10, núm. 44, photostat.

32. A recent account of Spanish politics during this period is Richard Herr, *The Eighteenth-Century Revolution in Spain* (Princeton, 1958), pp. 264ff.

33. Whitaker, *Spanish-American Frontier,* pp. 181-182.

34. Deposition of Cunningham, April 2, 1792, LC, Spanish transcripts, AHN, consejo, leg. 21,067.

35. ? to Aranda, Cádiz, Aug. 28, 1792, LC, Spanish transcripts, AHN, estado, leg. 3889 bis, expediente 10, núm. 40, photostat; Antonio de Faranco to Aranda, Madrid, Nov. 2, 1792, LC, Spanish transcripts, AHN, estado, leg. 3889 bis, expediente 10, núm. 47.

36. King, chiefs, and warriors of Creek Nation to Charles IV, Coweta Old Town, Oct. 24, 1792, LC, Spanish

transcripts, AHN, estado, leg. 3889 bis, expediente 10.

37. James Jackson to Edward Telfair, Savannah, April 8, 1793, in James Jackson, *The Papers of James Jackson, 1781-1798,* ed. Lilla M. Hawes (Savannah, 1955), p. 53; May 27, 1793, *ibid.,* p. 67; Alexander Cornel's talk, Tuckaubatchee, June 14, 1793, GDAH, Creek Indian Letters, 1705-1793, I, pp. 323-324.

38. Panton to Las Casas, Pensacola, Sept. 26, 1792, LC, ANC, Fla., leg. 1, expediente 5, núm, 33, Cuban transcript; an informative article is Arthur P. Whitaker, "Spain and the Cherokee Indians, 1783-98," *NCHR,* IV (July, 1927), pp. 252ff., though Whitaker does not indicate that the danger of Bowles's intrigues among the Chickamaugas was an important reason why Spain finally decided to give them presents and include them in the Spanish sphere.

39. Panton to Carondelet, Pensacola, Nov. 6, 1792, AGI, Cuba, leg. 203; John McDonald to Gov. White, Cherokees, Sept. 12, 1793, AGI, Cuba, leg. 211.

40. Las Casas to Alcudia, June 6, 1793, and enclosures, LC, Spanish transcripts, AGS, guerra, leg. 6928.

41. Carondelet to Francisco Montrevill, New Orleans, Dec. 13, 1792, in Lawrence Kinnaird, ed. and trans., *Spain in the Mississippi Valley, 1765-1794; Translations of Materials from the Spanish Archives in the Bancroft Library* (Washington, 1946), III, 100-101.

42. Timothy Barnard to Henry Gaither, Flint River, April 20, 1793, *ASP, IA,* I, p. 420; Simcoe to Clarke, Navy Hall, July 29, 1793, PRO, CO 42/96.

43. Benjamin Lincoln, "Journal of a Treaty Held in 1793, with the Indian Tribes North-West of the Ohio, by Commissioners of the United States," *Collections, Massachusetts Historical Society,* 3rd ser., V (1836), pp. 169ff.; Simcoe to Clarke, July 29, 1793, PRO, CO 42/96; Simcoe to Alexander McKee, Navy Hall, June 28, 1793, in

Cruikshank, *Correspondence of Simcoe*, V. p. 52.

44. Simcoe to Carondelet, Rapids of the Miamis River, April 11, 1794, PRO, CO 42/100.

45. John McDonald to McKee, Cherokees, April 10, 1794, PRO, CO 42/200; diary of John Hambly, June-Aug., 1794, B. Smith Papers, transcript, Lockey Collection, University of Florida Library.

46. Bowles to Duke de la Alcudia, cárcel real de la villa, Madrid, July 14, 1793, Add. MSS 37,873.

47. Dundas to Dunmore, Whitehall, Aug. 1, 1792, PRO, CO 72/27.

48. *Ibid*. Oct. 16, 1793, PRO, CO 23/32.

49. The definitive work on this treaty is Samuel F. Bemis, *Jay's Treaty;*

A Study in Commerce and Diplomacy (New Haven, 1962).

50. The most comprehensive treatment is Samuel F. Bemis, *Pinckney's Treaty; America's Advantage from Europe's Distress, 1783-1800* (New Haven, 1960).

51. Stephens, *Life of Bowles*, p. 26.

52. *Ibid.*, pp. 24-25; Bowles to Alcudia, July 14, 1793, Add. MSS 37,873.

53. Las Casas to Floridablanca, Havana, April 21, 1792, LC, Spanish transcripts, AHN, consejo, leg. 21,067.

54. Jorge Escobedas to Alcudia, Madrid, Dec. 12, 1793, LC, Spanish transcripts, AHN, estado, leg. 3889 bis, expediente 10, núm. 76, photostat; Campo to Aranda, London, July 31, 1792, AGS, estado, leg. 8148.

CHAPTER VI

1. Bowles to Grenville, June 5, 1798, AGI, Cuba, leg. 2371.

2. *Ibid*.

3. *Ibid*.

4. *Ibid.;* M. D. Guignes, "Observations on the Philippine Islands and the Isle of France," *A General Collection of the Best and Most Interesting Voyages and Travels in All Parts of the World* . . . ed., John Pinkerton (London, 1808-1814), XI, pp. 71ff.

5. Bowles to Reeves, Manila, Jan. 18, 1797, Add. MSS 37,876.

6. Bowles to Grenville, June 5, 1798, AGI, Cuba, leg. 2371.

7. *Ibid*.

8. *Ibid*.

9. Bowles to Reeves, Jan. 18, 1797, Add. MSS 37,876. Additional information about Reeves is in Gordon Goodwin's sketch in the *DNB*.

10. Bowles's diary, fragment, 1798, AGI, Cuba, leg. 2371.

11. Francisco Cerda to Francisco de Saavedra, Madrid, Sept. 28, 1798, LC, Spanish transcripts, AHN, estado, leg. 3889 bis, expediente 10, doc. 109, photostat; unsigned letter, Madrid, Aug. 30, 1798, LC, Spanish transcripts, AHN, estado leg. 3889 bis, expediente 10, doc. 110.

12. Unsigned letter, Madrid, Aug. 30, 1798, LC, Spanish transcripts, AHN, etstado, leg. 3889 bis, expediente 10, doc. 110.

13. J. B. G. M. Bory de St. Vincent, "Voyage to, and Travels through, the Four Principal Islands of the African Seas . . .," *A Collection of Modern and Contemporary Voyages and Travels. . .*, ed. Richard Phillips, II (London, 1805-1810), pp. 58ff.

14. Bowles to Juan Martinez, Mauritius, 1797, AGI, Cuba, leg. 2371.

15. Bowles to Master Wardens and Brothers of Lodges of Isle of France, no date, AGI, Cuba, leg. 2371; Martinez to Bowles, Oct. 16, 1797, AGI, Cuba, leg. 212B; ? to Bowles, Mauritius, Jan. 29, 1798, AGI, Cuba, leg. 212B.

16. Bowles to Grenville, June 5, 1798, AGI, Cuba, leg. 2371.

17. *Ibid.;* Bowles to French Captain, July 25, 1797 (draft), AGI, Cuba, leg. 2371.

18. London *Morning Post and Advertiser*, Nov. 5, 1798.

19. Bowles to Captain of French frigate, undated draft, AGI, Cuba, leg. 2371.

20. Zachary Macaulay to Chairman and

Court of Directors of the Sierra Leone Company, Freetown, June 5, 1798, PRO, CO 268/5.

21. Bowles to Grenville, June 5, 1798, AGI, Cuba, leg. 2371; Macaulay to Chairman, June 5, 1798, PRO, CO 268/5.

22. London *Morning Chronicle,* Aug. 21, 1798.

23. Stephens, *Life of Bowles,* pp. 27-28.

24. Plomer, *et al., Dictionary of Printers,* p. 31.

25. London *Morning Chronicle,* Aug. 21, 1798.

26. Bowles to Portland, Adelphi, Aug. 21, 1798, AGI, Cuba, leg. 2371; Pearson to Bowles, Leicester Square, Aug. 29, 1798, AGI, Cuba, leg. 212B.

27. Bowles to Portland, Aug. 21, 1798, AGI, Cuba, leg. 2371.

28. Bowles to Reeves, Portsmouth, March 1, 1799, Add. MSS 37,878.

29. Portland to Simcoe, Oct. 25, 1795, in Frederick J. Turner, ed., *Correspondence of the French Ministers to the United States, 1791-1797* (Washington, 1904), p. 990; Marqués de Casa Irujo to Timothy Pickering, Philadelphia, March 2, 1797, LC, Spanish transcripts, AHN, estado, leg. 3896 bis, apartardo 3, photostat.

30. Crown to Earl of Bute, Downing St., June 3, 1796, PRO, FO 72/41.

31. Arthur St. Clair to James Ross, Pittsburgh, Sept. 6, 1796, in William H. Smith, *The St. Clair Papers; The Life and Public Services of Arthur St. Clair, Soldier of the Revolutionary War; President of the Continental Congress; and Governor of the North-Western Territory* (Cincinnati, 1882), II, p. 411.

32. Robert Liston to Grenville, Philadelphia, March 16, 1797, PRO, FO 115/5; John Chisholm to Rufus King, London, Nov. 29, 1797, in Frederick J. Turner, ed., "Documents on the Blount Conspiracy, 1795-1797," *AHR,* X (April, 1905), pp. 596-597. Chisholm, following Dalton's and Bowles's example in 1789-1790, unsuccessfully tried to get Creek and Cherokee chiefs currently negotiating with the United States in Philadelphia to accompany him to London. Deposition of John Rogers, Germantown, Sept. 29, 1797, in *The Debates and Proceedings in the Congress of the United States . . . , Fifth Congress, 1797-1799* (Washington, 1851), pp. 2393-2394.

33. Liston to Grenville, Philadelphia, May 10, 1797, PRO, FO 115/5; *ibid.,* July 8, 1797, PRO, FO 115/5.

34. Robertson, *Miranda,* I, pp. 165ff.

35. James McHenry to St. Clair, War Office, May 1796, in Smith, *St. Clair Papers,* II, p. 395; Elijah W. Lyon, *Louisiana in French Diplomacy, 1759-1804* (Norman, 1934), p. 90.

36. Liston to Grenville, Philadelphia, April 2, 1798, PRO, FO 115/6.

37. Grenville to Liston, Downing St., June 8, 1798, PRO, FO 115/6; London *Morning Post and Gazetteer,* Oct. 26, 1798.

38. Hamilton to King, New York, Aug. 22, 1798, in Charles R. King, ed., *The Life and Correspondence of Rufus King; Comprising His Letters Private and Official, His Public Documents, and His Speeches* (New York, 1894-1900), II, p. 659; King to Pickering, London, Oct. 20, 1798, in *ibid.,* pp. 453-454.

39. Milfort, *Memoir,* pp. xiv ff.

40. Details of William Windham's career may be found in Earl of Rosebury, ed., *The Windham Papers; The Life and Correspondence of the Rt. Hon. William Windham, 1750-1810, A Member of Pitt's First Cabinet and the Ministry of "All the Talents," including Hitherto Unpublished Letters . . .* (London, 1913). Important Bowles letters are scattered throughout the Windham Papers in the British Museum.

41. British political conditions, divisions in the cabinet, and disputes whether to employ British forces primarily in Europe or against enemy colonies are recounted in John Steven Watson, *The Reign of George III, 1760-1815* (Oxford, 1960), pp. 376ff.

42. Bowles to Reeves, March 1, 1799, Add. MSS 37,878.

43. Reeves to Bowles, Nov. 10, 1798, AGI, Cuba, leg. 2371; *ibid.*, Feb. 4, 1799, AGI, Cuba, leg. 212B.
44. John Brickwood to Bowles, London, Jan. 30, 1799, AGI, Cuba, leg. 189-2.
45. John Leslie to Panton, London, Feb. 26, 1799, Cruzat Papers, University of Florida Library. George Chalmers was a distinguished historian and antiquarian who had left Maryland and returned to Britain in 1775. Though both Chalmers and Bowles were Maryland Loyalists it is doubtful this had any influence on the Board of Trade.
46. Dunmore to Pitt, Upper Berkeley Square, April 25, 1799, PRO, Chatham Papers, CXXXI.
47. Chalmers to Thomas Roker, Whitehall, April 22, 1797, Add. MSS 22,900.
48. Testimony of Mary Magdelin Henry Jones, Montreal District, Nov. 11, 1794, PRO, CO 42/102; Connolly to Duke of Kent, London, June 20, 1799, PRO, CO 42/88.
49. Joseph Hardcastle to Bowles, London, Dec. 24, 1798, AGI, Cuba, leg. 2372.
50. John Owen to Bowles, London, May 31, 1799, AGI, Cuba, leg. 183A.
51. J. W. Campbell to Bowles, Hammersmith, Nov. 1798, AGI, Cuba, leg. 189-2; Chevalier Ruspini to Bowles, Oct. 17, 1798, AGI, Cuba, leg. 216A.
52. Baynton to Bowles, Dunnamanaugh, Aug. 23, 1798, AGI, Cuba, leg. 2371.
53. Dalziel Hunter to Bowles, 1799?, AGI, Cuba, leg. 2371.
54. It is most probable that John Bowles was Carington Bowles's elder brother and William's first cousin. Even though John was a prolific and well-known pamphleteer, surprisingly almost nothing has been printed about his personal life. After an extensive, nearly fruitless search, the author has come to the conclusion that the definitive key to John Bowles's genealogy is still buried in English manuscript records.
55. Verses addressed to General Bowles, AGI, Cuba, leg. 192.
56. I. Browne to Bowles, Feb. 13, 1799, AGI, Cuba, leg. 216A.
57. John Genest, *Some Account of the English Stage, from the Restoration in 1660 to 1830* (Bath, 1832), VII, p. 405.
58. Hannah Brand to Bowles, Norwich, Feb. 17, 1799, AGI, Cuba, leg. 212B; Hannah Brand to Mrs. Browne, London, 1799?, AGI, Cuba, leg. 216A.
59. Townshend to Bowles, Oct. 30, 1798, AGI, Cuba, leg. 216A; *ibid.*, Dec. 25, 1798, AGI, Cuba, leg. 216A; T. Campbell to Bowles, no date, AGI, Cuba, leg. 216A.
60. Dunmore to Bowles, London, 1798?, AGI, Cuba, leg. 2371.
61. Brickwood to Bowles, London, Jan. 11, 1799, AGI, Cuba, leg. 192.
62. There is a convenient sketch of Thomas Phillips by R. E. Graves in the *DNB*.
63. Michael Flanagan to Bowles, HMS *Dover*, Deptford, Feb. 5, 1799, AGI, Cuba, leg. 189-2.
64. Reeves to Bowles, Feb. 4, 1799, AGI, Cuba, leg. 212B.
65. Pearson to Bowles, Leicester Square, Feb. 3, 1799, AGI, Cuba, leg. 212B.

CHAPTER VII

1. Brickwood to Reeves, London, Jan. 25, 1799, AGI, Cuba, leg. 212B; Bowles to Reeves, Portsmouth, March 1, 1799, Add. MSS 37,878.
2. A contemporary account of Portsmouth is George Pinckard, *Notes on the West Indies: Written During the Expedition under the Command of the Late General Sir Ralph Abercromby: Including Observations on the Island of Barbados . . .* (London, 1806), I, pp. 32ff.
3. Flanagan to Bowles, Feb. 5, 1799, AGI, Cuba, leg. 189-2.
4. Mrs. Browne to Bowles, Feb. 21, 1799, AGI, Cuba, leg. 216A.
5. Sabatier to Bowles, London, Feb. 28, 1799, AGI, Cuba, leg. 2371.

6. Hannah Brand to Bowles, Feb. 17, 1799, AGI, Cuba, leg. 212B.

7. Bowles to Reeves, Portsmouth, March 1, 1799, Add. MSS 37,878.

8. *Ibid.*, Pilgrim, April 17, 1799, Add. MSS 37,878.

9. *Ibid.* Brief descriptions of Bridgetown and Barbados are in *Lady Nugent's Journal*, pp. 10-11; and James A. Thome and J. Horace Kimball, *Emancipation in the West Indies. A Six Months' Tour in Antigua, Barbadoes, and Jamaica, in the Year 1837* (New York, 1838), pp. 53ff.

10. George Rickets to John King, Barbados, June 20, 1799, PRO, CO 28/65.

11. *Lady Nugent's Journal* gives the best contemporary account of affairs in Kingston and Jamaica.

12. Bowles to Reeves?, Kingston, June 16, 1799, Add. MSS 37,878. Napoleon was trying to re-establish France's American empire, and the former French colonies, Louisiana (including West Florida) and Haiti, whose economies complemented each other, were to be the nucleus.

13. Bowles to ?, Kingston, July 14, 1799, AGI, Cuba, leg. 212B.

14. Bowles to Reverend Sir, Kingston, July 28, 1799, AGI, Cuba, leg. 189-2.

15. Testimony of Hugh Ferguson, Pensacola, June 16, 1800, LC, ANC, Fla., leg. 1, expediente 24, núm. 10, Cuban transcript.

16. *Ibid.;* Bowles to ?, 1799 (draft), AGI, Cuba, leg. 2372; *Lady Nugent's Journal*, p. 18.

17. William Dowdeswell to Portland, Government House, Nov. 12, 1799, PRO, CO 23/39; Bowles to ?, Apalachicola, Nov. 27, 1799, AGI, Cuba, leg. 212B; Balcarres to Bowles, King's House, Jamaica, July 15, 1799, AGI, Cuba, leg. 2371.

18. Testimony of Ferguson, June 16, 1800, LC, ANC, Fla., leg. 1, expediente 24, núm. 10, Cuban transcript.

19. Bowles to Reeves?, June 16, 1799, Add. MSS 37,878.

20. Reeves to Bowles, Feb. 5, 1799, AGI, Cuba, leg. 2371.

21. *Bahama Gazette,* Aug. 20-23, 1799.

22. Dowdeswell to Portland, May 1, 1800, PRO, CO 23/39; Dowdeswell's answer to Forbes, June 22, 1799, Cruzat Papers, University of Florida Library; Dowdeswell to Bowles, Government House, Aug. 27, 1799, AGI, Cuba, leg. 2371.

23. Forbes to Panton, Nassau, Aug. 25, 1799, Cruzat Papers, University of Florida Library.

24. Andrew Ellicott, *The Journal of Andrew Ellicott, Late Commissioner on Behalf of the United States during Part of the Year 1796, the Years 1797, 1798, 1799, and Part of the Year 1800 . . .* (Philadelphia, 1814), pp. 177ff.

25. Miguel Joseph de Azanza to Mariano Luis de Urquijo, Mexico, July 27, 1799, AGI, estado, leg. 28-46.

26. *Bahama Gazette,* Aug. 30, 1799.

27. Forbes to Panton, Aug. 25, 1799, Cruzat Papers, University of Florida Library.

28. Bowles to ?, Nov. 27, 1799, AGI, Cuba, leg. 212B; *Bahama Gazette,* Nov. 15-19, 1799.

29. Declaration by Ellicott and Stephen Minor, Apalachicola, Aug. 15, 1799, Add. MSS 37,878.

30. Bowles to Reeves, Apalachicola, Nov. 26, 1799, Add. MSS 37,878; The Indians knew that Bowles had left London bound for Muskogee, and no doubt this strengthened their determination to oppose the Americans. See Jack D. L. Holmes, "The Southern Boundary Commission, the Chattahoochee River, and the Florida Seminoles, 1799," *FHQ,* XLIV (April, 1966), pp. 312ff.

31. Bowles to Ellicott, Fox Point, Sept. 22, 1799, Ellicott, *Journal,* pp. 227-228.

32. James Wooldridge to Ellicott, Fox Point, Sept. 22, 1799, in *ibid.,* pp. 226-227.

33. Ellicott to Hawkins, Apalachee, Oct. 9, 1799, in *ibid.,* p. 230.

34. *Ibid.,* pp. 232ff.

35. Manuel Garcia's diary, March 7, 1800, LC, ANC, Fla., leg. 1, ex-

pediente 24, núm. 5, Cuban transcript.

36. Bowles to Wooldridge, Perryman's, Oct. 23, 1799, AGI, Cuba, leg. 216A; Bowles to ?, Nov. 27, 1799, AGI, Cuba, leg. 212B.

37. Bowles to Wooldridge, Wekiva, Nov. 6, 1799, AGI, Cuba, leg. 216A.

38. Depositions on Bowles's arrival, in Enrique White to Marqués de Someruelos, St. Augustine, Nov. 2, 1799, AGI, Cuba, leg. 2355.

39. Dowdeswell to Bowles, Nassau, March 5, 1800, AGI, Cuba, leg. 183A.

40. Panton to Forrester, Pensacola, Dec. 9, 1799, Cruzat Papers, University of Florida Library.

41. Hawkins to Panton, Coweta Tallahassee, Oct. 9, 1799, AGI, Cuba, leg. 216A; *Bahama Gazette,* March 22-26, 1799.

42. Proclamation, Wekiva, Oct. 26, 1799, AGI, Cuba, leg. 2371.

43. Report of Emautlau Haujo, Coweta Tallahassee, Dec. 10, 1799, GDAH, Creek Indian Letters, 1794-1812, II.

44. Pedro Cevallos to Crown, London, May 24, 1803, AGS, estado, leg. 2631; Someruelos to Salcedo, Havana, Aug. 18, 1803, AGI, Cuba, leg. 2355.

45. A talk of one of the chiefs of Muskogee, Wekiva, Oct. 26, 1799, Add. MSS 37,878.

46. Bargain for Bowles's capture, St. Marks, Oct. 5, 1799, AGI, Cuba, leg. 2355.

47. Forrester to Panton, Apalachee, Oct. 1, 1799, Cruzat Papers, University of Florida Library; *ibid.,* Oct. 16, 1799, AGI, Cuba, leg. 203.

48. James Durouzeaux to Folch, Coweta, Nov. 9, 1799, AGI, Cuba, leg. 2355.

49. The best account of Hawkins and his dealings with the Indians is Merritt B. Pound, *Benjamin Hawkins, Indian Agent* (Athens, Ga., 1951).

50. Bowles to John Adams, Wekiva, Oct. 31, 1799, Add. MSS 37,878.

51. Bowles to Little Prince of the Broken Arrow, Achookwheethla, Nov. 30, 1799, AGI, Cuba, leg. 2371.

52. Marqués de Casa Irujo to Urquijo, Philadelphia, Jan. 13, 1800, LC, Spanish transcripts, AHN, estado, leg. 3897.

53. *Ibid.,* March 6, 1800, LC, Spanish transcripts, AHN, estado, leg. 3889 bis, expediente 10, núm. 142.

54. Bowles to Reeves, Nov. 26, 1799, Add. MSS 37,878.

55. A. G. to W. Lach, Downing Street, Dec., 1799, Cruzat Papers, University of Florida Library.

56. Portland to Dowdeswell, Whitehall, Jan. 25 1800, PRO, CO 24/14.

57. Henry Dundas' memorandum, Wimbledon, March 31, 1800, PRO, Chatham Papers, CCXLIII.

58. Liston to Grenville, Philadelphia, Dec. 13, 1799, PRO, FO 115/7.

59. Bowles to Capt. Neuville, Perryman's, Nov. 31, 1799, AGI, Cuba, leg. 216A.

60. Bowles to Ferguson, Thackiwithla, Jan. 28, 1800, LC, ANC, Fla., leg. 1, expediente 24, núm. 4, Cuban transcript.

61. Ferguson to Bowles, Jan. 28, 1800, LC, ANC, Fla., leg. 1, expediente 24, núm. 3, Cuban transcript.

62. Bowles to Reeves?, June 16, 1799, Add. MSS 37,878.

63. Miller to Reeves, Nassau, Jan. 30, 1800, Add. MSS 37,879.

64. Bowles's proclamation, Apalachicola, Nov. 26, 1799, Add. MSS 37,878; unsigned and undated letter, 1800?, AGI, Cuba, leg. 218.

CHAPTER VIII

1. *Bahama Gazette,* Feb. 7-11, 1800.

2. John Sevier's Executive Journal, Knoxville, Feb. 25, 1800, *ETHSP,* VI (1934), 110.

3. Manuel Rengil to Irujo, Savannah, March 31, 1800, LC, Spanish transcripts, AHN, estado, leg. 3889 bis, expediente 10, núm. 148, photostat; *Bahama Gazette,* April 11-15, 1800.

4. Leslie to Chalmers, Winchester St.,

May 21, 1800, Add. MSS 22,901.

5. Potato King to Bowles, Flint River, Feb. 14, 1800, AGI, Cuba, leg. 2372.

6. Details about the capture of Panton's warehouse are in AGI, Cuba, leg. 2372.

7. Hunter to Bowles, outside St. Georges Island, March 5, 1800, Greenslade Papers, University of Florida Library; Portell to Folch, San Carlos de Barrancas, June 7, 1800, AGI, Cuba, leg. 2355.

8. Portell to Folch, June 7, 1800, AGI, Cuba, leg. 2355; Muskogee Declaration of War, Estifunalga, April 5, 1800, AGI, Cuba, leg. 2372.

9. Many details of the siege are in LC, ANC, Fla., leg. 4, expediente 1, Cuban transcript.

10. Portell to Bowles, St. Marks, April 27, 1800, AGI, Cuba, leg. 2355.

11. Bowles to Hunter, St. Marks, June 9, 1800, AGI, Cuba, leg. 183A.

12. Folch to Marqués de Casa Calvo, Pensacola, June 2, 1800, AGI, Cuba, leg. 2355.

13. Portell to Folch, June 7, 1800, AGI, Cuba, leg. 2355.

14. Bowles to Portell, Camp before St. Marks, May 17, 1800, AGI, Cuba, leg. 2355.

15. Portell to Bowles, St. Marks, May 19, 1800, in Folch to Casa Calvo, June 2, 1800, AGI, Cuba, leg. 2355.

16. Folch to Casa Calvo, June 2, 1800, AGI, Cuba, leg. 2355.

17. Bowles to Hunter, June 9, 1800, AGI, Cuba, leg. 183A.

18. Bowles to Tostonee Opoie, Ft. St. Marks, May 22, 1800, GDAH, Creek Indian Letters, 1794-1812, II, p. 587.

19. Hawkins to Panton, Coweta, June 11, 1800, Cruzat Papers, University of Florida Library.

20. James Jackson to Hawkins, Louisville, Feb. 4, 1800, GDAH, Executive Minutes, Nov. 8, 1799 - Nov. 4, 1800.

21. Bowles to Jackson, St. Marks, June 6, 1800, GDAH, Creek Indian Letters, 1794-1812, II, p. 590.

22. Stephen Folch, journal of a voyage to the Creek Nation, 1803, AGI, Cuba, leg. 2372.

23. Irujo to Urquijo, Philadelphia, July 16, 1800, LC, Spanish transcripts, AHN, estado, leg. 3889 bis, expediente 10, núm. 154, photostat.

24. Félix Berenguer de Marquina to Crown, July 27, 1800, AGN, correspondencia de los virreyes, primera serie, tomo 203.

25. Portell to Folch, June 7, 1800, AGI, Cuba, leg. 2355.

26. Ferguson's testimony, June 16, 1800, LC, ANC, Fla., leg. 1, expediente 24, núm. 10, Cuban transcript.

27. Relación de la reconquista del fuerte de apalachee . . . , LC, ANC, Fla., leg. 2, expediente 21, Cuban transcript.

28. Bowles's proclamation, St. Marks, June 21, 1800, AGI, Cuba, leg. 183A.

29. Bowles to Spanish Commandant, St. Marks, June 23, 1800, AGI, Cuba, leg. 183A.

30. Bowles to Folch, St. Marks, June 23, 1800, AGI, Cuba, leg. 183A.

31. Folch to Garcia, Gavilon, June 19, 1800, LC, ANC, Fla., leg. 2, expediente 21, Cuban transcript.

32. Garcia to Casa Calvo, Leal, July 11, 1800, LC, ANC, Fla., leg. 2, expediente 21, Cuban transcript.

33. John Innerarity to Panton, St. Marks, July 5, 1800, LC, ANC, Fla., leg. 1, expediente 12, núm. 12, Cuban transcript.

34. Garcia to Casa Calvo, July 11, 1800, LC, ANC, Fla., leg. 2, expediente 21, Cuban transcript.

35. Bowles to ?, Miccosukee, Dec. 11, 1801, Add. MSS 27,859.

36. Relación de la reconquista del fuerte de Apalachee . . . , LC, ANC, Fla., leg. 2, expediente 21, Cuban transcript.

37. Bowles to ?, fragment, AGI, Cuba, leg. 2371.

38. Bowles to Folch, Miccosukee, July 2, 1800, AGI, Cuba, leg. 2372.

39. Folch to Bowles, St. Marks, July 4, 1800, AGI, Cuba, leg. 183A.

40. Hawkins to Panton, Ft. Wilkinson, July 10, 1800, LC, ANC, Fla., leg. 1, expediente 12, núm. 13, Cuban transcript.

41. Ibid., and enclosures. The broken days were a means of reckoning

time. If the Indians were to meet on a specified future day, native runners sent out to the villages to notify them each carried a bundle of sticks. One was broken each day, and when the last stick was broken it was the day the Indians were to be assembled.

42. Winthrop Sargent to John Marshall, Mississippi Territory, July 23, 1800, in Dunbar Rowland, ed., *The Mississippi Territorial Archives, 1798-1803, Executive Journals of Governor Winthrop Sargent and Governor William Charles Cole Claiborne* (Nashville, 1905), I, p. 263.

43. Franco-Spanish Treaty, San Ildefonso, Oct. 1, 1800, in Frances G. Davenport and Charles O. Paullin, eds., *European Treaties Bearing on the History of the United States and Its Dependencies* (Washington, 1917-1937), IV, pp. 181-182.

44. Casa Calvo to Urquijo, New Orleans, Oct. 19, 1800, LC, Spanish transcript, AHN, estado, leg. 3889 bis, expediente 10, núm. 179, photostat.

45. Sargent to Marshall, Mississippi Territory, Aug. 10, 1800, Rowland, *Mississippi Archives,* I, p. 266; White to Someruelos, St. Augustine, Nov. 14, 1800, AGI, Cuba, leg. 2355.

46. White to Someruelos, Nov. 14, 1800, AGI, Cuba, leg. 2355.

47. The standard account of the East

Florida rebellion is Richard K. Murdoch, *The Georgia-Florida Frontier, 1793-1796; Spanish Reaction to French Intrigue and American Designs* (Berkeley, 1951).

48. Bowles to Richard Lang, Ft. St. Marks, June 5, 1800, GDAH, Creek Indian Letters, 1794-1812, II, pp. 588-589; Thomas King to Jackson, St. Marys, Oct. 15, 1800, GDAH, E. and W. Fla., 1764-1850.

49. Lang got drunk on election day and left Bowles's letter lying out where it was discovered. To protect himself he wrote the Georgia governor and told him of Bowles's overtures, but this did not deter Lang or Jones, who were as often in Florida as in Georgia, from continuing to intrigue with Bowles about raising a force on the south side of the St. Marys River. Lang to Jackson, Camden Co., June 26, 1800, GDAH, Executive Minutes; King to Jackson, Oct. 15, 1800, GDAH, E. and W. Fla., 1764-1850; William Jones to Bowles, St. Marys, Aug. 17, 1800, GDAH, E. and W. Fla., 1764-1850.

50. Jackson's proclamation, Louisville, July 8, 1800, GDAH, Executive Minutes.

51. John King to ?, Coleraine, Oct. 16, 1800, GDAH, E. and W. Fla., 1764-1850; King to Jackson, St. Marys, Oct. 29, 1800, GDAH, E. and W. Fla., 1764-1850; White to Someruelos, St. Augustine, Nov. 14, 1800, LC, EF, 28B3.

CHAPTER IX

1. Miller to Hobart, Leicester Square, June 22, 1802, PRO, CO 23/42; Hunter and Walker to King Kinagie, Nassau, Feb. 10, 1801, AGI, Cuba, leg. 2372; Walker to Bowles, Hunter's Bay, July 8, 1801, AGI, Cuba, leg. 2372. Panton died early in 1801, and John Forbes became head of the firm.

2. John DeLacy to Bowles, Miccosukee, Dec. 9, 1801, Add. MSS 27,859; Bowles to Walker, Dec. 24, 1801, AGI, Cuba, leg. 2372.

3. Reeves to Miller, London, June

19, 1802, PRO, CO 23/42.

4. DeLacy to Bowles, Dec. 9, 1801, Add. MSS 27,859.

5. DeLacy to Bowles, March 11, 1802, AGI, Cuba, leg. 2372.

6. *Ibid.*

7. *Ibid.,* Bootle Johnson to Bowles, Nassau, March 12, 1802, AGI, Cuba, leg. 2372; John Ross to Bowles, Nassau, Nov. 20, 1802, AGI, Cuba, leg. 218; William Middleton and Smith to Bowles, Feb. 15, 1801, AGI, Cuba, leg. 218.

8. Irujo to Urquijo, Philadelphia,

Nov. 26, 1800, LC, Spanish transcripts, AHN, estado, leg. 3897, apartado 3, núm. 194, photostat.

9. John Harris to ?, Ft. Wilkinson, June 6, 1801, NA, Ft. Wilkinson, 1798-1806.

10. White to Someruelos, St. Augustine, Dec. 2, 1801, LC, EF, 28B3; Francis Fatio, Jr., to White, St. Augustine, Nov. 12, 1801, LC, EF, 197B16.

11. Dearborn to Hawkins, War Dept., April 6, 1802, NA, War Dept., Secretary's Office, Letters Sent, Indian Affairs, A:59.

12. Jacobo Dubreuil to Casa Calvo, St. Marks, March 29, 1801, AGI, Cuba, leg. 2355.

13. "State of Muskogee" presented for publication in *Nassau Gazette,* March 4, 1802, Cruzat Papers, University of Florida Library; a brief discussion of the Muskogee navy with accompanying documents is Lyle N. McAlister, ed., "The Marine Forces of William Augustus Bowles and His 'State of Muskogee,'" *FHQ,* XXXII (July, 1953), pp. 3ff.

14. Marine Articles of War to be Observed on Board All Vessels in the Service of the State of Muskogee, AGI, Cuba, leg. 2372; Muskogee Legal Proceedings, PRO, CO 23/42; instructions to Capt. Ward, Estifunalga, June 4, 1802, PRO, CO 23/42.

15. Muskogee Legal Proceedings, PRO, CO 23/42.

16. Juan Ventura Morales to Miguel Cayetano Soler, New Orleans, July 31, 1802, LC, Spanish transcripts, AGI, Santo Domingo, leg. 87-1-29, núm. 113.

17. Dubreuil to Casa Calvo, St. Marks, March 29, 1801, AGI, Cuba, leg. 2355; James Jones to Bowles, Nassau, June 2, 1801, AGI, Cuba, leg. 218; William Stanley to Bowles, copy made Nov. 14, 1800, LC, EF, 179B16.

18. John Forrester to White, Six Mile Creek, July 7, 1801, LC, EF, 116L9; "State of Muskogee," Cruzat Papers, University of Florida Library; minutes of Muskogee, 1801-1802, AGI, Cuba, leg. 218.

19. Bowles to Reeves?, Miccosukee, Dec. 11, 1801, Add. MSS 27,859.

20. *Ibid.*

21. *Ibid.*

22. Bowles to St. Marks' commandant, Miccosukee, June 4, 1801, AGI, Cuba, leg. 2372.

23. Irujo to Cevallos, Washington, March 24, 1802, LC, Spanish transcripts, AHN, estado, leg. 5630, núm. 266.

24. Dearborn to Hawkins, War Dept., April 6, 1802, NA, War Dept., Secretary's Office, Letters Sent, Indian Affairs, A:59.

25. Hawkins to Edward Wright, Creek Agency, July 16, 1801, NA, Ft. Wilkinson, 1798-1806.

26. Hawkins to Dearborn, Ft. Wilkinson, May 8, 1802, in Benjamin Hawkins, *Letters of Benjamin Hawkins, 1796-1806* . . . (Savannah, 1916), p. 418.

27. Dearborn to William Claiborne, War Dept., June 11, 1802, NA, Letters by Secretary of War, Indian Affairs, M-15.

28. Hawkins to Dearborn, Natchez, Nov. 14, 1801, in Hawkins, *Letters,* p. 396.

29. Bowles to Reeves?, Dec. 11, 1801, Add. MSS 27,859.

30. Miller to Portland, May 25, 1801, PRO, CO 23/40.

31. John Forbes to Halkett, Pensacola, March 8?, 1802, Cruzat Papers, University of Florida Library.

32. Minutes of Muskogee, Jan. 14, 1802, AGI, Cuba, leg. 218.

33. Irujo to Cevallos, March 24, 1802, LC, Spanish transcripts, AHN, estado, leg. 5630, núm. 266.

34. Bowles to St. Marks' Commandant, Camp before St. Marks, Jan. 23, 1802, AGI, Cuba, leg. 2372.

35. Bowles to My Lord (draft), 1802?, AGI, Cuba, leg. 183A.

36. Junta de Guerra, New Orleans, Feb. 12, 1802, AGI, Cuba, leg. 2355.

37. Treaty of Peace between Great Britain, France, Spain, and the Batavian Republic, Amiens, March 27, 1802, in Davenport and Paullin,

European Treaties, IV, pp. 187-188.

38. DeLacy to Bowles, Nassau, March 12, 1802, AGI, Cuba, leg. 2372.

39. Dubreuil to Salcedo, St. Marks, June 28, 1802, included with Juan Ventura Morales to Cayetano Soler, New Orleans, July 31, 1802, LC, Spanish transcripts, AGI, Santo Domingo, leg. 87-1-29, núm. 114.

40. Morales to Soler, July 31, 1802, LC, Spanish transcripts, AGI, Santo Domingo, leg. 87-1-29, núm. 115.

41. Morales to Soler, July 31, 1802, LC, Spanish transcripts, AGI, Santo Domingo, leg. 87-1-29, núm. 114 and 115.

42. DeLacy to Bowles, March 12, 1802, AGI, Cuba, leg. 2372.

43. John Ross to Bowles, Nassau, Nov. 20, 1802, AGI, Cuba, leg. 218.

44. Preliminary treaty of peace, St. Marks, Aug. 20, 1802, in Dubreuil to Folch, Aug. 22, 1802, AGI, Cuba, leg. 2355; Dubreuil's report on the Creek-Spanish Treaty, St. Johns River, Sept. 7, 1802, Cruzat Papers, University of Florida Library.

45. Benito Peres to Pedro Cevallos, Mérida, Aug. 15, 1802, AGI, estado, leg. 35-45.

46. DeLacy to Bowles, Nassau, March 10, 1802, AGI, Cuba, leg. 2372.

47. Court of Admiralty, Nassau, Sept. 14, 1802, AGI, Cuba, leg. 2372.

48. Halkett to Lord Hobart, Government House, Nov. 14, 1802, PRO, CO 23/42.

49. Halkett to John Sullivan, Oct. 13, 1802, PRO, CO 23/42.

50. Proceedings in Court of Admiralty, Bahama Islands, 1802, Cruzat Papers, University of Florida Library.

51. Halkett to John Milledge, Bahamas, Nov. 20, 1802, GDAH, Georgia, loose papers, transcript, Lockey Col.; Halkett to Someruelos, New Providence, Sept. 26, 1802, AGI, Cuba, leg. 2355.

52. Kinache's promise to pay $400 to Richard Powers in presence of William Harris and Bowles, Miccosukee, Sept. 20, 1802, AGI, Cuba, leg. 2372.

53. Windham to ?, Pall Mall, Nov. 3, 1802, in Rosebury, *Windham Papers,* II, pp. 201-202.

54. ? to Garcia, Aug. 28, 1802, LC, ANC, Fla., leg. 2, expediente 22, Cuban transcript.

55. Bowles to ?, Key Biscayne, Oct. 25, 1802, AGI, Cuba, leg. 2372; Bowles to Halkett, Camp Cape Florida, Oct. 25, 1802, AGI, Cuba, leg. 2372.

CHAPTER X

1. Thomas J. C. Williams, *A History of Washington County, Maryland, from the Earliest Settlements to the Present Time, including a History of Hagerstown* (Hagerstown, 1906), I, p. 135. See also W. C. Mallalieu's sketch of Key in the *DAB.*

2. Williams, *Washington County,* I, pp. 131, 144, 165, 177, 182, 561.

3. *Ibid.,* pp. 107, 182, 562.

4. James R. Jacobs, *Tarnished Warrior; Major-General James Wilkinson* (New York, 1938), p. 192.

5. John H. Frere to Lord Hawkesbury, Madrid, Jan. 27, 1803, PRO, FO 72/48.

6. Someruelos to White, Havana, April 17, 1803, LC, EF, 7A.

7. Estevan Folch, journal of a voyage

to the Creek Nation from Pensacola, 1803, AGI, Cuba, leg. 2372.

8. Order in Council, State of Muskogee, Tuchacefalle, March 18, 1803, AGI, Cuba, leg. 218.

9. Folch, journal of a voyage, 1803, AGI, Cuba, leg. 2372.

10. Hawkins to Jonathan Halsted, Creek Agency, March 24, 1803, NA, Ft. Wilkinson, 1798-1806.

11. Hawkins to James Madison, July, 1803, in Pound, *Hawkins,* pp. 194-195.

12. John Forbes, "A Journal of John Forbes, May, 1803; The Seizure of William Augustus Bowles," *FHQ,* IX (April, 1931), p. 282; Folch, journal of a voyage, 1803, AGI, Cuba, leg. 2372.

13. Ynstrucciones a que deve ceñirse el cadete con funciones de abanderado Don Estevan Folch, 1803, AGI, Cuba, leg. 2355.

14. "Journal of John Forbes," p. 282; Folch, journal of a voyage, 1803, AGI, Cuba, leg. 2372.

15. Dearborn to Hawkins, War Dept., May 24, 1803, NA, War Dept., Secretary's Office, Letters Sent, Indian Affairs, A:59.

16. Folch, journal of a voyage, 1803, AGI, Cuba, leg. 2372; "Journal of John Forbes," p. 287.

17. Hawkins to John Milledge, Creek Agency, June 8, 1803, *Georgia Republican,* June 23, 1803; Thomas S. Woodward, *Woodward's Reminiscences of the Creek, or Muscogee Indians, Contained in Letters to Friends in Georgia and Alabama* (Montgomery, 1859), p. 49.

18. Folch, journal of a voyage, 1803, AGI, Cuba, leg. 2372; "Journal of John Forbes," p. 287; Durouzeaux to Dubreuil, Coweta, June 29, 1803, AGI, Cuba, leg. 2372; J. D. Driesbach to Lyman C. Draper, Baldwin Co., Ala., July, 1874, Va. State Library, Draper MSS, Georgia, Alabama, and South Carolina Papers, V, microfilm.

19. Arthur P. Whitaker, *The Mississippi Question, 1795-1803: A Study in Trade, Politics, and Diplomacy* (New York, 1934), pp. 173-174.

20. Salcedo to Someruelos, New Orleans, June 11, 1803, AGI, Cuba, leg. 2355; Albert J. Pickett, *History of Alabama and Incidentally of Georgia and Mississippi, from the Earliest Period* (Sheffield, 1896), p. 471.

21. Salcedo to Someruelos, June 11, 1803, AGI, Cuba, leg. 2355.

22. Hawkins to Madison, July, 1803, in Pound, *Hawkins,* pp. 194-195.

23. Dearborn to Hawkins, War Dept., July 13, 1803, NA, War Dept., Secretary's Office, Letters Sent, Indian Affairs, A:59; General Anderson to David Meriwether, Aug. 18, 1803, *ASP, IA,* II, pp. 792-793.

24. Dubreuil to Folch, Apalachee, June 22, 1803, AGI, Cuba, leg. 2355.

25. Stephens, *Life of Bowles,* p. 31.

26. Young, *Revenge,* p. 7.

27. Conclusión fiscal, Havana, Jan. 11, 1805, LC, ANC, Fla., leg. 4, expediente 1, Cuban transcript; sentencia, Sept. 28, 1805, LC, ANC, Fla., leg. 4, expediente 1, Cuban transcript.

28. Miller to John Sullivan, Leicester Square, Jan. 14, 1804, PRO, CO 23/46.

29. Josef Antonio de Caballero to Captain General of Florida, San Lorenzo, Oct. 10, 1806, AGI, Cuba, leg. 1856.

30. *Gentleman's Magazine,* LXXVI (March, 1806), p. 281; *ibid.* (July, 1806), p. 676.

31. Someruelos to ?, Havana, April 29, 1805, AGI, Cuba, leg. 1717.

32. Bowles to Folch, 1800?, AGI, Cuba, leg. 183A.

33. Thomas Pinckney to Gov. Mitchell, Charleston, March 10, 1813, GDAH, Creek Indian Letters, 1813-1829, III, p. 769. For additional information on Bowles's Indian family see chap. 1, n. 30.

34. Arthur Wellesley, memorandum, Nov. 18, 1806, in Arthur Wellesley, First Duke of Wellington, *Supplementary Despatches and Memoranda of Field Marshal Arthur, Duke of Wellington, K.G. . . . ,* ed. Arthur R. Wellington (London, 1858-1872), VI, pp. 35-38; Wellesley Memorandum, Nov. 20, 1806, in *ibid.,* pp. 45-47; Prince of Peace to Viceroy of New Spain, Madrid, Dec. 4, 1806, AGN, historia, tomo 49, núm. 36.

35. A convenient study discussing British strategy in the Floridas and Louisiana, 1814-1815, from the American viewpoint is John S. Bassett, *The Life of Andrew Jackson* (Garden City, 1911), I.

36. Neither in Robertson's *Miranda* nor in the *Archivo del General Miranda* is there any indication that Bowles and Miranda ever cooperated or even knew each other.

Bibliography

I. MANUSCRIPTS

Archivo General de Indias, Seville.
  Cuba.
  Estado.
  Gobierno: Santo Domingo.
Archivo General de la Nación, Mexico.
  Correspondencia de los virreyes, primera serie.
  Correspondencia de los virreyes, segunda serie.
  Historia.
Archivo General de Simancas, Simancas.
  Estado.
  Guerra.
British Museum, London.
  Additional manuscripts:
    22,900-22,902 (George Chalmers Correspondence).
    27,859 (Francis Place Papers).
    37,873-37,879 (William Windham Papers).
Georgia Department of Archives and History, Atlanta, Georgia.
  Creek Indian Letters, Talks, and Treaties.
  Executive Minutes.
  East and West Florida, 1764-1850.
Library of Congress, Washington, D. C.
  Archivo Nacional de Cuba, Florida (transcripts).
  East Florida Papers.
  Personal Miscellaneous, accounts 5643 and 6662.
  Public Archives of Canada, Series C, Vols. 1905 and 1907 (photostats).
  Spanish transcripts and reproductions:
    Archivo General de Indias: Cuba and Santo Domingo.
    Archivo Histórico Nacional: Estado and Consejo.
Maryland Land Office, Annapolis, Maryland.
  BC and GS.
  Ledger and Journal, Commission for Confiscated British Property.
  Liber JK#T and JK#U.

National Archives, Washington, D.C.
    Ft. Coleraine, 1795-1797.
    Ft. Wilkinson, 1798-1806.
    Letters by Secretary of War, Indian Affairs.
    War Department, Secretary's Office, Letters Sent, Indian Affairs.

Public Record Office, London.
    Chatham Papers.
    Colonial Office 23 (Bahamas).
    Colonial Office 24 (Bahamas).
    Colonial Office 28 (Barbados).
    Colonial Office 42 (Canada).
    Colonial Office 137 (Jamaica).
    Colonial Office 217 (Nova Scotia).
    Colonial Office 268 (Sierra Leone).
    Foreign Office 4 (United States).
    Foreign Office 72 (Spain).
    Foreign Office 115 (United States).

University of Florida Library, Gainesville, Florida.
    Cruzat Papers.
    Maria T. Greenslade Papers.
    Joseph B. Lockey Collection.
    Lydia Parrish Papers (microfilm).

Virginia State Library, Richmond, Virginia.
    Lyman C. Draper Manuscripts (microfilm).

Washington County, Courthouse, Hagerstown, Maryland.
    Wills.

II. NEWSPAPERS AND CONTEMPORARY PERIODICALS

Bahama Gazette, 1785-1794; 1798-1800.
Daily Advertiser (London), 1790-1791.
Gazette of the State of Georgia, 1785-1792.
Gentleman's Magazine (London), 1730-1815.
Georgia Gazette, 1791-1803.
Georgia Republican, 1803; 1806.
Lucayan Herald and Weekly Advertiser (Bahamas), 1789.
Morning Chronicle (London), 1798-1799.
Morning Post and Advertiser (London), 1798-1799.
Morning Post and Gazetteer (London), 1798-1799.
Remembrancer (London), 1776-1781.
Royal Gazette (New York), 1778-1783.

III. PRINTED BOOKS AND ARTICLES

Abbott, Wilbur C. *New York in the American Revolution.* New York, 1929.

Abernethy, Thomas P. *The South in the New Nation, 1789-1819.* Baton Rouge, 1961.

Alden, John R. *The American Revolution, 1775-1783.* New York, 1954.

American Archives: Fourth Series. Containing a Documentary History of the English Colonies in North America, from the King's Message to Parliament, of March 7, 1774, to the Declaration of Independence by the United States, ed. Peter Force. 6 vols. Washington, 1837-1846.

American State Papers. Documents, Legislative and Executive, of the Congress of the United States, Indian Affairs. 2 vols. Washington, 1832-1861.

Armytage, Frances. *The Free Port System in the British West Indies; A Study in Commercial Policy, 1766-1822.* London, 1953.

Bassett, John S. *The Life of Andrew Jackson.* 2 vols. Garden City, 1911.

Baynton, Benjamin. *Authentic Memoirs of William Augustus Bowles, Esquire, Ambassador from the United Nations of Creeks and Cherokees, to the Court of London.* London, 1791. (Also reprinted in *The Magazine of History with Notes and Queries,* Extra No. 46 [1916], pp. 103-127).

Bemis, Samuel F. *Jay's Treaty; A Study in Commerce and Diplomacy.* New Haven, 1962.

———. *Pinckney's Treaty; America's Advantage from Europe's Distress, 1783-1800.* New Haven, 1960.

Black, Eugene C. *The Association; British Extraparliamentary Political Organizations, 1769-1793.* Cambridge, 1963.

Bowles, Carington. *The Artist's Assistant in Drawing, Perspective, Etching, Engraving, Mezzotinto-Scraping, Painting on Glass, in Crayons, in Water-colours, and on Silks and Sattins. . . .* 7th ed. London, 1787.

Boyd, Julian P. *Number 7, Alexander Hamilton's Secret Attempts to Control American Foreign Policy, with Supporting Documents.* Princeton, 1964.

Boyd, Mark F. "The Fortifications at San Marcos de Apalachee," *FHQ,* XV (July, 1936), pp. 3-34.

Brown, John P. *Old Frontiers; The Story of the Cherokee Indians from Earliest Times to the Date of Their Removal to the West, 1838.* Kingsport, 1938.

Browne, William H., Hall, Clayton C., and Steiner, Bernard C., eds. *Archives of Maryland.* Baltimore, 1883———.

Burson, Caroline M. *The Stewardship of Don Esteban Miró, 1782-1792.* New Orleans, 1940.

Burt, Alfred L. *The United States, Great Britain and British North America from the Revolution to the Establishment of Peace after the War of 1812.* New Haven, 1940.

Carter, Clarence E., ed. *The Territorial Papers of the United States.* Washington, 1934———.

Caughey, John W. *Bernardo de Gálvez in Louisiana, 1776-1783.* Berkeley, 1934.

———. *McGillivray of the Creeks.* Norman, 1959.

Coleman, Kenneth. *The American Revolution in Georgia, 1763-1789.* Athens, Ga., 1958.

Corbitt, Duvon C., ed. "Papers Relating to the Georgia-Florida Frontier, 1784-1800," *GHQ,* XX-XXV (1936-1941).

Corbitt, Duvon C. and Roberta, eds. and trans. "Papers from the Spanish Archives Relating to Tennessee and the Old Southwest," *ETHSP,* IX—— (1937——).

Corbitt, Duvon C., and Lanning, John T., eds. "A Letter of Marque Issued by William Augustus Bowles as Director General of the State of Muskogee," *JSH,* XI (May, 1945), pp. 246-261.

Cotterill, Robert S. *The Southern Indians; The Story of the Civilized Tribes before Removal.* Norman, 1954.

Craton, Michael. *A History of the Bahamas.* London, 1962.

Cruikshank, Ernest A., ed. *The Correspondence of Lieut. Governor John Graves Simcoe, with Allied Documents relating to His Administration of the Government of Upper Canada.* 5 vols. Toronto, 1923-1926.

Cubberly, Frederick. "Fort George (St. Michael), Pensacola," *FHQ,* VI (April, 1928), pp. 221-234.

Davenport, Frances G. and Paullin, Charles O., eds. *European Treaties Bearing on the History of the United States and Its Dependencies.* 4 vols. Washington, 1917-1937.

The Debates and Proceedings in the Congress of the United States . . . , Fifth Congress, 1797-1799. Washington, 1851.

Dictionary of American Biography. 20 vols. New York, 1928-1936.

Dictionary of National Biography. 24 vols. London, 1937-1939.

Dole, Esther M. *Maryland During the American Revolution.* Baltimore, 1941.

Douglass, Elisha P. "The Adventurer Bowles," *WMQ,* 3rd ser., VI (January, 1949), pp. 3-23.

Downes, Randolph C. "Cherokee-American Relations in the Upper Tennessee Valley, 1776-1791," *ETHSP,* VIII (1936), pp. 35-53.

———. "Creek-American Relations, 1782-1790," *GHQ,* XXI (June, 1937), pp. 142-184.

———. "Creek-American Relations, 1790-1795," *JSH,* VIII (August, 1942), pp. 350-373.

Ellicott, Andrew. *The Journal of Andrew Ellicott, Late Commissioner on Behalf of the United States during Part of the Year 1796, the Years 1797, 1798, 1799, and Part of the Year 1800. . . .* Philadelphia, 1814.

Farquhar, Thomas M. *The History of the Bowles Family. . . .* Philadelphia, 1907.

Faye, Stanley. "British and Spanish Fortifications of Pensacola, 1781-1821," *FHQ,* XX (January, 1942), pp. 277-292.

Fitzpatrick, John C., ed. *The Writings of George Washington from the Original Manuscript Sources, 1745-1799.* 39 vols. Washington, 1931-1944.

Forbes, John. "A Journal of John Forbes, May, 1803; The Seizure of William Augustus Bowles," *FHQ,* IX (April, 1931), pp. 279-289.

Ford, Paul L., ed. *Orderly Book of the "Maryland Loyalist Regiment," June 18th, 1778, to October 12th, 1778. . . .* Brooklyn, 1891.

Freeman, Douglas Southall. *George Washington, A Biography.* 7 vols. New York, 1948-1957.

Fundaburk, Emma Lila, ed. *Southeastern Indians: Life Portraits; A Catalog of Pictures, 1564-1860.* Luverne, 1958.

"General Bowles," *Public Characters of 1801-1802* (London, 1804), pp. 118-154.

Genest, John. *Some Account of the English Stage, from the Restoration in 1660 to 1830.* 10 vols. Bath, 1832.

Great Britain, Historical Manuscripts Commission. *Report on American Manuscripts in the Royal Institution of Great Britain.* 4 vols. London, 1904-1909.

Greenslade, Marie T. "William Panton," *FHQ,* XIV (October, 1935), pp. 107-129.

Guignes, M. D. "Observations on the Philippine Islands and the Isle of France," vol. XI, *A General Collection of the Best and Most Interesting Voyages and Travels in all Parts of the World . . . ,* ed. John Pinkerton. 17 vols. London, 1808-1814.

Haarman, Albert W. "The Spanish Conquest of British West Florida, 1779-1781," *FHQ,* XXXIX (October, 1960), pp. 107-134.

Hamer, Philip M. "The British in Canada and the Southern Indians, 1790-1794," *ETHSP,* II (1930), pp. 107-134.

Hartridge, Walter C., ed. *The Letters of Don Juan McQueen to His Family, Written from Spanish East Florida, 1791-1807.* Columbia, 1943.

Hawkins, Benjamin. *Letters of Benjamin Hawkins, 1796-1806. . . .* Savannah, 1916.

———. *A Sketch of the Creek Country, in 1798 and 99.* Savannah, 1848.

Herr, Richard. *The Eighteenth-Century Revolution in Spain.* Princeton, 1958.

Holmes, Jack D. L. "The Southern Boundary Commission, the Chattahoochee River, and the Florida Seminoles, 1799," *FHQ,* XLIV (April, 1966), pp. 312-341.

Humphreys, Frank L. *Life and Times of David Humphreys, Soldier-Statesman-Poet, Belov'd of Washington.* 2 vols. New York, 1917.

Jackson, James. *The Papers of James Jackson, 1781-1798,* ed. Lilla M. Hawes. Savannah, 1955.

Jacobs, James R. *Tarnished Warrior; Major-General James Wilkinson.* New York, 1938.

Johnson, Cecil. *British West Florida, 1763-1783.* New Haven, 1943.

Jones, E. Alfred. "The Real Author of the 'Authentic Memoirs of William Augustus Bowles,'" *Maryland Historical Magazine,* XVIII (December, 1923), pp. 300-308.

Jones, Thomas. *History of New York During the Revolutionary War, and of the Leading Events in the Other Colonies at That Period,* ed. Edward F. DeLancey. 2 vols. New York, 1879.

Kappler, Charles J., ed. *Indian Affairs. Laws and Treaties.* . . . Washington, 1903——.

King, Charles R., ed. *The Life and Correspondence of Rufus King; Comprising His Letters Private and Official, His Public Documents, and His Speeches.* 6 vols. New York, 1894-1900.

Kinnaird, Lawrence. "International Rivalry in the Creek Country, Part I, The Ascendancy of Alexander McGillivray, 1783-1789," *FHQ,* X (October, 1931), pp. 59-85.

————. "The Significance of William Augustus Bowles' Seizure of Panton's Apalachee Store in 1792," *FHQ,* IX (January, 1931), pp. 156-192.

————, ed. and trans. *Spain in the Mississippi Valley, 1765-1794; Translations of Materials from the Spanish Archives in the Bancroft Library.* 3 vols. Washington, 1946.

Lewis, William. *Commercium Philosophico-Technicum; or, the Philosophical Commerce of Arts; Designed as an Attempt to Improve Arts, Trades, and Manufactures.* London, 1763.

Lincoln, Benjamin. "Journal of a Treaty Held in 1793, with the Indian Tribes North-West of the Ohio, by Commissioners of the United States," *Collections, Massachusetts Historical Society,* 3rd ser., V (1836), pp. 109-176.

Lyon, Elijah W. *Louisiana in French Diplomacy, 1759-1804.* Norman, 1934.

————, ed. "Milfort's Plan for a Franco-Creek Alliance and the Retrocession of Louisiana," *JSH,* IV (February, 1938), pp. 72-87.

McAlister, Lyle N., ed. "The Marine Forces of William Augustus Bowles and His 'State of Muskogee,'" *FHQ,* XXXII (July, 1953), pp. 3-27.

————. "William Augustus Bowles and the State of Muskogee," *FHQ,* XXXX (April, 1962), pp. 317-328.

Mackenzie, Frederick. *Diary of Frederick Mackenzie, Giving a Daily Narrative of His Military Service as an Officer of the Regiment of Royal Welch Fusilers during the Years 1775-1781 in Massachusetts, Rhode Island and New York.* 2 vols. Cambridge, 1930.

McReynolds, Edwin C. *The Seminoles.* Norman, 1957.

Malone, Henry T. *Cherokees of the Old South; A People in Transition.* Athens, Ga., 1956.

Manning, William R. *The Nootka Sound Controversy. Annual Report of the American Historical Association for the Year 1904.* Washington, 1905.

Mattison, Ray H. "The Creek Trading House from Coleraine to Fort Hawkins," *GHQ*, XXX (September, 1946), pp. 169-184.

Milfort, LeClerc de. *Memoir; or, A Quick Glance at My Various Travels and My Sojourn in the Creek Nation*, ed. and trans. Ben C. McCary. Kennesaw, Ga., 1959.

Miranda, Francisco de. *Archivo del General Miranda*. 24 vols. Caracas, 1929-1950.

Murdoch, Richard K. *The Georgia-Florida Frontier, 1793-1796; Spanish Reaction to French Intrigue and American Designs*. Berkeley, 1951.

Nugent, Maria. *Lady Nugent's Journal, Jamaica One Hundred and Thirty-eight Years ago . . .* , ed. Frank Cundall. London, 1939.

Odell, George C. D. *Annals of the New York Stage*. 15 vols. New York, 1927-1945.

Palmer, William P., McRae, Sherwin, Colston, Raleigh E., *et al.*, eds. *Calendar of Virginia State Papers and Other Manuscripts. . . .* 11 vols. Richmond, 1875-1892.

Peters, Thelma. "The American Loyalists in the Bahama Islands: Who They Were," *FHQ*, XXXX (January, 1962), pp. 226-240.

———. "The Loyalist Migration from East Florida to the Bahama Islands," *FHQ*, XXXX (October, 1961), pp. 123-141.

Pickett, Albert J. *History of Alabama and Incidentally of Georgia and Mississippi, from the Earliest Period*. Sheffield, 1896.

Pinckard, George. *Notes on the West Indies: Written During the Expedition under the Command of the Late General Sir Ralph Abercromby: Including Observations on the Island of Barbados. . . .* 3 vols. London, 1806.

Plomer, Henry R., Bushnell, George H., and Dix, Ernest R. McC. *A Dictionary of the Printers and Booksellers Who Were at Work in England, Scotland, and Ireland from 1726 to 1775*. Oxford, 1932.

Pound, Merritt B. *Benjamin Hawkins, Indian Agent*. Athens, Ga., 1951.

Raymond, William O., ed. *Winslow Papers, A.D. 1776-1826*. St. John, 1901.

Renny, Robert. *An History of Jamaica. . . .* London, 1807.

Robertson, William S. *The Life of Miranda*. 2 vols. Chapel Hill, 1929.

Rosebury, Earl of, ed. *The Windham Papers; The Life and Correspondence of the Rt. Hon. William Windham, 1750-1810, A Member of Pitt's First Cabinet and the Ministry of "All the Talents" including Hitherto Unpublished Letters. . . .* 2 vols. London, 1913.

Rowland, Dunbar, ed. *The Mississippi Territorial Archives, 1798-1803, Executive Journals of Governor Winthrop Sargent and Governor William Charles Cole Claiborne*. Nashville, 1905.

St. Vincent, J. B. G. M. Bory de. "Voyage to, and Travels through, the Four Principal Islands of the African Seas . . . ," *A Collection of Modern and Contemporary Voyages and Travels . . .* , ed. Richard Phillips, II (London, 1805-1810), pp. 1-212.

Scharf, John T. *History of Western Maryland. Being a History of*

Frederick, Montgomery, Carroll, Washington, Allegany, and Garrett Counties from the Earliest Period to the Present Day. . . . 2 vols. Philadelphia, 1882.

Schoepf, Johann D. *Travels in the Confederation, 1783-1784,* ed. and trans. Alfred J. Morrison. 2 vols. Philadelphia, 1911.

Sevier, John. "Executive Journal," *ETHSP,* VI (1934), pp. 104-128.

Siebert, Wilbur H. "The Loyalists in West Florida and the Natchez District," *MVHR,* II (March, 1916), pp. 465-483.

Smith, Paul H. *Loyalists and Redcoats: A Study in British Revolutionary Policy.* Chapel Hill, 1964.

Smith, William H. *The St. Clair Papers; The Life and Public Services of Arthur St. Clair, Soldier of the Revolutionary War; President of the Continental Congress; and Governor of the North-Western Territory.* 2 vols. Cincinnati, 1882.

Starkey, Marion L. *The Cherokee Nation.* New York, 1946.

Stephens, Alexander, ed. *The Life of General W. A. Bowles, A Native of America—Born of English Parents in Frederick County, Maryland, in the Year 1764.* London, 1803.

Stryker, William S. *The Battle of Monmouth.* Princeton, 1927.

Swan, Caleb. "Position and State of Manner and Arts in the Creek, or Muscogee Nation in 1791," in Henry R. Schoolcraft, *Information Respecting the History, Condition and Prospects of the Indian Tribes of the United States. . . .* 6 vols. Philadelphia, 1851-1857, pp. 251-283.

Swanton, John R. *Early History of the Creek Indians and Their Neighbors.* Washington, 1922.

Thome, James A. and Kimball, J. Horace. *Emancipation in the West Indies. A Six Months' Tour in Antigua, Barbadoes, and Jamaica, in the Year 1837.* New York, 1838.

Turner, Frederick J., ed. *Correspondence of the French Ministers to the United States, 1791-1797.* Washington, 1904.

———, ed. "Documents on the Blount Conspiracy, 1795-1797," *AHR,* X (April, 1905), pp. 574-606.

———. "English Policy toward America in 1790-1791," *AHR,* VII (July, 1902), pp. 706-735 and VIII (October, 1902), pp. 78-86.

Watson, John Steven. *The Reign of George III, 1760-1815.* Oxford, 1960.

Watson, Samuel. "William Augustus Bowles," *American Historical Magazine,* V (July, 1900), pp. 195-199.

Wellesley, Arthur, First Duke of Wellington. *Supplementary Despatches and Memoranda of Field Marshal Arthur, Duke of Wellington, K. G. . . . ,* ed. Arthur R. Wellington. 15 vols. London, 1858-1872.

Wertenbaker, Thomas J. *Father Knickerbocker Rebels: New York City During the Revolution.* New York, 1948.

Whitaker, Arthur P. "Alexander McGillivray, 1783-1789," *NCHR,* V (April, 1928), pp. 181-203.

————. "Alexander McGillivray, 1789-1793," *NCHR*, V (July, 1928), pp. 289-309.

————, ed. and trans. *Documents Relating to the Commercial Policy of Spain in the Floridas, with Incidental Reference to Louisiana.* DeLand, 1931.

————. *The Mississippi Question, 1795-1803: A Study in Trade, Politics, and Diplomacy.* New York, 1934.

————. "Spain and the Cherokee Indians, 1783-98," *NCHR*, IV (July, 1927), pp. 252-269.

————. *The Spanish-American Frontier: 1783-1795; The Westward Movement and the Spanish Retreat in the Mississippi Valley.* Boston, 1927.

Williams, Thomas J. C. *History of Frederick County, Maryland, from the Earliest Settlements to the Beginning of the War Between the States.* 2 vols. Frederick, 1910.

————. *A History of Washington County, Maryland, from the Earliest Settlements to the Present Time, including a History of Hagerstown.* 2 vols. Hagerstown, 1906.

Woldert, Albert. "The Last of the Cherokees in Texas, and the Life and Death of Chief Bowles," *Chronicles of Oklahoma*, I (June, 1923), pp. 179-226.

Woodward, Grace S. *The Cherokees.* Norman, 1963.

Woodward, Thomas S. *Woodward's Reminiscences of the Creek, or Muscogee Indians, Contained in Letters to Friends in Georgia and Alabama.* Montgomery, 1859.

Worcester, Donald E., ed. and trans. "Miranda's Diary of the Siege of Pensacola, 1781," *FHQ*, XXIX (January, 1951), pp. 163-196.

Wright, J. Leitch, Jr., "British Designs on the Old Southwest: Foreign Intrigue on the Florida Frontier, 1783-1803," *FHQ*, XLIV (April, 1966), pp. 265-284.

Wylly, William. *A Short Account of the Bahama Islands, Their Climate, Productions, etc.* . . . . London, 1789.

Young, Edward. *The Revenge; A Tragedy,* in John Bell, ed., *British Theater.* London, 1791-1802. XXI.

Index

Addison family, 6

Alcide, captain lends barge to Bowles, 48

Alcudia, Duke of (see Godoy, Manuel de)

Allen, Benjamin, interpreter, 31

Allen, Levi, in London, 49

Allen, William, interpreter, 31

Aranda, Conde de, 80-81, 86

Augusta, Bowles spying at, 24

Avilés, Count of, 89

Bahama Gazette, 148; denunciations of Bowles, 34, 39; Muskogee proclamations in, 125

Balcarres, Earl of, and Bowles, 109-110

Barbados, Bowles at, 108

Barclay, John, 24

Baynton, Benjamin, 103; publishes Bowles's biography, 51

Beckwith, George, in New York, 45-46

Blount, William, 74, 82, 97-98, 120, 133, 138; correspondence with De-Lacy, 154

Bowles, Carington, 2-3, 52, 90, 95

Bowles, Carington, Jr., 95

Bowles, Catherine, birth, 3

Bowles, Chief, 13, 83, 147; death, 172

Bowles, Eleanor, 1, 3, 159, 171-172

Bowles, James, 159

Bowles, John, 2

Bowles, John (pamphleteer), 103

Bowles, John (William A. Bowles's brother), 79, 159, 171; birth, 3; in Florida, 69-70

Bowles, Mary, 13, 29, 34, 57, 116, 157, 162, 172; captured, 126

Bowles, Thomas, 2

Bowles, Thomas, Jr., 159, 171; birth, 3; possibly in Florida, 154

Bowles, Thomas, Sr., 1; arrival in Maryland, 2-3; on vestry of All Saints Anglican Church, 3; member Asso-

ciation for Frederick County and local Committee of Correspondence, 5; becomes Loyalist, 6; moves to Conocular Valley, 6; death, 52

Bowles, William ("little Billy"), 13, 29, 116, 158, 162, 173; chief of Paynes Town, 172

Bowles, William Augustus (Eastajoca, Director General of the Creek Nation, combined Creek-Cherokee nations, or Muskogee), birth, 1, 3; childhood in Frederick Town, 3-4; volunteers in British army, 6-7; at Battle of Monmouth, 9; resigns commission, 11; re-commissioned, 14; in New York, 16-18, 19; attempts to establish trade with Indians, 26-28; comparison with McGillivray, 29-30; commissioned by Indians to go to London, 37-38; pictures of, 38, 51, 105, 163; Canadian negotiations, 42-48; reception at Whitehall, 49-50; negotiations with Grenville, 52-54; linguistic ability, 58; at Indian council at Coweta, 58-59; negotiations with the United States, 62; seizes Panton's warehouse, 65-66; at New Orleans, 71-75; wrote account of life, 77; imprisoned in Spain, 80-87; Manila exile, 89-92; escape attempt, 93; return to England, 95-106; in Barbados, 108-109; in Jamaica, 109-111; reception at Nassau, 111-115; confers with Ellicott, 115-116; re-elected Director General, 118, 120; surprised by Garcia, 126; captures Ft. St. Marks, 127-131; abandons Ft. St. Marks and retires to Micco-sukee, 136-137; resumes siege of Ft. St. Marks, 152-153; attends council at Hickory Ground, 162-167; capture compared with that of Duc d'-